SPORTS GOVERNANCE HANDBOOK

Amanda Bennett, Kevin Carpenter
and Rob Wilson

icsa

The Governance
Institute

First published 2019
Published by ICSA Publishing Ltd
Saffron House
6–10 Kirby Street
London EC1N 8TS

Additional material for this Work authored by Kevin Carpenter.

Typeset by Paul Barrett Book Production, Cambridge
Edited by Sheida Heidari
Cover designed by Anthony Kearney

British Cataloguing in Publication Data
A catalogue record for this book is available from the British Library.

ISBN 978-1-86072-765-8

Contents

About the authors

Kevin Carpenter

Kevin Carpenter is a sports lawyer with an international reputation as regards governance, integrity and regulatory issues in sport, having advised on these areas across a diverse range of sports. He has worked with a range of stakeholders in the sector including international federations, national governing bodies, clubs, players' unions, inter-governmental organisations and other public bodies. At the same time as practising, Kevin has always had a passion for research, writing and teaching, and has contributed to a variety of both undergraduate, postgraduate and professional courses for institutions based in the UK and overseas.

Amanda Bennett

Amanda is a governance and diversity specialist working in the sport and charity sectors. She has worked with more than 100 organisations' including the International Paralympic Committee, the Football Association and local voluntary bodies, helping them to build effective leadership models and create robust, inclusive governance structures.

Before establishing FairPlay Ltd, Amanda was Head of Governance at UK Sport and Chair of European Women and Sport. She also served as a board member with Sport Wales. Amanda is currently an Independent Non-Executive Director with England Handball, Non-Executive Director at Saracens Women Ltd and serves on the RFU Game Development Sub-Committee. She is also a qualified mentor, supporting elite coaches and senior executives.

Rob Wilson

Rob is the Head of Department for Finance, Accounting and Business Systems at Sheffield Hallam University and an expert in sport finance. With 20 years' experience in higher education in a variety of roles, ranging from quality enhancement to external relations, Rob has significant teaching and research experience in the sport business field. His main teaching and research interests are in the finance and economics of sport, with his PhD focusing on the factors affecting financial performance in professional team sports.

He has published five books including two on finance: *Finance for Sport and Leisure Managers: An Introduction* and *Managing Sport Finance*; as well as contributing numerous chapters on finance and financial management in sport to books and more than 30 peer reviewed outputs. In addition, he serves on the editorial boards of several international journals. He is a regular commentator in the national and international media (including BBC, Al Jazeera, Bloomberg and ESPN).

Introduction

Sport as a sector has never faced such scrutiny about how it operates. This has been as a result of a critical mass of scandals that have put into sharp focus the lack of even awareness of good modern governance practices, meaning many governing bodies and other sport organisations, can no longer cite the 'autonomy of sport' as a cloak of protection from long overdue reform. After all, good governance engenders trust between all stakeholders – allowing sport to flourish competitively and commercially. Therefore, only the highest possible standards of ethics and governance can now suffice.

It is not all doom and-gloom, however, as being in this position means sport organisations can also adopt good practice from other sectors who have already been through governance reform and tailor it to them in a proportionate manner. Much of this handbook draws from practices outside of the sport sector to first raise awareness, then apply those practices to some of the specificities found in sport.

Overall, this stand alone handbook is a comprehensive analysis and practical companion for all stakeholders with either an obligation or an interest in how their sport and organisation is, and should be, run. The handbook not only covers traditional governance topics such as the role of the board, funding and conducting meetings, but moves understanding on to more 'soft skills' topics such as ethics, culture and the duty of care – all of which have made the role of working in a sports organisation undoubtedly more challenging.

Whatever stakeholder group you are from, or whatever level of a sports organisation you work in, this handbook is a must-have resource which will both add value to your understanding and role, save time and above all make your role in your sport even more enjoyable.

Kevin Carpenter
May 2019

Acronyms and abbreviations

ABP	Athlete biological passport
ACT	Ann Craft Trust
ADO	Anti-doping organisation
ADRVs	Anti-Doping Rule Violations
AGM	Annual general meeting
AIOWF	Association of International Olympic Winter Sports Federations
ARISF	Association of IOC Recognised International Sports Federations
ASOIF	Association of Summer Olympic International Federations
BAC	British Athletes Commission
BAME	Black, Asian and minority ethnic
BBBofC	British Boxing Board of Control
BEIS	Department for Business, Enterprise and Industrial Strategy
BHA	British Horseracing Authority
BITC	Business in the Community
BJA	British Judo Association
BPA	British Paralympic Association
CA	Companies Act 2006
CAS	Court of Arbitration for Sport
CASC	Community Amateur Sports Club
CEO	Chief executive officer
CFO	Chief financial officer
CIMPSA	Chartered Institute for the Management of Sport and Physical Activity
CIO	Charitable Incorporated Organisation
CIRC	Cycling Independent Reform Commission
CLG	Company limited by guarantee
CLS	Company limited by shares
CPSU	Child Protection in Sport Unit
CSF	Combat Sports Federation
CSP	County Sports Partnership
CSPL	Committee on Standards of Public Life
CSR	Corporate social responsibility
DBS	Disclosure and Barring Service
DCMS	Department for Digital, Culture, Media and Sport
DTRs	Disclosure and Transparency Rules
DPO	Data protection officer
EC	European Commission

ECB	England and Wales Cricket Board
ECHR	European Convention on Human Rights
EGM	Extraordinary general meeting
EJU	European Judo Union
EPO	Erythropoietin
ESSG	Elite Sport Sub-Group
FA	Football Association
FAW	Football Association of Wales
FCPA	Foreign Corrupt Practices Act
FIFA	Fédération Internationale de Football Association
FIL	Federation of International Lacrosse
FRC	Financial Reporting Council
FRS	Financial Reporting Standards
GAISF	Global Association of International Sport Federations
GDPR	General Data Protection Regulation
GLFW	Governance and Leadership Framework for Wales
HMRC	Her Majesty's Revenue & Customs
HNSC	Home nation sports council
IAAF	International Association of Athletics Federations
ICC	International Cricket Council
ICCSC	International Standard for Code Compliance by Signatories
ICF	International Canoe Federation
IF	International federation
IFRS	International Financial Reporting Standards
IoD	Institute of Directors
IOC	International Olympic Committee
IPC	International Paralympic Committee
IPED	Image and performance-enhancing drug
IRM	Institute of Risk Management
ISU	International Skating Union
IWG	International Working Group on Women and Sport
LFA	London Football Association
LOCOG	London Organising Committee of the Olympic Games
LTA	Lawn Tennis Association
NADO	National Anti-Doping Organisation
NAKMAS	National Association of Karate and Martial Art Schools
NCVO	National Council for Voluntary Organisations
NED	Non-executive director
NF	National federation
NGB	National governing body
NGO	Non-governmental organisation
NOCs	National Olympic Committees
OC	Olympic Charter

OSCR	Office of the Scottish Charity Regulator
PIDA	Public Interest Disclosure Act 1998
POCA	Proceeds of Crime Act 2000
PFA	Professional Footballers Association
PGG	IOC Principles of Good Governance
RAG	Red/Amber/Green
RFU	Rugby Football Union
SBIU	Sports Betting Intelligence Unit
SGBs	Scottish Governing Bodies of Sport
SGSA	Sports Grounds Safety Authority
SID	Senior independent director
SME	Small to medium-sized enterprise
SORP	Statement of Recommended Practice
SRA	Sport and Recreation Alliance
SRUK	Sports Resolutions UK
SSAP	Statement of Standard Accounting Practice
UCI	Union Cycliste Internationale
UFC	Ultimate Fighting Championship
UK GAAP	Generally Accepted Accounting Principles
UKA	UK Athletics
UKAD	UK Anti-Doping
WADA	World Anti-Doping Agency
WCP	World Class Programme

1

General principles of sports governance

Introduction

In this chapter, we shall briefly outline the basic concepts of governance. We shall address the fundamental questions of what governance is and why it is important in sport.

Defining governance in sport

Simply put, governance is the process by which decisions are made. If a decision, either positive or negative, requires an action to be taken by an organisation, then governance also encompasses how that decision is implemented. Strategically, governance encompasses the system(s) of oversight in place for an organisation and the approach used to achieve specific goals.

Governance is a well-known concept in most sectors of society, particularly in corporate ones, but historically sport has lagged behind in this aspect. In the past few years, the issue of good governance in sport has moved towards the top of the agenda not only of sports organisations themselves, but also non-governmental organisations (NGOs) (such as Transparency International, Play the Game), governments and intergovernmental organisations (such as the Council of Europe) following a number of recent high-profile scandals.

A key concept which drives governance in sport, both for Olympic and non-Olympic sports, is the autonomy of sport. This has principally been developed by the International Olympic Committee (IOC) and is one of the Fundamental Principles of Olympism, as set out in the Olympic Charter:

> Recognising that sport occurs within the framework of society, sports organisations in the Olympic movement chart the rights and obligations autonomy, which include freely establishing and controlling the rules of sport, determining the structure and governance of their organisations, enjoying the right of elections free from any outside influence and the responsibility for ensuring the principles of good governance be applied.

The autonomy of sport principle typifies the sport movement's belief that it alone understands best how to govern and regulate itself and is a hangover from when sports were run by volunteers who were only concerned with satisfying their members. This belief manifests itself in a resistance to government or other outside interference in the governance of the sector.

Governing organisations of sport can often forget and/or underestimate that the bottom levels of the pyramid (grass roots and amateur clubs) form the foundation of the pyramid as they offer sport for all and foster generations of new participants, including players, referees, coaches or simply fans/supporters. However, by adopting good governance principles, sports organisations substantially lessen the real risks from poor practices (including corruption).

Governance versus management

The distinction between governance and management is an important one. In contrast to what governance encompasses, management involves the day-to-day running of an organisation. The UK Corporate Governance Code states this distinction succinctly:

> Corporate governance is therefore about what the board of a company does and how it sets the values of the company. It is to be distinguished from the day to day operational management of the company by full-time executives.

The functions of management focus on achieving an organisation's objectives within a framework established by the governance organs. The governance organs will then oversee the performance of the executive organs of the organisation.

Principles of good governance

The importance of good governance in achieving organisational objectives

Any organisation should identify and institute goals and objectives. The organisation's governance should be geared towards those objectives. Sports organisations also need to have credible and good governance structures in place which are comprehensive yet proportionate, and implemented effectively.

However, until sports organisations are accountable to their stakeholders and transparent, they will ultimately not have the authority to tackle the challenges facing sports organisations (corruption, doping, match-fixing and so on), and thus risk losing their stakeholders' trust.

Good governance is often talked of in relation to certain key principles. Such principles can be found in much corporate and academic literature, often with overlap between them. It is important to put such governance concepts into a practical framework which can be understood and implemented at all levels of the sports organisation.

Fairness

Fairness is a concept linked to ethical behaviour and integrity.

In a sporting context, the group who are of principal concern are usually the members. However, a sports organisation should also be fair in the treatment of all of its interested participants and stakeholders including (but not limited to) coaches, match officials, volunteers, communities and administrators.

The fairer the sports organisation entity can be to all its interested stakeholder groups, the more likely it is that it can manage diversity of interests and develop an organisation with wide-reaching impact, effectiveness and legitimacy.

Accountability and responsibility

Good governance is ultimately about developing trust between all stakeholders, particularly in the people who run the sports organisation itself. To develop trust in this group, who are required to run the sport in a responsible manner, it is vital that they have accountability (are responsible) for their performance in relation to what should be transparent objectives.

If transparent and reasonable objectives are not set by the sports organisation, there is no way to make the people who run the sport accountable.

Holding a sports organisation's board accountable can be achieved in a number of ways.

Fiscal accountability

Fiscal accountability refers to the formal mechanisms of control over funding. When it comes to high performance sport, particularly in the UK, this is perhaps the most powerful form of accountability, as national governing bodies (NGBs) depend on public funding. This is an increasingly precarious strategy, given major cuts in public spending. UK Sport and Sport England have placed good governance at the heart of the conditions attached to funding with the implementation of their new Code for Sports Governance.

Legal accountability

International bodies and their employees must abide by the laws of relevant jurisdictions in which those laws apply. Despite concepts unique to sport, such as the autonomy and specificity of sport, organisations in the sector are subject to a multitude of laws, depending on the countries/jurisdictions in which they are based and operate.

Both the IOC and the Fédération Internationale de Football Association (FIFA) have made fundamental changes to their governance structures and procedures due to high-profile civil and criminal legal action taken by authorities in the US.

Market accountability

Market accountability is the potential power that commercial partners have to influence the governance of a sport through market mechanisms. Traditionally, sponsors and commercial partners of sporting organisations have been reluctant to speak publicly about the governance of sports they support. However, given the pressures applied upon the sponsors themselves by their own shareholders and other stakeholder groups, they have been far more proactive in holding sport accountable. Recently FIFA's sponsors, including Coca-Cola and Visa, spoke out against the corrupt governance practices which had been revealed.

At a time when public funding for sport is decreasing, governing bodies will aim to fill the gap by turning to commercial organisations; therefore, as part of their offerings, sports organisations will have to have good governance in place.

Peer accountability

The evaluation of organisations by their peer institutions is closely related to supervision, particularly in sport, given that primarily supervision comes from within the sector (their peers). Some 'independent' organisations that have taken more of an interest in sports governance and accountability in recent years include Transparency International, Play the Game and the Council of Europe.

Public reputational accountability

The reputation of an organisation as a mechanism of accountability has been perhaps the most effective and yet damaging for sport in recent years. Governing bodies are under much higher levels of scrutiny from both the media and the general public than ever. This has manifested itself in the UK through numerous scandals emerging in relation to athlete welfare issues (such as bullying and sexual offences).

Transparency

Transparency means that those affected by decisions of an organisation should know not only the basic facts and figures, but also the mechanisms and processes.

A central principle of the rule of law is that each participant within a state must know their rights and any restrictions on those rights imposed by the law. In sport, this means that the governing body must make all rules and policies available both in print and online when requested. These must be easy to locate on the governing body's website. As a matter of best practice, all disciplinary and appeal rulings should also be published.

Principle 3 (Communication) of the new UK Sport & Sport England Code of Sports Governance states the following:

> 3.1 Each organisation shall publicly disclose information on its governance, structure, strategy, activities and financial position to enable stakeholders to have a good understanding of them.

The commentary to this requirement once again supports the steps outlined above: 'Transparency enables stakeholders to have timely access to important information about the organisation, thereby improving the accountability of the organisation, and helping with stakeholder engagement'.

Co-operation and collaboration

Sports organisations should collaborate with organisations in other sectors that are further advanced in their governance practices so as to expedite the pace of governance change.

A lack of public funding should also drive co-operation and collaboration between sports so as to share the time and financial burden of putting in place robust governance practices, policies and frameworks.

None of this necessarily has to be done formally; even discussing the relevant issues informally will help learning and spread good practice between sports.

Proactivity

Being proactive means creating or controlling a situation rather than just responding to it after it has happened. Elements of acting proactively would include a sports organisation having open channels of communication, following up thoroughly on any information received and inviting external scrutiny of the organisation's governance practices.

When setting up a governance structure for a sports organisation, it is important that the organisation chooses the right legal form and complies which the legal requirements of that form. This chapter outlines the main advantages and disadvantages of each type of organisational form available in the UK.

Sports organisations and governance structures in the UK

Roles of different types of sports organisations

UK Sport

UK Sport was established in 1996 and is the UK's high-performance sports agency investing in Olympic and Paralympic sport. It funds and works with its partner sporting organisations, primarily NGBs, to lead sport in the UK to world-class success: winning medals primarily at the Olympic and Paralympic Games.

UK Sport is funded by money from the National Lottery and HM Treasury. UK Sport must decide how best to strategically invest these monies to support athletes with credible medal potential within the high-performance system.

Investment decisions are made on a four-year basis wherever possible to cover a complete Olympic/Paralympic cycle, but are focused on an eight-year performance development model, which is based on the following nine 'investment principles':

1. Olympic and Paralympic impact;
2. international medal success;
3. investing in athletes;
4. investing in sports;
5. investing in people;
6. performance pathway;

7. the cost of Olympic and Paralympic success;
8. a culture of responsibility, accountability and partnership; and
9. a culture of 'world class'.

In addition to funding athletes, UK Sport has other responsibilities including: bidding for and staging major sporting events; increasing sporting influence internationally; and promoting the highest standards of governance, sporting conduct, ethics and diversity in society.

One way in which UK Sport seeks to meet these responsibilities is by strategic investment into the World Class Programme, which accounts for approximately 70% of its spend.

UK Sport supports more than just athletes. It recognises that investment is also needed into the elements that support athletes, including coaching, governance, talent identification and sports science, medicine and technology.

The other key area in which UK Sport provides financial support is bidding for and staging sporting events in the UK. In doing this, UK Sport is supporting the preparation of British athletes for the Summer/Winter Olympic Games by hosting important qualification events on home soil, as well as providing economic and social benefits for the UK.

Those who have applied for UK Sport funding know that it is a rigorous process that should not be embarked upon lightly. National governing bodies and athletes are aware of the time and resource commitment it takes to make an application, but have very little sense of their chances of success until the final decision is made.

Even if funding is awarded, the its success and the compliance with any conditions is strictly monitored as part of UK Sport's controversial 'no compromise' approach whereby, when it comes to individuals, funding is awarded solely on the likelihood to medal at the Olympic Games, with no other factors taken into account (for example, an athlete's development).

Home Country Sports Councils

The development of sport at the grass-roots level is the remit of the individual Home Country Sports Councils for the UK: Sport England, Sport Wales, sportscotland and Sport Northern Ireland.

Each body focuses on community sport in their respective parts of the UK by increasing participation levels; however, they have autonomy as to the strategies they create and implement to achieve this.

For example, Sport England has seven investment programmes for the five-year period 2016–21 to 'increase the number of people getting active':

1. *Tackling inactivity* – helping the 28% of people in England who don't do any sport or physical activity.
2. *Children and young people* – to work with children from the age of five to increase children's basic competence and enjoyment of sport and physical activity.

3. *Volunteering* – focusing on the motivations and needs of the volunteers so that volunteering in sport attracts more people from a wider range of backgrounds.
4. *Taking sport and activity into the mass market* – focusing on the sports and activities that have mass appeal and can get large numbers of people active.
5. *Supporting sport's core markets (including talented athletes)* – supporting those who already have a strong affinity for sport in a more efficient and sustainable way.
6. *Local delivery* – exploring new ways of working locally by investing in up to ten specific areas to pilot new, more joined-up approaches to getting people active.
7. *Creating welcoming sports facilities* – with a new Community Asset Fund, and continuing its successful Strategic Facilities Fund, prioritising multi-sport facilities and, wherever possible, co-locating them with other local services.

sportscotland has approached its work in a different way, with its 2015–19 corporate plan *Raising The Bar* outlining three focused priority areas for improvement:

1. equalities and inclusion
2. people development
3. collaboration and impact.

National governing bodies

There is one official NGB for each sport, which is formally recognised by the international federation (IF), giving NGBs a monopolistic position in UK sport. NGBs regulate all general matters within their sport and represent their members in the continental federations and IF. They also organise national championships and act as regulatory bodies.

NGBs delegate some of their powers/responsibilities down the pyramid to area/county/regional governing bodies/organisations, including the management of finances for that area or disciplinary matters (other than for the most serious offences, such as doping).

In the UK, the government takes a non-interventionist approach to the regulation of NGBs, despite their actions and decisions being of great interest to the public. This further reinforces the autonomy of sport in the UK.

However, they are not completely free from such intervention, which can come in three forms:

1. *direct intervention* – legislation and/or regulatory measures – examples: public safety (stadiums); public order (hooliganism); protected list of sports events for public broadcasting;
2. *exhortation* – putting pressure on NGBs to act in a certain way (the threat of legislative intervention) – examples: public inquiries into football governance and doping in cycling; and

3. *indirect intervention* – using the leverage that comes from control over access to public funding – this is increasing due to the belief that this form of 'partnership' with NGBs must accord with the usual public standards of transparency, equity and accountability – examples: UK Sport, Home Country Sports Councils, UK Anti-Doping.

It is settled law in the UK that NGBs are not public bodies, despite many of them receiving significant amounts of public funding. As a result, legal recourse cannot be sought through the efficient and powerful avenue of judicial review.

However, the civil courts of the land do have 'supervisory jurisdiction' over the actions and decisions of NGBs. This means the sport's members (including regional governing bodies, clubs, athletes and/or other participants) can bring claims against NGBs (and indeed have done so) as regards the following causes of action:

- *NGB acted outside of its own regulations and/or the law* – such as imposing a sanction which is outside what is allowed by the relevant regulations and amounts to an unlawful restraint of trade;
- *NGB's decision was based on errors of fact* – any decision made must have a sound evidential basis;
- *NGB took into account irrelevant considerations when making its decision;*
- *NGB acted contrary to the rules of natural justice* – this concept encompasses a variety of elements, for example, the right to be informed of the charge, right to a hearing, right to legal representation;
- *NGB acted contrary to a legitimate expectation* – for example, concrete promises about the renewal of a contract;
- *NGB reached its decision under the influence of bias;*
- *NGB acted unreasonably, irrationally, arbitrarily or capriciously* – this is a high threshold for the challenger to overcome;
- *NGB breached a contract* – either an express or implied obligation; or
- *NGB acted negligently* – such as failure to provide proper guidelines to deal with serious injury.

National sports organisations

There are other important national sports organisations/agencies. They often focus on matters of importance which cut across all sport, in particular issues regarding integrity.

UK Anti-Doping (UKAD) is responsible for ensuring sports bodies in the UK comply with the World Anti-Doping Code through implementation and management of the UK's National Anti-Doping Policy. UKAD is the National Anti-Doping Organisation (NADO) for the purposes of the World Anti-Doping Agency (WADA) Code, and its functions include:

- a prevention through education programme;
- intelligence-led athlete testing across more than 40 Olympic, Paralympic and professional sports;

- investigations; and
- being the exclusive results management authority for the determination of Anti-Doping Rule Violations (ADRVs).

Another UK body dealing with a serious threat to the reputation and integrity of sport is the Child Protection in Sport Unit (CPSU). The CPSU was founded in 2001 to work with UK Sports Councils, NGBs, County Sports Partnerships (CSPs) and other organisations to help them minimise the risk of child abuse during sporting activities.

The overall mission of the CPSU is to build the capacity of sports to safeguard children and young people in and through sport, and to enable sports organisations to lead the way in keeping children safe from harm. The CPSU tries to achieve this by:

- being a lead voice, champion and pioneer, both UK-wide and internationally;
- providing expert safeguarding and child protection advice to sports organisations;
- contributing safeguarding knowledge to policies, procedures and programmes;
- developing and delivering sports-specific training, resources and guidance;
- coordinating, lobbying and advocating on behalf of the sports sector in response to government consultations;
- commissioning and supporting research into a range of issues, developing understanding and an evidence base;
- consulting with children and young people; and
- working with international organisations to promote safeguarding work with other countries.

Regional bodies

Regional bodies of sport are the next level down in the pyramid below NGBs. They will have certain functions devolved to them to exercise in the region for which they are responsible. The reason for having regional bodies is usually a combination of practicality and history.

One example of a regionalised UK sport is professional boxing. The British Boxing Board of Control is the NGB, with seven 'Area Councils' sitting below it: Scottish, Northern Ireland, Welsh, Northern, Central, Southern and Midlands.

Regulatory responsibilities given to regional bodies include having jurisdiction over certain disciplinary matters, taking participant licensing decisions, managing the safety of events and training new match officials.

Clubs and leagues

Clubs are the lifeblood of many sports as they bring together a collection of individuals with common interests who wish to take part in a particular sport, be it competitively or socially. Almost all clubs are membership associations operated for the benefit of those members. Sports clubs are the primary place where grass-roots sport is developed and they are one of the main sources of increased participation. They are also often tied very closely to the local community and can provide facilities that will benefit the wider community.

The clubs are themselves members of a governing body and also usually a competition or league, with the latter in professional sport (the Premier League and Premiership Rugby, for example) having increasing influence in the overall order due to their commercial clout. Many of the significant regulatory sports developments have come from clubs (and their leagues) challenging the decisions of governing bodies in relation to promotion, the development of their stadiums or the registration or treatment of their participants. All of these clubs therefore play an extremely important role in the UK sporting pyramid and its success.

Organisations that use sport to achieve social and community outcomes

Numerous sporting organisations in the UK are operated wholly or partially to further social and community development. This may be by:

- targeting certain underrepresented groups, such as female participation, black, Asian and Middle East participation;
- seeking to engage a broader audience for a particular sport;
- helping in the education and well-being of young people; or
- raising funds through sport for charitable projects.

Such organisations are often supported by a variety of potential funding sources, both public and private, as there is little doubt as to the multitude of benefits that sport brings to society, such as physical, mental, teamwork and so on.

Governance structures in UK sport

The governance of sports in the UK follows the pyramid structure prominent in European sport. In the UK, NGBs sit near the top; regional bodies (where applicable) are below, then leagues, with amateur/grass-roots organisations at the bottom. However, even UK NGBs are not wholly autonomous, with European and then international federations sitting above them in the pyramid. None of these levels of governance within the pyramid operates within a complete autonomous vacuum.

This system cannot work effectively if there are competing/rival governing bodies at any level of the pyramid. Mechanisms are in place to prevent any outside bodies impinging on this exclusive governance model.

One way in which governing bodies seek to achieve and then maintain their authority and autonomy is to require participants to be involved only in competitions sanctioned by the NGB, meaning that they are played subject to the rules and regulations of that sport.

Theory in action

The most recent 'breakaway' threat to the status quo of so-called 'sanctioned' events/competitions heard in a formal legal process came in the Olympic sport of short track speed skating.

In June 2014, two prominent Dutch speed skaters, Mark Tuitert (Olympic Champion) and Niels Kerstholt (World Champion), filed a competition law complaint against the International Skating Union (ISU) with the European Commission.

In doing so they also published an open letter to the European Commissioner for Competition, the key extracts of which were:

'We work in an economic sector that is mostly regulated by international sports federations. More often than not, those rules are disconnected from the interests of those that matter the most: the athletes...If we would participate in such events we can expect to be banned for life from all ISU competitions (including Olympic Games, World Championship, etc.). As such, the federation effectively denies our right to participate in alternative events that do not conflict with the official ISU competition calendar...The far-reaching restrictive effects of this prohibition became manifest when an independent organizer, Icederby International, took the initiative to organize out-of-season international speed skating events. Such new initiatives are welcome opportunities for speed skaters to make a better living out of their profession. The numbers speak for themselves: an individual short track speed skater winning all the ISU competitions in a typical season would earn around 25.000 EUR. This is less than what the same skater would receive for merely appearing in a single, two-day Icederby event! The ISU, however, prevents us from seizing this and any other future opportunity without any valid justification... The ISU's abuse of its worldwide monopoly position can only be tackled at a supranational level. And the stakes are high. This is not just about speed skating. In numerous other sports, international federations impose similar restrictions on athletes. The European Commission now has the chance to set an important precedent that would put an end to these abusive practices once and for all.'

In response to the complaint and the letter, the European Commission opened a formal investigation in October 2015 saying, 'The Commission has decided to pursue this investigation because it raises specific allegations of breaches of competition law at the international level rather than wider issues of internal governance or rule-making in a sport federation'.

The European Commission's decision came in December 2017 and stated that the ISU rules imposing severe penalties on athletes participating in speed skating competitions that are not authorised by the ISU were in breach of EU antitrust law.

The key findings by the Commission were:

- Under the ISU eligibility rules, in place since 1998, speed skaters participating in competitions that are not approved by the ISU face severe penalties up to a lifetime ban from all major international speed skating events. The ISU can impose these penalties at its own discretion, even if the independent competitions pose no risk to legitimate sports objectives, such as the protection of the integrity and proper conduct of sport, or the health and safety of athletes.
- By imposing such restrictions, the ISU eligibility rules restrict competition and enable the ISU to pursue its own commercial interests to the detriment of athletes and organisers of competing events. In particular, the Commission considers that the ISU eligibility rules restrict the commercial freedom of athletes who are prevented from participating in independent skating events. As a result of the ISU eligibility rules, athletes are not allowed to offer their services to organisers of competing skating events and may be deprived of additional sources of income during their relatively short speed skating careers.
- The ISU eligibility rules prevent independent organisers from putting together their own speed skating competitions because they are unable to attract top athletes. This has limited the development of alternative and innovative speed skating competitions, and deprived ice-skating fans from following other events.

The consequences of this decision were that the ISU to stop its 'illegal conduct' within 90 days. To comply the ISU had to abolish or modify its eligibility rules so that they were based only on legitimate objectives (explicitly excluding the ISU's own economic interests) and that they were inherent and proportionate to achieve those objectives.

Incumbent sports governing bodies in the UK also benefit from the fact that as already noted, they are not public bodies, or exercising public powers, and are therefore not subject to judicial review, which can be a powerful tool for aggrieved parties. The courts in the UK are in any event reluctant to interfere in issues between governing bodies, its members and/or other stakeholders, preferring to leave disputes to be decided by either internal quasi-judicial processes, or specialist sports tribunals/alternative dispute resolution services such as Sport Resolutions UK or the Court of Arbitration for Sport, depending on what the constitution of the particular sport allows.

Legal forms of sports organisations in the UK

Sports governing bodies and organisations in the UK are naturally not all the same in terms of their size, objectives and many other factors. A central distinction can be seen between professional and amateur sporting bodies. The laws in the UK reflect this with different legal structures available. There are advantages and disadvantages to each.

Unincorporated association

The majority of amateur sports organisations (clubs and governing bodies) are 'unincorporated associations'. This is when no formal legal steps have been taken to set up the organisation, and the individuals are bound together by the constitution or rules of the organisation, which is run by one or more committees. The members bind the organisation into contracts on behalf of the club. There is great flexibility in this form of sporting organisation and little cost or formal administration is required.

However, members can be held personally liable for contracts and legal claims made against the organisation (such as personal injury claims) and the club does not own any of its own assets; these are owned by the individual who enters into the contract.

Company limited by guarantee

Another prevalent form of legal structure in UK sport is the company limited by guarantee (CLG). These are particularly common in amateur sports as CLGs can only really be used for clubs who operate on a not-for-profit basis, given each member pays only a small sum (usually £1) if the club becomes insolvent, thereby providing the key advantage over an unincorporated association, as the members have limited legal liability. However, a CLG must file forms at Companies House by defined deadlines, or face fines.

Company limited by shares

Across all sectors, a company limited by shares (CLS) is the most common company. The owners of a CLS are its shareholders and crucially are protected by limited liability, like members of a CLG. Shares in the company can be bought and sold (subject to restrictions in the constitutional documents of the company) and attract a dividend payment when sufficient profits are made by the sporting association. For these reasons, CLSs are usually only formed for large sports governing bodies and organisations.

There is a risk to the sport in that a CLS can be controlled strategically and operationally by any shareholder or group of shareholders with a common objective, who owns over 50% of the voting rights, with little legal protection for minority shareholders.

There is even greater risk where an individual or group of shareholders owns over 75% of the shares, as they can pass special resolutions and thereby change the constitution of the organisation. This can be mitigated by protectionist provisions being inserted into the Articles of Association and/or a shareholders' agreement.

Community Amateur Sports Club status

Any unincorporated sporting organisation or sporting company that is a club can acquire Community Amateur Sports Club (CASC) status, which offers significant tax relief, including business rates relief and Gift Aid. A CASC's main purpose must be to provide facilities for and promote participation in one or more eligible sports (a club can have a number of sports provided by the CASC).

To be eligible for CASC status, an organisation must:

- *be open to all of the community* – membership must be open and cannot discriminate except when a certain level of physical ability is needed to take part in a sport;
- *offer affordable membership and costs of participation* – no more than £1,612
- *provide facilities for eligible sports and encourage people to take part* – at least 50% of the members must take part in the sport(s);
- *be organised on an amateur basis* – this means the club must not make a profit, unless this is reinvested in the club, and not pay more than £10,000 in total to all players in a year; and
- *be managed by 'fit and proper persons'* – as determined by Her Majesty's Revenue & Customs (HMRC) on each individual's personal history.

Charitable legal structures

Unincorporated associations and CLGs can also be charities, making fundraising easier and offering significant tax advantages even greater than those for CASCs.

A club or sporting organisation can only be charitable in nature if its constitution promotes amateur sports and/or other healthy amateur recreations as set out in the Charities Act 2011. In all cases, the club must exist for the public benefit.

One potential downside to obtaining charitable status for a sports club is that membership is open to all; all members must play, be amateur and cannot simply be 'social members'. There are also additional administration costs involved in registering with the Charity Commission.

There is also a specific charitable legal structure open to sports organisations called the Charitable Incorporated Organisation (CIO). Again, it must meet the charitable requirements in the Charities Act 2011, but it is a flexible, low-cost structure with limited liability.

However, a CIO may have more difficulties raising finance given that the Charity Commission does not provide a searchable register of charges. This increases the risk for an organisation that could provide finance for a sports club in the form of debentures or secured investments.

▒ The impact of poor governance on sports organisations

Strategic failure

A strategy is a plan of action designed to achieve a long-term or overall aim. For a sporting organisation, the long-term aim could mean a number of things, including:

- achieving the maximum number of medals (UK Sport);
- commercial success (NFL);
- winning the maximum number of trophies (Paris St Germain football club);
- increasing participation (This Girl Can campaign); or
- getting public funding back (British Basketball).

Strategy can originate from anywhere within an organisation. However, any change in leadership is likely to have a major impact.

Business failure and financial loss

Business failure refers to a company ceasing operations following its inability to make a profit or to bring in enough revenue to cover its expenses.

It is vital for any sports organisation to budget well so as not to succumb to business failure. In amateur sports organisations, budgeting may be done by the treasurer. Regardless of who prepares the budgets, whether for the financial year ahead or a particular project, they should be reviewed and scrutinised closely by both the board and the members.

With the new Code for Sports Governance having been recently introduced by UK Sport and Sport England, poor governance practices will result in restrictions being placed on any public funding received.

Theory in action

At the Table Tennis England AGM on 8 July 2017, the board put forward a proposal to meet the standards of governance required by the Code. That proposal needed 75% of support from leagues and counties to be accepted. It received 74.93% and therefore failed. As a result, Sport England froze any further funding from the £9 million that Table Tennis England were due to receive between 2017 and 2021. The Table Tennis England board warned that this would have implications on the organisation's ability to service the members. Less than a month later, at an extraordinary general meeting (EGM), the same proposal was passed with an overwhelming majority of 96.96% of the organisation's members in favour – more than the 75% needed for the changes to go through. The members also agreed that the organisation should undertake a thorough and wide-ranging review of all governance and board structures to ensure table tennis is fit for purpose for the future, to comply with the Code.

Reputational damage

Reputation is an intangible asset for an organisation; it is hard to establish but very easy to lose.

With ever-evolving technology comes increasing media interest and scrutiny in the behaviour of organisations. When decisions are made, and if they are unpopular or controversial, much of the way they will be reported cannot be controlled by the organisation once it is in the public domain. Untold reputational damage can be caused to an organisation by poor governance practices.

This is even more true in the sports sector, where an organisation will undoubtedly be in the public interest and spotlight. Each instance of poor governance practice by an organisation will soon be on social media and each retweet or Facebook view will damage the brand of the organisation.

Being proactive is vital, both to lessen the risk and keep control of the flow of information. This can be achieved by having a communications plan, if an organisation has the expertise to put one in place.

Theory in action

Allegations were made to the press by some members of British Cycling's World Class Programme (WCP) about the toxic culture and poor governance in the organisation. In particular, there were allegations of bullying and sexism by the senior coaches. This brought a great deal of negative publicity to the sport, given that it had won a large number of medals at the Olympic Games since Beijing 2008, and currently receives public funding of nearly £26 million from UK Sport for the four-year period leading up to Tokyo 2020.

To repair some of the reputational damage, and to discover whether fundamental governance changes needed to be made, British Cycling and UK Sport's response to the allegations was to commission jointly an independent panel to look at the culture and ethical behaviour within British Cycling's WCP.

The panel proposed five key recommendations based on its findings. From a governance perspective, Recommendation 1 stated that the leadership within the British Cycling board and WCP needed to change, recognising that accountability and example-setting must begin at the top of any organisation. This meant the new CEO and Performance Director having appropriate leadership, communication and behavioural skills not only to lead their own programmes but also to work together and with UK Sport to implement the Recommendations. Recommendation 3 noted that, for the staff working on the WCP, there was a need for professional development to be offered, not only in coaching and course-attendance in their core disciplines but also in terms of equality and discrimination. In addition, an evolution of interpersonal (especially communication) skills also needed to be focused on for coaching staff within the WCP.

Legal challenges

A sports organisation can face a range of legal challenges as a result of poor governance practices, including:

- a failure to act lawfully;
- a failure to act in accordance with its own rules;
- a failure to act fairly in a procedural sense (natural justice);
- taking into account irrelevant considerations when making a decision;
- acting contrary to a member's legitimate expectations; or
- acting in a way that is objectively unreasonable, irrational, arbitrary or capricious.

Protracted legal proceedings could spell major disaster for an organisation; many sports have now improved their internal disciplinary proceedings and provide an appeals process to an independent specialist tribunal, such as Sports Resolutions UK or the Court of Arbitration for Sport (CAS).

Theory in action

A Disciplinary Panel of the British Horseracing Authority (BHA), chaired by Mr Matthew Lohn (senior partner of Fieldfisher LLP solicitors), imposed a penalty of four years' disqualification on trainer Mr Jim Best following allegations he had deliberately ordered the stopping of two horses, contrary to the Rules of Racing in respect of manipulation.

Mr Best appealed against the decision of the Disciplinary Panel on five grounds, the principal of which was that the original hearing was conducted in a way that was substantially unfair and prejudicial to him, because of the apparent bias of the chairman.

There was no allegation of actual bias against Mr Lohn, who has sat as one of the legally qualified members of the Disciplinary Panel for some ten years. The question of bias arose because it was discovered, following the conclusion of the hearing, that Mr Lohn had described the BHA, in an internet video to promote his firm, as one of his 'clients'.

It subsequently transpired that between February 2014 and October 2015, Mr Lohn and his firm had done legal work for the BHA, the fee invoices for which totalled more than £50,000. These invoices were not in relation to payments made for Mr Lohn's services for acting as a member of the Disciplinary Panel.

By letter dated 13 May 2016, the BHA informed Mr Best's solicitors that it would not oppose this ground of his appeal, and conceded that 'Mr Lohn's position gave rise at the time of the hearing before the Disciplinary Panel to an appearance of bias within the meaning attributed to that phrase in *Porter v Magill* [2001] UKHL 67'. The BHA accepted that the Disciplinary Panel's decision and findings should be quashed, and the matter remitted to a different Panel for a fresh inquiry.

Loss of people and knowledge

The most important asset for any sport is its people, including athletes, administrators, volunteers and others who give their time and have a passion for the particular sport. There is a delicate balance to be struck to utilise their knowledge and passion, while not allowing them to stymie progression and the evolution of the sport.

If you operate in team sports, you will also want to ensure top-class personnel (such as coaches, physios) do not leave for a rival (unless otherwise agreed), taking their knowledge and skills with them. This may require some legal protections (confidentiality and restrictive covenant clauses, for example) and action to be taken (such as cease and desist letters and then litigation).

Reform/modernisation in the sport sector to address poor governance practice

Despite the success of UK athletes in recent years, given record levels of public funding under the New Labour government, a variety of stakeholders have voiced concerns about the decline in sports participation across the UK given competing attractions and activities for people's leisure time, and the way in which sport is funded by public bodies in times of austerity.

Some complaints raised against the current practices of sports governance include the following:

- Having distinct funding bodies for elite and grass-roots sport has led to a funding gap for sports and athletes who sit between those two levels in the pyramid, which has ultimately led to a lack of joined-up strategic thinking.
- UK Sport's 'no compromise' policy has led to certain sports constantly getting elite funding (such as athletics, rowing and cycling), meaning others do not receive any.
- An over-reliance on the requirement to 'medal' at the Olympics/Paralympics to determine funding decisions results in rampant short-termism in governance.
- There is a disparity between the funding for individual sports and team sports as it costs far less to achieve success in the former, at the expense of the many other benefits of team sports.
- Not enough funding is available to participants other than athletes (such as coaches or match officials).

The increasing clamour for reform of sport in the UK at all levels saw UK Sport make the first public move with a strategic review and consultation. The outcome of that consultation was published in a report in January 2015. One of the key themes was the strategic changes that UK Sport could make to improve on their success, including:

- a stronger narrative of social, political and economic benefits of high performance sport;

- a clearer strategy to attract commercial and private philanthropic sponsorship of high-performance sport;
- separate strategic approaches for team and Paralympic sports to reflect the different contexts in which they operate;
- further work on the long-term care of athletes, with a clear ethical framework; and
- practical improvements in terms of better communication with stakeholders to manage expectations, and formal vehicles for knowledge and resource sharing between NGBs.

Following the publication of the consultation report, the UK Sport board made a statement as to how the responses would affect its approach to performance investment for the Tokyo Cycle 2017–21 for the Tokyo 2020 Olympics and Paralympics. Regrettably for many of those who had fed back into the consultation, the status quo remained, with other factors (such as supporting a broader range of sports) being a clear secondary issue and only if there are sufficient finances remaining (which is unlikely, as the government has already indicated that money given to sport will decrease significantly in the coming years).

This stance softened first in October 2018, when DCMS announced that a £3 million Aspiration Fund was to be established for Olympic and Paralympic sports outside the World Class Programme to be able to bid to UK Sport for additional investment to help more talented athletes compete at Tokyo 2020. Then in early 2019, UK Sport released its *Future Investment Strategy*, to come into force in April 2021, covering the Paris 2024 and Los Angeles 2028 Olympic and Paralympic cycles, and contains a new funding tier called 'Progression', with investment to enable sports and athletes to take the first step on the performance pathway.

Given this situation for the time being, the Home Nation Sports Councils (HNSCs) say they are now a 'funder of last resort' and have recommended that sports organisations in the UK pursue 'partnership funding'. Therefore, when applying for a HNSC grant, one should also try to secure some local funds or finance. By doing this, with local partners supporting the project, the case for investment from the HNSC will be stronger.

The Sport and Recreation Alliance (SRA) has recommended using performance indicators/targets to give a measurable indication as to the success of a strategy or the governance of the organisation. There are many different types of possible indicators (quantitative, qualitative, practical, directional, actionable, financial , to name just a few), but whichever combination of indicators a sports organisation chooses, the indicators should be SMART: Specific, Measurable, Attainable, Relevant and Timed.

In an organisation, to improve governance at all levels of the sport, continuing professional development/training should be carried out for all board members, other executives and volunteers. In embarking on such a programme, a training needs assessment should take place to determine whether specific training for certain individuals is required or more general training, or (more likely) a combination of the two. There are sporting organisations that can assist with this; however, looking externally to other sectors and training providers may provide different perspectives and drive innovation with the governance of the sport.

Chapter summary

- Governance in any sector is fundamentally about decision making. This is particularly important in the sports sector, given the pervading principle of the autonomy of sport.
- Governance and management are different but related. In your sports organisation, it will be important to explain this distinction to colleagues so that they are fully aware of their responsibilities and how to implement the principles of good governance.
- The five principles of good governance (fairness; accountability and responsibility; transparency; co-operation and collaboration; and proactivity), if implemented correctly and proportionally to your organisation, will ensure that you satisfy any requirements demanded by your members or by any funding bodies.
- Considering the ways in which your organisation may be held accountable will assist in formulating good governance strategies and policies based on the other four principles.
- The sports governance framework in the UK is characterised by a pyramid hierarchy. The level of the pyramid at which your organisation sits will determine the degree of autonomy and responsibility you have for that sport within the UK.
- A great amount of importance has been placed on obtaining public funding from either UK Sport or the Home Country Sports Councils. However, in continuing times of austerity, clubs, athletes and other stakeholders have to be more creative when financing their operations and growth. One area organisations may wish to look at is their legal form, with different options carrying potential fundraising and tax benefits.
- Poor governance can have a number of impacts on a sports organisation, which can in certain cases be fatal to an organisation's long-term sustainability.

2
Approaches to sports governance

Introduction

There are a variety of approaches that can be taken to achieve good governance in any sector. This chapter outlines the five main theories of governance, which range along a spectrum from being principally focused on rules and value creation to balancing the interests of all stakeholders in your sport. An overview is provided of the Nolan Principles, which were published in 1995 and have remained relevant to organisations in the public and voluntary sectors as the required standards of conduct for leaders. Also covered in this chapter is legislation which sports organisations must consider, including the Companies Act 2006, Charities Act 2011 and Equality Act 2010.

General approaches to governance

Rules-based approach

A rules-based approach to governance is the simplest, and therefore most prevalent, across all sectors. This is particularly true in sport which, as we have already discussed, is not as advanced in its governance systems and practices compared to many other sectors.

With this approach, the rules are prescriptive, with defined sanctions for transgressions. For sports organisations, such rules, and the sanctions, can most commonly be found in various pieces of legislation including the Data Protection Act 2018, Companies Act 2006, Employment Act 2008, Bribery Act 2010 and Equality Act 2010. Each Act has its own penalties to impose if the legislation is not followed. You and the employees/volunteers of your organisation must be aware of the key laws and provisions that apply to your sport.

The rules-based approach has the advantage of providing a set of minimum governance practices that must be followed by all organisations, and therefore some uniformity. In addition, there is clarity as regards potential liability.

The major drawback is that a strict adherence to this approach encourages form over substance (in other words, causing a 'box-ticking' approach) and makes organisations focus on legal liability rather than wider stakeholder interests, which is not good for engendering trust.

Principles-based approach

A principles-based approach requires an organisation to adhere to the spirit, rather than the letter, of any applicable governance code(s). The most prominent example of a principles-based governance code in sport is the Code for Sports Governance for those organisations under the remit of UK Sport and Sport England.

An organisation must either comply with the provisions of a code or explain why it has not. This is done by providing written reports to the appropriate body overseeing the particular code. These explanations must also be supplied to your members. However, the principles-based approach does not mean that organisations have a choice not to adhere. It just means you can temporarily explain why it has not.

UK Sport and Sport England have already taken some significant actions against sports for non-compliance with the Code for Sports Governance, including suspending funding until the necessary governance changes have been made. In addition, compliance by the executives of the sports organisation can be done by the members, as they have the ultimate power to vote an individual(s) off the board of an organisation, as well as non-executive independent board members.

The principles-based approach has a number of advantages over the rules-based approach:

- Because the executives of the sport report on the circumstances of their own company, the report should be more meaningful than one based on specific detailed requirements.
- A code of governance practice can be changed much more easily than statutory requirements, meaning that such a code can be updated to respond to changing conditions and changing expectations of stakeholders.
- A principles-based approach encourages the executives to follow the spirit of a particular governance code, whereas a rules-based approach may result in a 'tick-box' mentality.

However, given that the leaders of the sport must report on their own organisation, the effectiveness of the code relies significantly on their honesty, integrity and commitment to good governance. Also, it is possible that the principles in a code may be so broad that they are of very little use as a guide to best governance practice, which can make compliance difficult.

Stakeholder approach

An alternative approach to the requirements of good organisational governance is based on stakeholder theory. This argues that the aim of sound governance is not just to meet the objectives of shareholders/members, but also to have regard for the interests of other individuals and groups impacted by the performance and conduct of an organisation, including the public at large. This thinking is a comparatively new approach in the corporate governance and regulatory landscape; however, in sport, this has perhaps always been true given that most sports organisations do not have profit maximisation as their main objective.

From a 'stakeholder view', governance is concerned with achieving a balance between economic and social goals, and between individual and communal goals. Sound governance for sports organisations should recognise the economic imperatives they face in an increasingly tough economic environment and should encourage the efficient use of resources through sound decision making.

This approach also requires accountability from the executives/board of an organisation to the members, who should ensure the stewardship of those resources. Within this framework, the aim should be to recognise the interests of other stakeholder groups, including individuals, international federations, sponsors, broadcasters and society at large, in the decisions and activities of the company.

Selected advantages of a stakeholder-oriented system include the active integration of stakeholder knowledge, increased commitment for strategic decisions and a longer-term view on performance.

A problem with the stakeholder approach is that, if your organisation is incorporated, company law gives certain rights to shareholders and there are some legal duties on the board of directors towards their company. These often trump the interests of other stakeholders, whose rights are not reinforced to any great extent by company law, other than for employees and now s. 172 of the Companies Act 2006 (see below). However, other aspects of the law do offer more specific protection to the organisation's wider stakeholders – for instance, specific employment laws and health and safety law (for example, fans attending matches).

The success of a stakeholder approach ultimately relies upon the directors/ executives fostering cooperative and productive relationships and achieving the 'buy-in' of the organisation's membership. This can be a delicate balancing act.

The enlightened shareholder approach

The enlightened shareholder approach to corporate governance is that the executives of an organisation should pursue the interests of their shareholders/ members, but in an enlightened and inclusive way. It is a form of compromise between the agency view (that the executives act as the agents of the members) and the stakeholder view. In essence, this approach focuses on generating shareholder/member value, while having regard to the long-term external impacts of the commercial drivers and decisions made by the board.

The organisation, and its directors/executives should look to the long term, not just the short term; they should also have regard to the interests of other company stakeholders, not just the shareholders.

This trickles down to the managers within your organisation, who should be aware of the need to create and maintain productive relationships with a range of stakeholders having an interest in your sport.

This theory can be found for the first time in English and Welsh company law in s. 172 of the Companies Act 2006 regarding the directors' duty to promote the success of the company:

172 Duty to promote the success of the company
    (1) A director of a company must act in the way he considers, in good faith, would be most likely to promote the success of the company for the benefit of its members as a whole, and in doing so have regard (amongst other matters) to –
        (a) the likely consequences of any decision in the long term,
        (b) the interests of the company's employees,
        (c) the need to foster the company's business relationships with suppliers, customers and others,
        (d) the impact of the company's operations on the community and the environment,
        (e) the desirability of the company maintaining a reputation for high standards of business conduct, and
        (f) the need to act fairly as between members of the company.
    (2) Where or to the extent that the purposes of the company consist of or include purposes other than the benefit of its members, subsection (1) has effect as if the reference to promoting the success of the company for the benefit of its members were to achieving those purposes.

Integrated stakeholder-inclusive approach

A final approach to governance which can be applied to sports organisations stems from the King Code or King Report, developed by the Institute of Directors (IoD) in South Africa. It is currently in its fourth incarnation (King IV) and advocates a stakeholder-inclusive approach, which is what King IV believes is a key part of 'integrated thinking'.

This approach means that a governing body takes account of the legitimate and reasonable needs, interest and expectations of all material stakeholders in the execution of its duties in the best interests of the organisation over time. In doing so, your organisation will be giving parity to all sources of value creation, including social and relationship capital as represented by stakeholders.

Being 'stakeholder-inclusive' involves the board balancing competing interests in the sport over time. This is far from straightforward, and is a dynamic and ongoing process which must at all times be done in the best interests of the organisation over the long term. The engagement and quality of relationships with the sport's stakeholders will affect your organisation significantly.

When considering the above, although the enlightened shareholder and the stakeholder-inclusive models both take the view that the board should consider the interests and expectations of stakeholders other than shareholders, the two models differ significantly in their emphasis. With the former, stakeholders are only considered in so far as it would be in the interests of shareholders to do so. With the latter, the board of directors considers the legitimate interests and expectations of stakeholders on the basis that this is in the best interests of the company, and not merely an instrument to best serve the interests of the shareholders.

Sport-specific codes of governance

A broad range of codes and other tools are available to aid you in governing your organisation and sport. Some are voluntary, while others need to be complied with in order to obtain public funding, which is often the lifeblood to operate and sustain many sports organisations. The key to the success of your organisation from a governance perspective will not be just to know the codes and principles, but to use the tools to identify the areas where your organisation requires improvement to become 'fit for purpose'.

Code for Sports Governance (UK Sport/Sport England)

In December 2015, the UK Government published its strategy 'Sporting Future', which included an announcement that a new governance code was to be developed and agreed by September 2016. The UK Sports Governance Code was to be mandatory for all sports bodies seeking public funding, and those that did not meet the requirements of the code would not be eligible for public funding.

The Code for Sports Governance was launched in October 2016 and was to have effect for those who ask for Government and National Lottery funding from April 2017. The Code sets out the levels of transparency, accountability and financial integrity that will be required to obtain public funding.

The Code is designed around five key principles:

1. *Structure* – sports organisations must have a clear and appropriate governance structure, led by a board which is collectively responsible for the long-term success of the organisation and exclusively vested with the power to lead it. The board shall be properly constituted, and shall operate effectively.
2. *People* – organisations shall recruit and engage people with appropriate diversity, independence, skills, experience and knowledge to take effective decisions that further the organisation's goals.
3. *Communication* – organisations shall be transparent and accountable, engaging effectively with stakeholders and nurturing internal democracy.
4. *Standards and conduct* – organisations shall uphold high standards of integrity, and engage in regular and effective evaluation to drive continuous improvement.
5. *Policies and processes* – organisations shall comply with all applicable laws and regulations, undertake responsible financial strategic planning and have appropriate controls and risk management procedures.

Each of these principles are supported by a set of requirements and then detailed commentary to aid implementation of the Code.

The Code will apply differently to your organisation depending on its size and/ or the amount of funding received, and you will be placed into one of three tiers as follows.

Tier 1

This is the minimum level of mandatory governance requirements in the Code. All organisations seeking funding will need to meet at least the basic governance requirements of Tier 1. Your organisation will be categorised as Tier 1 if it is granted on a one-off basis (for example, for a specific project which has a finite life) and the total amount of funding is less than or equal to £250,000.

Tier 2

Investments will be placed into Tier 2 where UK Sport and/or Sport England require organisations to go further than the requirements in Tier 1, but not as far as full compliance with Tier 3. The exact Tier 2 requirements to be met, and the timeline for compliance, will depend on the nature of the investment and the circumstances of the organisation. Investments falling into Tier 2 are likely to be in the region of £250,000–£1 million.

Tier 3

This tier represents the top level of mandatory governance requirements in this Code. The requirements in this tier seek to ensure high governance standards because of the significant public investment. Such requirements will have to be made within defined time frames. An investment will be categorised as Tier 3 if it is intended to be granted over a period of years and the total amount of funding is greater than £1 million.

This tiered approach has been taken by UK Sport and Sport England to achieve some form of proportionality with the regulation and avoid unnecessary administrative, and consequently financial, burdens.

If you are having difficulty applying and implementing the Code despite the guidance, UK Sport and Sport England should provide support to achieve the standards.

Governance and Leadership Framework for Wales

In late 2014, Sport Wales and the Sport and Recreation Alliance began to facilitate a move by Welsh governing bodies to create a structured programme of leadership and governance development. Following six months of consultation with over 50 NGBs, a framework was produced and published in April 2015; this sets out what Sport Wales believes to be the minimum standard of governance and the expected leadership behaviours of those running sports in the country.

The Framework is designed to be flexible, simple and not prescriptive. It provides the principles of good governance, effective behaviours, practical recommendations and minimum expectations for sports organisations in Wales.

Unlike the Code, the Framework is not mandatory. However, by signing up to it, your organisation will be making a long-term commitment to aspire to good governance and leadership and to integrate the principles and behaviours across your organisation. They are a guide and hopefully stimulus to both improve and then maintain the governance of your organisation. It is then left to each individual organisation as to how to implement the principles of the Framework and develop them.

The seven principles of the Framework are as follows:

1. *Integrity*: this means acting as guardians of the sport, recreation, activity or area. The board must uphold the highest standards of integrity not only in what it does but also in the wider environment of its sport, recreation, activity or area.
2. *Defining and evaluating the role of your board*: the board needs to understand and evaluate the role it plays and the way it contributes to the organisation.
3. *Setting vision, mission and purpose*: the board should set the strategy and vision of the organisation and ensure that it is followed without becoming involved in the operational delivery.
4. *Objectivity*: the board should be balanced, inclusive and skilled. It should be made up of individuals with the right balance of skills, knowledge and experience to meet the needs of the organisation. This includes independent expertise and representation of the diversity of the sport and the communities that the organisation serves.
5. *Standards, systems and controls*: the board needs to be conscious of the standards it should operate to, and of its role in exercising appropriate and effective control of the organisation.
6. *Accountability and transparency*: the board needs to be open and accountable to its athletes, participants and members, and its actions should stand up to scrutiny.
7. *Understanding and engaging with the sporting landscape:* the board needs to be aware of the international and domestic sporting environment, and position its organisation appropriately.

Each of the principles contains the following sections:

- minimum expectations
- other considerations
- success indicators
- effective behaviours
- ineffective behaviours ('I do not').

Sport Wales and the Sport and Recreation Alliance have developed an online support programme including guidance, toolkits and workshops to help you embed the principles and behaviours in your organisation.

Northern Ireland Code of Good Governance for the Voluntary and Community Sector

There is no specific governance guidance for sports organisations based in Northern Ireland. However, the Charity Commission for Northern Ireland has produced the Code of Good Governance for the Voluntary and Community Sector (NI Code), which can be applied to grass-roots sports organisations.

The NI Code was reviewed in 2014 with a revised code launched in 2016 by the Developing Governance Group. The Code is widely accepted in the country as the set of standards for governance in the voluntary and community sector.

The revised NI Code now contains five overarching principles, each deliberately broad and generic so that organisations of any size or type can use it. The five principles are equally important.

The NI Code says that an effective board will provide good governance and leadership by:

- understanding its role and responsibilities;
- working well both as individuals and as a team;
- ensuring delivery of organisational purpose;
- exercising appropriate control; and
- behaving with integrity and being open and accountable.

There are a number of complementary practical resources to help your organisation apply and implement the NI Code. These include a 'governance health check' and practical resources on the 'diycommitteeguide' website (www.diycommitteeguide.org). There is also reference to the Sport & Recreation Alliance's Voluntary Code of Good Governance for the Sports and Recreation Sector.

The NI Code is proactive and positive in that it tells organisations that are working to adhere to it that they should publicise this in their annual reports and other materials.

Scottish Governing Bodies' Governance Framework

Scotland's Home Country Sports Council, sportscotland, has produced the Scottish Governing Bodies Governance Framework (SGB Framework). When making investment decisions, sportscotland wants to ensure that the relationship between performance, development and good governance is fully integrated strategically and operationally and that the decisions are based on robust integrated plans with a clear focus on agreed outcomes.

sportscotland makes it clear in the SGB Framework that, as a publicly funded body, it has a high degree of accountability and is required to have high standards of governance. As a result, it expects all the organisations it invests in to be 'fit for purpose', well organised and well structured. In addition, organisations must make efficient and effective use of resources.

sportscotland states that the overarching aim of the SGB Framework is:

> to enhance governance in Scottish Governing Bodies of Sport (SGBs) ensuring they are well led; robust and legally compliant; and are effective and efficient in their operations, fostering strong partnerships. SGBs will be investment ready, positioned for growth and best placed to deliver outcomes for the sport. They will provide real results and return on investment to their members, sportscotland and other strategic partners.

Each of the 12 principles of good governance from the SGB Framework links into one of the following areas: well led; robust organisations; and strong networks. The principles for SGBs in Scotland to adhere to are as follows.

Well led
1. Commitment to implementing the Nolan Principles
2. Commitment to continuous improvement
3. Strategic planning framework
4. Appropriate board composition
5. Succession planning

Robust organisations
6. Effective performance management systems
7. Clear roles and responsibilities
8. Legally compliant
9. Effective control environment
10. Appropriate operational structure

Strong networks
11. Positive relations and partnerships
12. Proactive GB and home country engagement

Each of the principles provides the following information/guidance to answer the following questions:

- What does it look like?
- How will we know we've achieved it?
- Where can I find out more?

The Principles of Good Governance for Sport and Recreation
The Sport and Recreation Alliance (SRA) is a membership body providing advice, support and guidance to grass-roots organisations in the UK sports sector. It has 320 members (largely sports governing bodies) and speaks up on your behalf, represents your views and provides services which assist with the governance

of your sport. As part of the SRA's stated remit to provide advice, support and guidance to sport to help it grow, thrive and be fit for the future, it has taken a keen interest in good governance.

This began in 2011 when it published its first Voluntary Code of Good Governance for the Sports and Recreation Sector, an aspirational target for good governance in sport and recreation, which was then revised in 2014. This has now been superseded by the SRA's new Principles of Good Governance for Sport and Recreation (Principles) which were launched in May 2017, carrying on the same message of gold-standard good governance of the Voluntary Code while taking account of updates in the sports sector and providing additional resources and support.

The SRA says that the Principles represent best practice in governance, developed through its experience working with organisations across the sector. Adopting these principles is the first step towards a sustainable and successful future for your organisation.

Each of the seven Principles is accompanied by a list of recommended actions to achieve better governance. The Principles are intended to be applied flexibly and proportionally, according to the size and structure of your organisation. They are targeted principally at the board of your organisation, and each Principle provides both 'supporting governance actions' and 'guidance notes'.

The seven Principles are as follows:

1. *Integrity*: the board should uphold the highest standards of integrity within the organisation by embedding values and good practice, and promoting high ethical standards.
2. *Organisation's vision and mission*: the board is responsible for identifying and reviewing the values of the organisation, and should strive to achieve its vision and mission by creating a strategic plan that is best suited to maintaining the long-term stability of the organisation.
3. *Leadership and role of the board*: every organisation should have effective leaders and a board which has the right balance of skills and expertise needed for the long-term success of the organisation and its growth.
4. *Board structure*: the board must ensure its composition is balanced, inclusive and skilled, and reflects the diversity of the community it serves. Appropriate recruitment policies should be adopted to help ensure the right balance of individuals is elected to achieving their mission.
5. *Controls and compliance*: directors must understand and comply with the legal and regulatory requirements and be aware of their fiduciary duties, financial and risk obligations as part of their role.
6. *Accountability and transparency*: as guardians of the sport, the board is accountable to its stakeholders. To ensure an open and transparent culture, boards should engage with the wider sector as often as possible.
7. *Engaging with the sport and recreation landscape*: directors represent their organisation outside of their boardrooms and therefore must engage and

maintain strategic relationships with key stakeholders and other governing bodies.

In addition to the Principles, there is a helpful section regarding effective board behaviours that you can implement in your organisation:

- *Protect integrity*: this applies both to the board as a collective and the individual members; both must act objectively and with complete independence. Conflicts of interest within sport boards are particularly sensitive matters and must be managed proactively and transparently.
- *Encourage understanding*: all board members must have a thorough understanding of their organisation and be united in implementing and demonstrating the organisation's shared visions and values.
- *Create an effective environment*: this is all about communication with the board and between the board and the rest of the organisation – you must be prepared to challenge, and be challenged, in a positive and constructive way. This will create a rigorous, improved decision-making process.
- *Respect the process*: there is a saying that 'preparation prevents poor performance'; the same is true of being an effective board member. There has to be a culture within the board of constructive feedback and continuous improvement.

Better Boards, Stronger Sport toolkit

The project that led to the Better Boards, Stronger Sport toolkit was led by the SRA. However, rather than focusing on the UK, the toolkit was a European Commission-funded project aimed at 'promoting innovative approaches to strengthen the organisation of sport in Europe' as part of the EU funding for Preparatory Action in the Field of Sport 2011.

After much consultation with the sports movement across Europe, the toolkit was created, and is designed to:

- identify and agree the key features and requirements for an effective sports board across Europe;
- promote the importance of strategic leadership and the role of the board in sports organisations; and
- empower sports organisations to take responsibility for governing their future successfully.

Crucially, being a toolkit, it was designed to be used selectively and adapted to the needs and make-up of any sports organisation.

The toolkit is organised into three key sections:

1. features
2. case studies
3. tools and resources.

The first section of the toolkit comprises the ten 'features', which reflect the concepts that sports organisations in Europe believe to be critical to the development of good governance:

1. *Act in the best interests of the sport*: the board should behave with high ethical standards of honesty and fairness, and manage conflicts of interest to protect the reputation of the sport and the organisation.
2. *Define the role of the board and evaluate their performance*: the board as a whole and individual board members should have clearly defined roles.
3. *Establish a balanced competency-based board*: the board should be recruited from individuals with the right balance of skills and backgrounds to meet the needs of the organisation.
4. *Set the vision and mission and prove leadership on the strategy*: the board should prepare and consult on the vision, mission and strategy for the organisation, and then oversee the implementation of that strategy.
5. *Establish effective controls*: the board should ensure the organisation has controls in place to be legally compliant. In addition, it should be aware of best practice and oversee the development of efficient and effective controls.
6. *Act with transparency and be accountable to stakeholders*: the board should be open and accountable to its membership and stakeholders. The actions of the board should stand up to scrutiny.
7. *Engage with sporting and non-sporting bodies*: the board should understand and perform its role within the domestic and international sporting world, and seek opportunities with the non-sporting sector to develop initiatives for the benefit of sport.
8. *Work as a team*: the board should be effective as a team to support each other.
9. *Focus on membership*: the board should actively engage with members and enable their voices to be heard.
10. *Promote good governance throughout the sport:* the board should work with affiliated and regional sporting organisations and clubs to establish good governance at all levels.

For each Feature, the toolkit explains why it is both important and a challenge.

Ten case studies are included to illustrate each Feature; the Toolkit gives the key learning points, which are that implementing good governance leads to an increased chance of funding, change can be viewed as a threat to individuals within the organisation and other stakeholders, and that to overcome this threat, communication is key.

The latter two relate to the culture of an organisation. Whatever sector you work in, there will likely be significant resistance to cultural change. You must plan for this in particular because although it will often not be an issue of money, the strength of the emotional connection of individuals or groups involved in the running of your sport, with good intentions or otherwise, will make implementation even more prolonged and fraught. Great patience and communication skills will be imperative to achieve successful cultural and governance change.

The final piece of the toolkit is the 'tools' themselves. These are intentionally broad and adaptable, yet have great practical application for any sports organisations. They include:

- annual report
- board competencies
- board member appraisals
- board performance evaluation
- board skills audit
- code of conduct and ethics
- communication plan
- conflicts of interest policy
- conflicts of interest register
- defining vision, mission and strategy
- engaging non-sporting bodies
- financial procedures
- induction programme for new board members
- lobbying government
- membership management
- operational plan
- list of policies
- role descriptions for board members
- strategic plan
- team-building activities.

The tools you will use from this list will depend on the governance needs of your organisation and the sources of funding that apply to your organisation.

The IOC's Basic Universal Principles of Good Governance of the Olympic and Sports Movement & Olympic Agenda 2020

The IOC is arguably the most influential sports organisation globally, as all international sport federations have to comply with the provisions of the Olympic Charter (OC) to take part in the Olympic Games. Consequently, these requirements filter down the sporting pyramid to regional, national and local sports organisations. Therefore, you need an awareness and understanding of the approach and policies coming from the IOC.

Good governance is part of the Fundamental Principles of Olympism found at the start of the OC.

'Recognising that sport occurs within the framework of society, sports organisations within the Olympic Movement shall apply political neutrality. They have the rights and obligations of autonomy, which include freely establishing and controlling the rules of sport, determining the structure and governance of their organisations, enjoying the right of elections free from any outside influence and the responsibility for ensuring that principles of good governance be applied.' (Current edition in force from 9 October 2018).

Article 2.1 of the OC also states that one of the IOC's roles is, 'to encourage and support the promotion of ethics and good governance in sport'.

As part of the IOC's role in promoting that, each member of the IOC has to comply not only with the OC, but also with its Code of Ethics. Article 11 of the Code of Ethics (2018 edition) states that 'The Basic Universal Principles of Good Governance of the Olympic and Sports Movement, in particular transparency, responsibility and accountability, must be respected by all Olympic constituents'.

The IOC's Principles of Good Governance (PGG) were launched at a seminar on Autonomy of the Olympic and Sport Movement in February 2008. The PGGs are broken down into seven sections, each containing individual themes (with 38 themes in total), some of which are described below:

1. *Vision, mission and strategy.*
2. *Structures, regulations and democratic processes*: powers and size of each organ within a governing body – decision making – dealing with conflicts of interest – limited terms of office – avenue of appeal.
3. *Highest level of competence, integrity and ethical standards*: number of signatories for financial matters – internal management – communication and coordination – risk management process – selection and appointment of management.
4. *Accountability, transparency and control*: introduction of clear and measurable objectives and standards – application of internationally recognised standards to financial matters – ongoing training and education programme for staff.
5. *Solidarity and development*: clear and transparent policy for the allocation of resources underpinned by the need for them to be distributed in a fair and efficient manner – criteria for choosing event venues should be fair and transparent.
6. *Athletes' involvement, participation and care*: right of athletes to participate should be protected – refrain from discrimination – protect young athletes from exploitation and mistreatment – codes of conduct – protect athletes health – fight against doping – insurance – fairness and fair play – athlete education and career management.
7. *Harmonious relations with government while preserving autonomy*: cooperation, coordination and consultation towards common goals for both parties.

The PGG is a more holistic view of governance, very much reflecting the Fundamental Principles of Olympism approach. One example from the themes described above is the protection of athletes' health; this is increasingly important with the prevalence of legal actions being brought for issues such as doping and concussion.

Olympic Agenda 2020 is the strategic roadmap for the future of the Olympic Movement, which was agreed was unanimously agreed at the 127th IOC Session held in December 2014. It contains 40 recommendations covering a variety of areas. Recommendation 27 addressed the need for all organisations belonging to the Olympic Movement to accept and comply with basic principles of good governance, in particular, the PGG:

- Such compliance to be monitored and evaluated. Supporting tools and processes can be provided by the IOC in order to help organisations become compliant with the principles of good governance, if necessary.
- Organisations to be responsible for running self-evaluation on a regular basis. The IOC to be regularly informed of the results of the organisations' self-evaluations. In the event of missing such information, the IOC to request such an evaluation at its discretion.
- The PGG to be updated periodically, emphasising the necessity for transparency, integrity and opposition to any form of corruption.

Most recently in December 2016, in furtherance of Recommendation 27, the IOC produced a detailed and comprehensive document called *The consolidated minimum requirements for the implementation of the basic principles of good governance* which are also at the disposal of the NOCs (accessible here: https://stillmed.olympic.org/media/Document%20Library/OlympicOrg/IOC/ What-We-Do/Leading-the-Olympic-Movement/PGG-Implementation-and-Self-Evaluation-Tools-23-12-2016.pdf). This includes a self-evaluation tool which it would be useful for board members of a sports organisation to become familiar with. In particular, it can be used for evaluating the governance needs of an organisation.

The Seven Principles of Public Life

One set of principles that has been adopted by different sectors is the Nolan Principles. These can be applied to individuals in sports leadership roles and sports bodies.

Background to the Nolan Principles

Following ethical concerns regarding the conduct of some Westminster MPs in 1994, the then Prime Minister, John Major, set up the Committee on Standards in Public Life (CSPL).

The first Chair of the CSPL was Lord Nolan, and the principles set out in the first report have since become embedded in public life in Britain. They are often referred to as the Nolan Principles.

Committee on the Standards in Public Life

The CSPL is an independent advisory non-departmental public body funded by the Cabinet Office and its main purpose is to examine current concerns about standards of conduct of all holders of public office.

Individuals to whom Nolan Principles apply

The seven Principles of Public Life apply to anyone who works as a public office-holder including those in the civil service, local government and non-departmental public bodies (including sports councils).

While officers of British sports bodies operate in the voluntary sector, many organisations choose to adopt these principles on the basis that they reflect the values and standards expected of their leaders.

The seven Principles of Public Life

The seven Nolan Principles are as follows:

1. *Selflessness*: holders of public office should act solely in terms of the public interest. They should not do so in order to gain financial or other benefits for themselves, their family or their friends.
2. *Integrity*: holders of public office should not place themselves under any financial or other obligation to outside individuals or organisations that might seek to influence them in the performance of their official duties.
3. *Objectivity*: in carrying out public business, including making public appointments, awarding contracts, or recommending individuals for rewards and benefits, holders of public office should make choices on merit.
4. *Accountability*: holders of public office are accountable for their decisions and actions to the public, and must submit themselves to whatever scrutiny is appropriate to their office.
5. *Openness*: holders of public office should be as open as possible about all the decisions and actions that they take. They should give reasons for their decisions and restrict information only when the wider public interest clearly demands it.
6. *Honesty*: holders of public office have a duty to declare any private interests relating to their public duties and to take steps to resolve any conflicts arising in a way that protects the public interest.
7. *Leadership*: holders of public office should promote and support these principles by leadership and example.

Application of Nolan Principles to sports organisations

Members and stakeholders of sports organisations can reasonably expect the same standards of board members and senior executives as those listed in the Nolan Principles. This is why many sports bodies, including NGBs, have adopted the principles, as they provide a sound basis for ethical leadership.

How the Nolan Principles support organisational values

The Nolan Principles can provide a helpful guide to voluntary bodies regardless of their legal status or size. Specifically, the principles assist in setting the standards of behaviour expected of an organisation's leaders – whether this is a club, regional body or NGB. As sports organisations come under increasing scrutiny, the adoption of trusted principles can help build the confidence of stakeholders. These principles can be aligned with organisational values that all board members, staff and volunteers are expected to demonstrate. For example, England Athletics values are pride, integrity and inclusivity, while England Hockey values are teamwork, pride, respect and openness.

Adopting the Nolan Principles within governance frameworks

In 2000, the Scottish Executive identified nine key principles underpinning public life in Scotland, which determine the key behaviours of public bodies, their board members and officers.

In 2014 sportscotland, the Scottish Sports Council integrated the principles into its SGB Governance Framework. The rationale for this decision was that, as a publicly funded body, sportscotland expected all the organisations it invested in to be 'fit for purpose', well organised and well structured, and to make efficient and effective use of resources at their disposal.

The 12 principles of good governance for SGBs in Scotland start with a commitment to implementing the Nolan Principles. The SGB Governance Framework sets out how SGBs can demonstrate this commitment.

Table 2.1: SGB Governance Framework – Principle 1

Principle 1 **Area:** Well led
What does it look like? The SGB is recognised by sportscotland and its peers as conforming to the highest principles of integrity, honesty and openness in public service, respected by members, partners and stakeholders. Board members understand the value of implementing the Nolan Principles in all they do, embedding ethical standards in the policies, practices and culture of their organisation.
How will we know we've achieved it? • Analysis through the Development Audit • Commitment to deliver against an equality policy • Bye laws include description and requirement for board members to adhere to an agreed code of conduct • Regular review of procedures • Board members sign up to a conflict of interest register • Board members act in a way that reflects the Nolan Principles

The Nolan Principles are also visible in the Code for Sports Governance, Governance and Leadership Framework for Wales and the Northern Ireland Code of Good Governance for the Voluntary Sector. Table 2.2 shows an example.

Table 2.2: Application of Nolan Principles to sports governance codes and frameworks

Nolan Principles	Sports governance code	Code text
Integrity	Code for Sports Governance	**Standards and conduct** Organisations shall uphold high standards of integrity, and engage in regular and effective evaluation to drive continuous improvement.
	Governance and Leadership Framework for Wales	**Integrity** The board must uphold the highest standards of integrity not only in what it does but in the wider environment of its sport, recreation, activity or area.
	Northern Ireland Code of Good Governance for the Voluntary Sector	**Principle 5** An effective board will provide good governance and leadership by behaving with integrity and by being open and accountable.

Applying the Nolan Principles to board members

Taking the example of integrity, a code of conduct can make clear to all leaders the ways in which integrity is demonstrated and the consequences of any failures in meeting the standards required.

Relevant legislation

UK Charities Acts

Not all sports organisations are registered charities but those who are, in England in Wales, are subject to the Charities Act 2011. The key aim of this Act was to simplify and clarify the law. The Charity Commission is the independent regulator in England and Wales and is responsible for registering and regulating charities in England and Wales.

In Scotland, the Charities and Trustee Investment (Scotland) Act 2005 provides the regulatory framework designed to support and encourage charitable activity in Scotland. The Office of the Scottish Charity Regulator (OSCR) was established to register and regulate charities.

The Charity Commission for Northern Ireland was established under the Charities Act (Northern Ireland) 2008 (amended 2013). Its core functions include the registration of charities, facilitating better administration of charities and investigating misconduct.

The Commissions' priorities are generally to register and support charities, and to ensure compliance and accountability.

Charities are organisations established with purposes that are exclusively charitable; these must be set out in the objects clause of the governing document. These objects must fall under one of the Charities Act's charitable purposes, and 'the advancement of amateur sport' is listed as a charitable purpose. To achieve and maintain charitable status, sports bodies must demonstrate how their purposes benefit the public. The objects are contained in the organisation's articles and must also be reflected in any strategy or business plan.

All charitable organisations registered under charity law in England and Wales must publicise their charitable status on all written material. This is to ensure that anyone supporting it knows that it is properly regulated and that any money donated will be correctly used as per the stated objectives of the charity.

If a registered charity has gross income in excess of £10,000, it must clearly state the organisation's charitable status in all:

- notices;
- advertisements and other documents issued by or on behalf of the charity and soliciting money or other property for the benefit of the charity;
- bills of exchange, promissory notes, endorsements, cheques and orders for money or goods purporting to be signed on behalf of the charity; and
- bills rendered by it and in all its invoices, receipts and letters of credit.

Charities registered under company and charity law must show the following information on their stationery:

1. the full charity name;
2. the place of registration, such as England and Wales;
3. the company registration number;
4. the address of its registered office; and
5. the words Registered Charity.

This applies to all formats in which these documents are produced, including hard copy and electronic.

Duties of trustees

Section 177 of the Charities Act 2011 defines trustees as 'the persons having the general control and management of the administration of a charity'. The Charities Commission requires trustees to fulfil all their duties in the Act and to apply good practice in running their charities.

The duties below have been drawn from the Charities Act 2011. If your organisation is a registered charity in England and Wales, whatever its size or capacity, you must comply with them.

Ensure the charity is carrying out its purposes for the public benefit
Trustees must:

- ensure they understand the charity's purposes as set out in its governing document;
- plan what the charity will do, and what they want it to achieve;
- be able to explain how all of the charity's activities are intended to further or support its purposes; and
- understand how the charity benefits the public by carrying out its purposes.

For example, a club that has local youth development enshrined in its objects must be able to demonstrate through its activities that it is using its resources to engage and develop young people.

Comply with the charity's governing document and the law
Trustees must:

- make sure that the charity complies with its governing document; and
- comply with charity law requirements and other laws that apply to your charity.

An effective induction will help new trustees understand the charity's objectives and how it benefits the public through its activities.

Act in the charity's best interests
Trustees must:

- decide how to best enable the charity to carry out its purposes – this is a fundamental role of the board as a whole and cannot be delegated;
- make balanced and adequately informed decisions, thinking about the long term and short term;
- avoid putting themselves in a position where the duty to the charity conflicts with personal interests or loyalty to any other person or body; and
- not receive any benefit from the charity unless it is properly authorised and is clearly in the charity's interests; this includes anyone who is financially connected to a trustee, such as a partner, dependent child or business partner.

Individual trustees in sports organisations, particularly if they have been elected by a constituent group, may find themselves in a situational conflict. For example, members in a designated region may elect a trustee because they believe the trustee will act in that region's best interests. The law is clear on this point: individuals will pay due regard to the needs of stakeholders, including members; however, they must act in the best interests of the charity as a whole.

Manage the charity's resources responsibly

Trustees must:

- make sure the charity's assets are only used to support or carry out its purposes;
- avoid exposing the charity's assets, beneficiaries or reputation to undue risk;
- not over-commit the charity;
- take special care when investing or borrowing; and
- comply with any restrictions on spending funds or selling land.

This might include developing a suite of policies in respect of data protection, fraud and whistleblowing. Robust business planning and risk management also underpin sound resource management.

Act with reasonable care and skill

Trustees must:

- use reasonable care and skill, making use of their skills and experience and taking appropriate advice when necessary; and
- give enough time, thought and energy to the role, for example, by preparing for, attending and actively participating in all trustees' meetings.

Ensure your charity is accountable

Trustees must:

- be able to demonstrate that the charity is complying with the law and is well run and effective;
- ensure appropriate accountability to members, if the charity has a membership separate from the trustees; and
- ensure accountability within the charity, particularly where particular tasks or decisions are delegated to staff or volunteers.

Well-run sporting charities will consider governance as a priority and will regularly review their policies, practices and programmes to ensure they are implementing best practice. The adoption of governance codes, such as the Code for Sports Governance, provides direction and guidance that will create sound governance processes.

In July 2017, the revised Charity Governance Code was launched. This is the third edition of the governance code for the charity sector and, although it remains a voluntary framework, sporting charities should give consideration to the principles and guidance therein.

Companies Act 2006

The Companies Act 2006 (CA 2006) was brought into force in stages, and has been subject to additions and amendments since the first provisions were enacted in 2006. The Act provides a comprehensive code of company law for the UK. The key provisions are as follows.

Formation of a company

- Companies may be incorporated online.
- A new format memorandum states that the subscribers declare their wish to form a company and agree to take the stated number of shares.
- The statement of proposed officers remains the same, but directors must now supply an address.
- No company secretary is required for private companies.

Members and management

- The minimum age for directorship is 16 years.
- Every company must have a director who is a natural person (a human being).
- Directors' duties are codified in statute.

Decision making – meetings and resolutions

- Annual general meetings (AGMs) are no longer required for private companies unless the companies wish to hold them or their articles require them to. Members may still require their directors to call a general meeting.
- The minimum notice of meetings is 14 days for private companies.
- Minutes of general meetings and records of written resolutions must now be kept for a minimum of 10 years.
- Special resolutions require 21 days' notice and can only be passed by a 75% majority.

Accounts and audit

- The time limit for filing accounts with Companies House is reduced to nine months for private companies.
- Directors have a duty not to approve accounts unless they give a true and fair view of the company's financial position.
- Accounts must be signed by a director.
- The general prohibition against a company indemnifying its auditor against claims for negligence remains. However, there is a new provision enabling auditors to make a 'liability limitation agreement' with a client company.

This is a summary of the provisions as applied to private companies. Sports bodies should review and assure themselves that they have sufficient grasp of their legal obligations. As noted above, directors' duties are now codified in the Act, and individuals who accept the position of director should quickly acquaint themselves with these duties before joining a board.

Duties of directors

Directors have certain legal duties; these are to the company itself, not to its shareholders, its employees or any person external to the company. The duties of directors were introduced into UK statute law by CA 2006 (ss. 171–77).

The duties apply to non-executive directors as well as to executive directors, and are listed below.

Duty to act within powers

A director must act within their powers in accordance with the company's constitution; they should only exercise these powers for the purpose for which they were granted.

Duty to promote the success of the company

A director, in good faith, must act in the way they consider would be most likely to promote the success of the company for the benefit of its members as a whole. A director must also have regard, among other matters, to the:

- likely long-term consequences of any decision;
- interests of the company's employees;
- need to foster the company's relationships with its customers, suppliers and others;
- impact of the company's operations on the community and the environment;
- desirability of the company maintaining its reputation for high standards of business conduct; and
- need to act fairly between members of the company.

There is no requirement that any one factor is given precedence over another, but the board must demonstrate it has at least considered the needs of stakeholders in its decisions. In addition, there is nothing in the Act that suggests one stakeholder should have greater significance than another. The organisation's constitution should be properly constructed to ensure directors fully understand their duties, including those to members.

Duty to exercise independent judgement

The duty to exercise independent judgement applies to all directors whether or not they are considered independent for the purpose of relevant governance codes.

Directors with a particular interest should set aside any representative function and make final decisions on their own merits. All directors, regardless of how they are appointed, must demonstrate independent judgement.

Duty to exercise reasonable care, skill and diligence

No directorship is an honorary position, even for volunteers. It is a serious position and the law requires directors to use reasonable care, skill and diligence in carrying out their tasks.

There is a double test within the Act. First, the objective standard – a board member must have the knowledge, skill and experience that would reasonably be expected to anyone doing that job. This is a basic level of competence expected from all directors. Second, the subjective standard – a director has to perform according the knowledge, skill and experience they actually have. This is a higher standard expected of those with special skill or experience – for example, a qualified accountant. They will be expected to use that expertise for the company's benefit and will be judged by the higher standard.

Duty to avoid conflicts of interest

Board members have a duty to avoid conflicts of interest; however, this duty is not breached if the director declares to the board their interest in a transaction and the interest is approved by the board.

A director might have a direct or indirect interest in a contract, for example, a volunteer director who is an employee of another company with which the sports organisation is planning to sign a business contract. Such a contract is not illegal, although the company may choose to cancel it.

The Companies Act 2006 recognises certain situations in which an actual or potential conflict of interest may arise. These include situations where a director sits on two boards and the duties to each may conflict. This can occur in sport as NGB directors may also be board members of affiliated bodies, trustees of a related charity or nominated by another organisation with its own constitution and legal identity.

All of the situations above can amount to a breach of duty if they are not declared and managed in a transparent manner by the board.

Duty to declare interests in proposed transactions with the company

For example, a director may own a sports clothing company that wants to supply kit for teams at an event.

Proposed transactions do not necessarily create a conflict of interest, but they must be declared, and be subject to approval by the rest of the board. There should be a robust conflict of interest policy which sets out how individual directors and the board will manage such situations. Establishing a transparent tendering or bidding process will also ensure the organisation can secure suppliers that provide the best available product and value for money.

Duty not to accept benefits from third parties

It is not uncommon for board members and senior executives to be offered tickets to major sporting events in an effort to foster good relations between organisations. CA 2006 says that a director must not accept a benefit from a third party that was offered because of the director's position or because of anything they may do as a director. In the sporting world, it would be regarded as reasonable to accept an invitation to a sector-specific awards ceremony or a sporting event. However, sports board members must be mindful that they may be perceived as seeking and enjoying benefits in excess of those that would be deemed reasonable.

Equality Act 2010
Background
The Equality Act 2010 brings together all previous equality legislation in England, Scotland and Wales. The Act covers exactly the same groups of individuals that were protected by the previous legislation including the Race Relations Act (1975), Equal Opportunities Act (1976) and Disability Discrimination Act (1996).

The Act aims to protect people who share certain characteristics and prevent all forms of discrimination. The protected characteristics are age, disability, gender reassignment, marriage and civil partnership, pregnancy and maternity, race, religion or belief, sex and sexual orientation.

In Northern Ireland, s. 75 of the Northern Ireland Act 1998 requires public bodies to have due regard to the need to promote equality of opportunity between persons of different religious belief, political opinion, racial group, age, marital status, sexual orientation, men and women generally, persons with a disability or persons without, and persons with dependants and persons without.

Discrimination happens when a person treats, or proposes to treat, another person less favourably because they possess a particular characteristic as recognised in law. A person may also be discriminated against because they associate with someone who has the particular attribute.

The board is required to ensure their organisation complies with the Act as the duty to avoid discrimination also extends to the provision of goods, services and facilities. In the case of disability, sports bodies are required to adapt their services and facilities.

Provisions relating to private members' clubs
Although it is not possible to cover all aspects of the legislation in this study text, certain provisions have specific relevance to sport. The Act includes private members' clubs but contains a number of potential exemptions, provided that the club meets the definition of 'association' in the Act, which is an association of persons which has at least 25 members, and admission to membership of which is regulated by the association rules and involves a selection process.

An association will be able to allow members only from a specific protected characteristic (such as a specific sex, race, sexual orientation). However, where an association does allow members from different protected characteristics, it must treat all members equally. For example, a club that has both male and female members would not be allowed to restrict female members' use of the facilities to certain days or to restrict access to certain parts of the club house.

Gender reassignment in sport
Under the Equality Act 2010, transsexual people cannot be directly or indirectly discriminated against, nor can they be harassed.

Gender reassignment is not a protected characteristic covered under s. 75 of the NI Act; however, the Gender Reassignment Regulations (Northern Ireland)

1999 makes it unlawful to discriminate on grounds of gender reassignment (sex change) in employment and training.

In 2004, the International Olympic Committee (IOC) published its policy on the participation of transsexual people in the Olympic Games. This was known as the Stockholm Consensus. Following a number of high-profile cases involving transsexual, intersex and androgyne athletes, the IOC amended its position in November 2016.

Health and safety
Health and Safety at Work Act (1974)
Board members are collectively responsible for the health and safety of employees, volunteers and members of the general public who visit buildings when engaging with the organisation's activities. The Health and Safety at Work Act (1974) is the main legislation for health and safety, and there is a large and complex body of statutory regulation concerning health and safety. While this study text can only provide a brief introduction, sports boards must be sufficiently familiar with their obligations. This might involve taking external advice.

The Health and Safety Executive, along with the Institute of Directors, has published guidance which states that boards should:

■ set the direction for effective health and safety management – that is, develop and communicate a policy;
■ introduce management and practices that ensure risks are dealt with sensibly, responsibly and proportionately;
■ monitor and report with health and safety appearing on board agendas; and
■ undertake a formal boardroom view of health and safety performance.

Sports Grounds Safety Authority
Major spectator sports face unique health and safety challenges in creating the conditions for safe and enjoyable experiences for spectators at sports grounds. The Sports Grounds Safety Authority (SGSA) was established to carry out a range of statutory functions in relation to football in England and Wales and advisory functions in relation to other sports. The agency's statutory functions are set out in the Football Spectators Act 1989 and the Sports Ground Safety Authority Act 2011.

The SGSA provides a range of services to sports bodies and facility managers including:

■ stadium inspections;
■ advice on capacity calculations;
■ Green Guide compliance for new stadia;
■ training for stadium safety staff at all levels;
■ conference presentation and organisation; and
■ advice on the development of operations manuals and other documentation.

Employment legislation
Board members' employment responsibilities
Employment legislation applies to full-time, part-time, casual and temporary employees, and board members must be clear about those individuals who would be classed as employees under legislation. A self-employed person is not an employee and has no obligation beyond the specific piece of work for which they are contracted. In sport, a number of clubs and NGBs appoint coaches, instructors and others on a contract basis.

In general, employees have a right to certain benefits and conditions in the areas of leave, pay and conditions. These include (but are not limited to) rights to:

- not be discriminated against;
- equal pay;
- if part-time workers, be treated no less favourably than full-time workers;
- take leave in certain circumstances, including maternity leave;
- pay, including the minimum wage, statutory sick pay, sick pay, etc;
- not be unfairly dismissed; and
- protection when making disclosures of wrongdoing to the employer.

Board members must ensure that there are policies for recruitment ensuring applicants are treated fairly. They should also establish processes for appraisal, support, probationary periods and remuneration that are proportionate to the size of the organisation.

Chapter summary

- A rules-based approach to governance provides a set of minimum standards, but can be overly prescriptive.
- A principles-based approach encourages the executives of a sport to follow the spirit of a particular governance code and is therefore a more flexible approach.
- A stakeholder approach to governance is concerned with achieving a balance between economic and social goals, and between individual and communal goals. It is becoming a more common way in which to manage a sporting organisation.
- The enlightened shareholder approach focuses on generating value for members, while having regard to the long-term external impacts of the commercial drivers and decisions made by the organisation's board.
- The UK Sport/Sport England Code for Sports Governance sets out the levels of transparency, accountability and financial integrity that will be required to obtain public funding. There are also other applicable governance guides for Scotland, Wales and Northern Ireland.
- There are seven Principles of Good Governance for Sport and Recreation, each of which is accompanied by a list of recommended actions to achieve better governance.

- The IOC's Olympic Agenda 2020 Recommendation 28 addresses adapting and further strengthening the principles of good governance and ethics to changing demands. Subsequently, they have also produced a detailed document called 'The consolidated minimum requirements for the implementation of the basic principles of good governance' which includes a self-evaluation tool that can be used by any sports organisation.
- The Nolan Principles were published in 1995 and established the seven Principles of Public Life. These principles have been integrated into sports governance codes and individual sports organisations' codes of conduct.
- The Charities Act 2011 is the main piece of legislation affecting charities in England and Wales, and the Charity Commission is the independent regulator. In Scotland the Charities and Trustee Investment (Scotland) Act 2005 provides the regulatory framework and the Office of the Scottish Charity Regulator oversees Scottish charities. The Charity Commission for Northern Ireland was established under the Charities Act (Northern Ireland) 2008. Action 77 of the Charities Act 2011 sets out the six duties of trustees.
- The Companies Act 2006 sets out the duties of directors. Sections 171–77 set out the duties that apply to both non-executive and executive directors.
- Sports organisations are subject to a range of legislation including the Equality Act 2010, Freedoms Act 2012 and Health and Safety at Work Act 1974. Trustees and directors bear ultimate responsibility for their organisations meeting legal obligations.

3
Governance and business challenges in sport

▥ Introduction

This chapter outlines the ways in which boards can demonstrate ethical leadership and address governance risks. The sport sector faces new challenges to its integrity with corruption and illegal gambling, which have affected consumer and stakeholder confidence. International federations have a critical role to play in governing sports at the international level, and we shall explore their influence on NGBs.

▥ Governance challenges in the sport sector

The governance challenges facing sports organisations are multiple and complex, including doping and match fixing. Both of these have created significant threats to the integrity of the sector as a whole.

Doping

Doping refers to the use of banned substances and prohibited methods to improve athletic performance and it has become a significant risk to the integrity of sport. In 1999, to combat the rise in the use of prohibited drugs, the World Anti-Doping Agency (WADA) was established as an international agency composed and funded equally by the sports movement and world governments.

One of WADA's most significant achievements is the development of the World Anti-Doping Code, first published in 2004. The Code aims to harmonise anti-doping policies, rules and regulations within sports organisations and among public authorities. In order for sports to be included on the Olympic and Paralympic Games programmes, international federations and Olympic and Paralympic Committees must demonstrate compliance with the Code. There is usually a National Anti-Doping Agency that creates national anti-doping policies, but some smaller nations work as part of a Regional Anti-Doping Division. Each national anti-doping policy is wholly aligned with the Code to ensure that the same standards, rules, regulations and sanctions apply as athletes progress from national to international competition. NGBs must demonstrate compliance with the national policy to receive public funding.

Doping scandals have caused significant harm to the integrity and reputation of sport. In the 1998 Tour de France, none of the riders were caught doping by any of the ordinary doping controls at the time. Nevertheless, police searches and interrogations proved the existence of organised doping by the Festina and TVM teams, which consequently had to withdraw from the race. Years later, retrospective tests and rider confessions confirmed that erythropoietin (EPO) was something the majority of riders had been using. In 2013 Lance Armstrong, who had won seven Tours, was stripped of his titles and banned from cycling for life after admitting the use of performance-enhancing drugs (PEDs).

Following an investigation into the mishandling of doping tests and corruption at the International Association of Athletics Federations (IAAF) and reports from investigative journalists, Richard McLaren was commissioned by WADA to investigate allegations of systematic doping by Russian authorities. His report, presented in 2016, concluded that it was 'beyond reasonable doubt' that Russia's Ministry of Sport and WADA-accredited laboratory had 'operated for the protection of doped Russian athletes'. Russian sport and ministerial authorities rejected the report's conclusions; however, the entire Russian athletics team was suspended from all competitions by the IAAF. Individual Russian athletes who could demonstrate they had trained outside of Russia under a robust anti-doping regime were allowed to compete under a neutral flag. In addition, the International Paralympic Committee (IPC) voted to ban all Russian athletes from the Rio Paralympic Games. The IOC allowed international federations to decide on Russia's inclusion in their respective sports at the Rio Games.

Committing an anti-doping rule violation (ADRV) means that an athlete, coach or athlete support person could be liable for a sanction which may include a ban from the sport. The sanction for intentional cheating is a four-year ban for the first offence, and individuals are likely to receive at least a two-year ban for inadvertent doping. If banned, the athlete, coach or athlete support person cannot participate either in their sport or any other sport that follows WADA rules, including non-Olympic sports.

Sports and media commentators have suggested that drug-testing techniques do not evolve as quickly as PED development. This means, as demonstrated on the Tour de France in 1998, that testing alone will not necessarily identify athletes who take PEDs. Subsequently, the IOC, IPC and international federations have introduced retrospective testing that applies new techniques to samples from previous events. Several athletes have been banned because their samples tested positive, including medallists from the Beijing and London Olympic Games.

National anti-doping organisations, such as UK Anti-Doping (UKAD), have turned to specialists outside the world of sport to enhance intelligence gathering on doping. Although doping in sport is not a criminal offence in the UK, UKAD is increasingly drawing on legal and law enforcement expertise to identify the ways in which PEDs are sourced and supplied. Intelligence is also applied to the testing programmes, with some sports prioritised over others. This policy relates to the physical requirements of the sport and historical testing results – for example, weightlifting, track sprinting and endurance events are deemed high-risk sports when compared to golf or archery.

International federations have sought to control doping through the establishment of sport-specific integrity units. The international federations for athletics and rugby have created such units with online platforms that enable confidential reporting of suspected doping.

Gambling

Online gambling has created a significant shift in public engagement with betting on a range of sports. Moreover, individual sportsmen and women and officials have become targets for illegal gambling as the potential for financial gains increase.

Spot betting, also known as spot fixing, involves betting on a small detail that may occur in a contest, for example, the exact timing of the first no-ball in a cricket, or whether the first serve in a tennis match is a double fault. In several cases, players have placed bets themselves and contrived to ensure the named event occurred. These include Southampton footballer Matt Le Tissier in a game against Wimbledon in 1995. With bookmakers predicting that the ball would go out of play for the first time after a minute, Le Tissier conspired to find touch almost immediately after kick-off and then make money having 'bought' under one minute; however, a team mate managed to keep the ball in play.

In 2011, members of the Pakistan national cricket team were convicted of taking bribes from bookmaker Mazhar Majeed to under-perform deliberately at certain times in a test match against England. The plan was for bowlers Mohammad Amir and Mohammad Asif to bowl no-balls at specific points in an over. This information was used by gamblers to place bets and, when the no-balls were bowled, secure big wins. A *News of the World* undercover operation exposed Majeed, Amir, Asif and another bowler, Salman Butt. They were all suspended by the International Cricket Council (ICC) and, following criminal investigations, given prison sentences.

Match fixing consists of dishonestly determining the outcome of a contest. In order to win a bet, gamblers approach players and officials and offer bribes to perform poorly on purpose so that they or their team loses the contest. This is problematic in team sports because it is difficult to involve the majority of the players and also managers and officials.

In 2013 Europol announced it had been investigating gambling in football. A total of 680 matches in 30 countries were investigated, 13,000 emails were analysed and 425 suspects identified, of whom 50 were arrested. The breadth of the investigation was unprecedented and helped to highlight the scale of the problem facing sport.

The IOC and a number of international federations have set up integrity units to monitor, investigate and manage gambling-related issues. These include the International Tennis Union and the ICC. In the UK, the Gambling Commission has also established the Sports Betting Intelligence Unit (SBIU) to help protect the integrity of sport and betting. The Commission has set up a confidential intelligence line to encourage alerts and has the power to bring prosecutions regarding criminal offences under S. 42 of the Gambling Act 2005.

This work is further supported by the Sports Betting Group, chaired by the Sport and Recreation Alliance, which brings together sports, player representative groups and experts to provide leadership and share good practice.

Governance corruption and ethical leadership

The national and international bodies that oversee different sports must ensure that the core values on which sport is founded are clearly communicated and upheld. The IOC, for example, highlights that one of its primary roles is 'to encourage and support the promotion of ethics and good governance in sport'. Creating robust policy frameworks and internal control systems assures members, athletes and other stakeholders that the board acknowledges and accepts this responsibility.

The organisers of international events are required to make decisions that have billion-dollar implications and affect a wide range of stakeholders. They are responsible for the selection of the host country and venue, the concession of broadcasting rights to TV networks and the negotiation of sponsorship deals with multinational organisations. Facing significant pressure from different stakeholders, sports bodies have not always been able to manage these relations properly and failed to prevent corruption taking hold.

In 2016, four senior IAAF officials were banned for life following an investigation into corruption, blackmail and extortion. An independent ethics commission found that the senior officials had conspired to conceal anti-doping violations in return for significant sums of money. The IAAF President's son, Papa Massata Diack, was one of the banned officials and the President, Lamine Diack, was also investigated for his involvement in corrupt practices. These investigations were undertaken at the same time as FIFA officials were being arrested and tried for corruption, creating a perception of sports leadership that was more about money and power than fair play.

In 2016 the IAAF approved constitutional changes that introduced greater checks and balances to eliminate the ability of the President to take major decisions alone, as was previously the case under Lamine Diack.

Clubs, community groups, NGBs and international federations have a board or executive committee that is tasked with setting the vision and values of the organisation. Board members are also required to demonstrate consistently the values if others in the organisation are to do the same.

Safeguarding

The Protection of Freedoms Act 2012 established the Disclosure and Barring Service (DBS), which processes criminal records checks and manages the Barred

Children's and Barred Adults' Lists of unsuitable people who should not work in regulated activities with these groups. If someone, whether paid or unpaid, is in regulated, face-to-face contact with children under 18 years of age or vulnerable adults, it is highly likely they will need a DBS check. This might mean that everyone from the referee to the physiotherapist may require a check – whether that be basic, enhanced or just a self-declaration form.

Sports boards should ensure that the organisation has assessed the level of check required for each role and that these are comprehensively managed. Safeguarding should be listed on the risk register with policies, procedures and accountability established and reviewed regularly. Further guidance is available from the NSPCC and Child Protection in Sport Unit (CPSU).

It is likely that safeguarding will appear in the organisation's risk register as, while processes and education will assist in mitigating the likelihood of a safeguarding incident, the impact will always be high. With this in mind, sports are expected to prioritise their safeguarding strategies.

Standards for Safeguarding and Protecting Children in Sport
All organisations across the UK must meet safeguarding standards in order to receive sports council funds. The Standards for Safeguarding and Protecting Children in Sport were launched in 2002 and their purpose is to:

- help create a safe sporting environment for children and young people and protect them from harm;
- provide a benchmark to assist those involved in sport to make informed decisions; and
- promote good practice and challenge practice that is harmful to children.

The Standards for Safeguarding and Protecting Children in Sport are available on the CPSU website: https://thecpsu.org.uk/media/1040/english-standards.pdf.

The CPSU is a partnership between the NSPCC, Sport England, Sport Northern Ireland and Sport Wales. In Scotland there is a similar partnership between Children 1st and sportscotland.

The Ann Craft Trust (ACT) receives funding from Sport England for the Safeguarding Adults in Sport project to help NGBs, regional partnerships and sports clubs to develop best practice in safeguarding adults at risk. The ACT also provides sport-specific guidance and training to sports bodies.

Equality, diversity and inclusion
The Equality Act 2010, covered in Chapter 2 (pages 45 and 46), sets out the organisation's legal duties. Discrimination in sport is illegal and widely condemned by stakeholders. Widening access can increase participation, membership and the number of volunteers and coaches; a more diverse board brings broader perspectives, skills and expertise to decision making, and inclusive organisations are more likely to secure public funds.

There have been several high-profile examples of sex discrimination in sport; for example, Lucy Ward successfully pursued an unfair dismissal and sex discrimination case against Leeds United football club in April 2016. Ward argued that she had been sacked in 2015 by the club's owner Massimo Cellino because she was the partner of former manager Neil Redfearn. The club was ordered to pay her £290,000, having claimed she was sacked for taking too much annual leave. The judge agreed with Ms Ward's legal team that the club had taken a 'sexist' view.

Football has faced several claims of institutional racism and sexism; however, the London Football Association (LFA) announced in August 2017 that it would overhaul its board as it aimed to better reflect the diversity of London. While retaining six directors with footballing experience, the LFA advertised for four independent directors with an emphasis on diversity in its search. The LFA is one of the few county football associations with a female CEO.

Within the Code for Sports Governance, one requirement for Tier 3 organisations funded by Sport England and UK Sport is to achieve at least 30% female representation on the board. Where the majority of a sport's board is female, at least 30% males are required. The governance challenge facing sports in meeting this requirement is the need to increase the number of women elected from within the sport. With less disposable time and income, greater caring responsibilities and lower participation rates, there are fewer female volunteers in sport than men. This reduces the talent pool available and can adversely affect the nomination process for board positions. Yet the requirement will have implications for the governance of sports bodies including NGBs, clubs and community organisations.

Equality Standard for Sport

The Equality Standard for Sport was launched in 2004, and by 2017 more than 240 sports organisations across the UK were implementing the Standard framework. The Standard is owned by the five sports councils and is endorsed by the Equality and Human Rights Commissions. All funded organisations must meet relevant levels of the Standard. The first organisation to achieve all four levels was the London Organising Committee of the Olympic Games (LOCOG), which had made visible commitments to diversity in all aspects of the planning and delivery of the 2012 Games.

The Standard has also been implemented by organisations that do not receive funding, including the National Association of Karate and Martial Art Schools (NAKMAS) and the British Gliding Association. It helps ensure the organisation has in place the necessary policies and procedures to meet legal obligations.

It also assists in creating positive action schemes to attract more diverse participants, volunteers and decision-makers. One example is the Us Girls scheme run by Street Games. The project focused on 50 disadvantaged areas across England with over 34,000 young women taking part in the initial sessions.

It was presented, promoted and organised on the basis of what teenage girls wanted from activity and has been successfully replicated in Wales.

The sports councils have created a website that provides the background, requirements and resources associated with the Equality Standard: www.equalityinsport.org.

Volunteers

With 3.2 million volunteers across the country, volunteering in sport is the biggest single sector. Join In, the scheme that aims to increase the number of volunteers in community sport, reported in 2014 that seven in ten sports clubs are looking for volunteers. The economic, health and social impacts of sports volunteering are reported in Join In's 2014 *Hidden Diamonds* report. The findings show that:

- sports volunteers have higher self-esteem, emotional well-being and resilience than those who have never volunteered;
- sports volunteers are 15% less likely to worry; and
- one volunteer creates the capacity for 8.5 more people to play, acting as a catalyst for multiplying benefits in their communities.

More information is available on the Join In website: www.joininuk.org.

Websites such as those of Sport England Clubmark and Sport Wales's Club Solutions offer practical guidance on the recruitment and retention of volunteers. By developing a clear plan, organisations can identify skills gaps, target under-represented groups and develop effective communications to attract new volunteers.

One of the legacies from the 2012 Games was the creation of the Spirit of 2012 charity that invests in national and international sports development projects. Included in the range of eligible projects is volunteering, and all Spirit-funded projects make use of volunteers in some capacity. Spirit of 2012 has developed a set of volunteering principles with which Spirit-funded projects must align. More information on these principles is available at www.spiritof2012trust.org. uk/our-volunteering-principles.

In 2015, the Social Action, Responsibility and Heroism Act 2015 came into force in England and Wales. Its purpose is to provide a greater degree of reassurance and protection to good Samaritans, volunteers and those who may be deterred from participating in socially useful activities due to worries about risk or liability. While the Act does not change the legal framework around claims in negligence, it will consider the context in which alleged negligence occurs and whether the individual (such as a volunteer) demonstrated a predominantly responsible approach and was acting for the benefit of others. In a sporting context, this may provide assurance to club and community volunteers who might be deterred by risk or liability when volunteering.

Financial and commercial challenges

Public funding for most NGBs is the primary source of revenue and often features on organisational risk registers, as the loss of public and National Lottery support would have significant impacts on the sport as a whole. There is now a requirement to co-fund sports programmes and this is enshrined in UK Sport funding Principle 7, which states that:

> To secure the long-term financial sustainability of the high performance system, we will expect National Governing Bodies to 'co-fund' the World Class Programme, and will release resources only where there is evidence of financial need.

Sport England, in its strategy *Towards an Active Nation*, also places greater emphasis on the sector itself generating new sources of income. Investment Principle 7 states:

> In future that investment will be more limited and we will encourage the sector to diversify its funding from both private and other public sector sources. We will also encourage them to use their assets – including data – to generate income, and to reduce costs, for example, by sharing services.

The challenge is clear, and to assist in generating revenue from alternative sources, sports are seeking individuals with commercial expertise for their boards. Ultimately, public monies available to NGBs are not likely to reach the heights experienced around the London 2012 Games, so the board will have to give greater consideration to commercial strategies. Therefore, board appointments, especially open recruitment of independent board members, are increasingly seeking individuals with commercial experience as sports build commercial strategies to complement existing funding streams.

Negotiating the complex legal and regulatory environment

The first step for any board member in negotiating the complex legal and regulatory environment is to understand the board's role and its duties. These are covered in Chapter 2 (pages 42 to 44) and Chapter 4 (pages 68 to 73). The nature of the duties should be captured initially in the role description, and new board members should receive a full induction that expands on their legal responsibilities.

The Companies Act 2006 includes regulations relating to:

- the preparation and auditing of annual financial statements, for approval by the shareholders;
- the powers and duties of directors;
- other disclosures to shareholders, such as the requirement for companies to publish a strategic report in their annual report and accounts;
- the disclosure of information about directors' remuneration;

- general meetings of companies, and shareholder rights to call a general meeting; and
- shareholder voting rights at general meetings, including the right to re-elect directors and have a binding vote on the company's remuneration policy.

Organisations should appoint individual board members with governance knowledge and expertise and also appoint a company secretary. Unlike public companies, private companies are not legally required to appoint a company secretary and should check their Articles of Association to see if there is an express requirement to do so. If no company secretary is appointed, the tasks will still need to be completed.

The company secretary plays a central role in the governance of an organisation's affairs. They provide essential practical support to the directors, ensuring that statutory and regulatory requirements are met for the conduct and running of board meetings. They will also ensure that the statutory and regulatory requirements are met, particularly in relation to CA 2006.

The role of the company secretary is covered in more detail in Chapter 5 (pages 98 and 99).

All charities must comply with:

- the Charities Act 2011, which replaced most of the Charities Act 2006 and Charities Act 1992;
- the Charities (Protection and Social Investment) Act 2016, which strengthens the powers of the Charity Commission;
- the Trustees Acts 1925, 2000: the most recent Act concerns the powers of trustees regarding investments and delegation;
- Charity Commission regulation: requires compliance (depending on annual income) on the submission of annual returns, reports and accounts;
- the Statement of Recommended Practice (SORP) 2015, published by the Charity Commission;
- laws on trading, political activities and fundraising; and
- regulation covering people who are disbarred from acting as trustees under the Charities Act 1993 or the organisation's memorandum and articles.

Charities should also consider the appointment of someone with appropriate expertise to undertake the necessary regulatory tasks including the filing of accounts.

▨ Influence of sporting federations over membership bodies

Governance of sport globally

Sport can bring the world together through major events and it generates significant economic value. The SRA reports that the sport economy contributes £6 billion to HM Treasury. International development through sport has been established as an effective means of engaging and empowering disadvantaged communities across the world, and it can help address the fourth biggest cause of mortality, physical inactivity, as reported by the World Health Organization.

Despite the enormous potential of sport, international sports governance has faced significant challenges in recent years. The investigation by Richard McLaren into institutional doping led to the banning of the entire Russian Paralympic team from the Rio Games; in 2015, US federal prosecutors indicted a number of FIFA officials on cases of corruption which ultimately led to the resignation of FIFA President Sepp Blatter; and successive studies have reported governance failings by a number of international federations.

Sports governance is under greater scrutiny than ever, and organisations that run sport are under pressure to meet higher standards of conduct and leadership. Codes govern specific aspects of international sport, including the Olympic Charter. This is the codification of the principles of Olympism, rules and by-laws adopted by the IOC. It governs the organisation, action and operation of the Olympic Games. International federations, national Olympic committees and Olympic Games host cities must comply with the Charter, which is a governing document of significant reach and influence.

International federations

The organisation of each sport at the global level is the responsibility of international federations (IFs). Some have existed for more than a hundred years – for example, FIFA was founded in 1904 – while others have only recently been established, such as the Boccia International Sports Federation, which was formed in 2012. Regardless of their history, IFs are non-governmental organisations that mostly fulfil similar functions. These include:

- responsibility for the integrity of their sport on the international level;
- affiliation of national federations administering sport at the national level;
- establishing statutes, practices and activities that conform to umbrella organisation standards, including the Olympic Charter;
- managing and monitoring the everyday running of the sport's disciplines;
- governing the sport at world level to ensure its promotion and development;
- supervising the development of athletes practising the sport at every level; and
- representing the sport.

As an example, the international federation for sailing, World Sailing, sets out its main responsibilities as follows.

World Sailing is responsible for:

- the promotion of the sport internationally;
- managing sailing at the Olympic and Paralympic Games;
- developing the Racing Rules of Sailing and regulations for all sailing competitions;
- the training of judges, umpires and other administrators;

- the development of the sport around the world; and
- representing the sailors in all matters concerning the sport.

In order for a UK NGB to be recognised as the sole body responsible for governing an Olympic or Paralympic sport, it will need to apply and receive recognition from the relevant IF for their sport. The NGB must meet certain criteria in terms of membership, structure and autonomy, and must commit to be bound by the statues, rules and systems established by the IF. IFs will only recognise one national federation in each country and it is through this body that administration of the sport, communication, democratic representation and the organisation of competitions are managed.

Although there is no single governance model for IFs, most will appoint members of the executive committee or board through democratic election processes. The International Canoe Federation is an example of this model:

> The International Canoe Federation (ICF) is a membership organisation that is responsible for the global sport of canoeing and comprises of five Continental Associations (CA) and 163 National Federations (NF). The ICF is the recognised international body for paddle sport and has representatives for nine (9) separate disciplines on its Board.

> The ICF's bi-annual congress, which is comprised of voting delegates from each of the NFs, is the supreme authority and is where rules, governance decisions and elections for the President, Vice Presidents (3), Treasurer (1) and Standing Committee Chairs (11) take place. The term for each of the ICF elected positions is four years.

> The appointed President is the chairperson for the Congress, Board of Directors and Executive Committee. The Board of Directors is collectively responsible for the strategic direction of the sport, whilst the five (5) members of the Executive Committee ensure the decisions of the Congress and Board of Directors are implemented.

> The five continents (Africa, America, Asia, Europe and Oceania) are also represented on the ICF Board with each electing Continental Representatives and a President during their respective Continental Congress.

> In addition to the ICF Board of Directors, the nine (9) disciplines each have technical committees responsible for rules and international competition delivery – for example world championships and world cups. There is also an Athletes' Committee and Medical and Anti-Doping Committee. These committees are collectively referred to as Standing Committees (11).

International sports federations form an integral part of the Olympic and Paralympic movements. Each Olympic sport is represented by its IF, which in turn helps administer its respective events during the Games. For a sport to become an Olympic sport, its IF must be recognised by the IOC. There are 35 recognised IFs.

Likewise, an IF must be recognised by the International Paralympic Committee (IPC) for its sport to become a Paralympic sport, although several Paralympic sports are governed the IPC itself. For example, disability track and field athletics is governed by the IPC under the name World Para Athletics.

In order to discuss common problems and decide on their events calendars, federations have formed associations including the Association of Summer Olympic International Federations (ASOIF), the Association of International Olympic Winter Sports Federations (AIOWF) and the Association of IOC Recognised International Sports Federations (ARISF).

The autonomy of sport is recognised by the United Nations and its specificity is enshrined in the Lisbon Treaty signed by all EU states in 2007. In essence, governments are discouraged from interfering in sporting affairs at the international or national level unless it is a pure economic activity, in which case it falls outside the scope of the 'specificity' provision. Under Rule 25 of the Olympic Charter of 1949, being 'independent and autonomous' became a requirement for recognition of the national Olympic committees by the IOC. Thus sport is self-regulating.

Representative bodies

There is a wide range of international sports organisations that represent federations including the Global Association of International Sport Federations (GAISF), the umbrella organisation for all Olympic and non-Olympic international sporting federations. The GAISF has strict membership criteria and, for non-Olympic sports, especially new sports such as parkour and skateboarding, GAISF membership is a significant step towards sole recognition at world level.

Equality and inclusion are important at the international level and sports bodies have received particular criticism for the lack of female representation in decision making. The organisation that has created the greatest impact on gender equality internationally is the International Working Group on Women and Sport (IWG). The IWG, at its first World Conference on Women and Sport in 1994, created the Brighton Declaration, a set of 10 principles for governmental, non-governmental, international, national and local organisations. By 2017, 441 organisations had signed the Brighton Declaration including the IOC, World Badminton Federation, Arab Women and Sport Association and Sport England.

The impact of Olympic and Paralympic status on the growth and development of sports

Olympic recognition can have a significant effect on sports, with inclusion on the Olympic programme considered to be the pinnacle for most. In 2016, rugby returned to the Olympic arena for the first time since 1924. World Rugby, the IF, had lobbied intensively to be reinstated with rugby sevens (the short form of the game involving seven players on each team) as the preferred format. Olympic policy states that no new sports or disciplines can be introduced unless they are offered to both men and women, and Rio hosted the first women's rugby competition in Olympic history.

IFs must meet certain criteria for the sport to be considered for inclusion in the Olympic programme. When rugby was announced for the Rio Olympics, sporting superpowers like the USA and China increased funding and playing numbers. Governments and national Olympic committees invested in the game and, for many countries, rugby was taught in schools for the first time. Rio was a game changer for the sport.

World Rugby has reported record participation growth since sevens was awarded an Olympic place in 2009. In 2016, the total number of registered players increased from 2.82 million to 3.2 million while the total number of non-registered rugby players rose from 4.91 million to 5.3 million. Olympic status is credited as a major influence on this growth.

Charged with setting the strategic direction of the sport that will be sustainable and generates growth, boards of some non-Olympic sports include the achievement of Olympic status in their long-term plans. World Squash and the International Roller Sports Federation continue to invest their IF's resources into bidding for Olympic status (even though they have failed on more than one occasion), as this could reap great benefits for their sports.

Through Agenda 2020, the IOC's strategic roadmap, the Olympic Movement is attempting to reach a younger audience. With this in mind, five new sports will be introduced to the Tokyo Olympic Games programme, four of which are new – skateboarding, karate, sport climbing and surfing. The decisions were taken even though disputes remain over the recognised IFs for surfing and skateboarding. It remains to be seen if Olympic status helps these sports as it did for rugby.

The advantages and disadvantages of hosting major sporting events

'Inspire a generation' was the promise made in Singapore in 2005 when London was awarded the right to host the 2012 Olympic and Paralympic Games. Since then, the various benefits of London 2012 have been analysed extensively, creating a large body of research on the subject. Most studies of the impact of hosting major sporting events focus on four key areas: economic, social, political and sporting.

Economic

The initial London 2012 bid was based on total estimated costs of £3.4 billion, which later escalated to £9.35 billion. However, in 2013, the official government report stated that the final cost was £528 million under budget.

Professor Simon Shibli, Head of the Sports Industry Research Centre at Sheffield Hallam, stated that events like 2014's Open Golf Championships can make a big difference to the local economy – to the tune of £75 million in the case of host region Liverpool and the Wirral. Similarly, the Ryder Cup was held in Wales in 2010 and generated over £84 million for the Welsh economy, with 69% of spectators coming from outside Wales.

Conversely, the long-term economic impact is not always positive. Montreal made an estimated loss of £692 million from the 1976 Olympic Games, with the Olympic stadium very underused after the event.

A significant benefit is the long-term investment which comes from preparing for a major event. The city/country will often have a legacy of improved sporting venues. Also, cities may have to invest in infrastructure and transport to cater for visitors at the event.

Social

The feelgood factor, which is often mentioned but difficult to measure, has consistently been linked to sporting events. From Super Saturday at London 2012 to Wales's men's football team's progress through the UEFA Euro 2016 Championships, national pride is most visible through television audiences and social media activity.

Political

For a country like China with a controversial human rights record, hosting a major sporting event can help gain greater international acceptance. When South Africa hosted the rugby World Cup and later the football World Cup, it was a defining moment in highlighting the new, post-apartheid South Africa. Such opportunities are rare in any other field, such as the arts, which do not necessarily generate the same global interest across so many population demographics.

Sporting

Most bids are now required to demonstrate how sports will be developed, in particular in legacy. By 2015 only three Olympic sports had seen an increase in participation in England, and figures released in 2016 showed an overall drop in participation. Only Wales has seen an increase in children's and adults' participation in recent years, so all sports councils expect major events to be linked to development programmes.

Workforce development and volunteering

These are important for many sports in the UK, and hosting a sporting event can provide a significant catalyst for recruitment and skills development. Over 10,000 people applied for the 4,000 volunteer positions, known as Runners, for the World Athletics Championships in London in 2017. At a time when finding paid work is challenging, especially for young people, offering quality volunteering opportunities that provide skills development can be invaluable.

UK Sport is a strategic investor in major events in the UK. It developed, in partnership with the Sport Industry Research Centre at Sheffield Hallam, the Event

Impacts toolkit of resources to help event organisers improve their evaluation of the impacts associated with staging sporting events. These include:

- attendance
- economic
- social
- environmental
- media.

More information is available on the UK Sport Event Impacts website: www.eventimpacts.com.

Whether it is for a local festival or regional championship, the planning process is complex. Effective governance, including risk management, financial controls and rigorous project management, will be needed to ensure a safe, successful and sustainable event.

How national sports organisations can achieve international influence

As discussed on pages 57 and 58, sport is governed globally by international bodies. For NGBs in the UK, a positive relationship with international and European federations can bring additional benefits – for example, winning the right to host a major event.

Individuals in senior IF positions can significantly influence decisions on changes to the Olympic and Paralympic programme. For example, track cycling rule changes introduced prior to London 2012 meant only one rider from each nation could compete in the keirin and sprint events, reducing British Cycling's potential medal chances.

British NGBs will actively seek appointments onto IF and European committees in order to contribute to such decisions and protect British interests. Having a strong voice is also essential to ensure that NGBs can engage effectively with the international community and contribute to the good governance, development and leadership of world sport. Recognising the value of international influence, UK Sport funds attendance at congresses, representation on IF committees and support for promising British sports administrators.

Such is the importance of international influence, the Code of Sports Governance includes an exception to the requirements on term limits for board members. Specifically, the commentary under Principle 1 states that a director may serve on the board for a maximum of 12 years if appointed as chair of the organisation or to a senior position with an IF. In the case of an NGB executive director being appointed to an IF position, they would have to relinquish this role if they left the NGB. Exceptions would apply if they were later appointed in a non-executive role.

While not all sports bodies will necessarily prioritise representation at higher levels in the sport, effective stakeholder management is a board responsibility.

Moreover, CA 2006 states that directors must foster the company's business relationships with suppliers, customers and others. In a sporting context, this would include international partners.

Chapter summary

- The World Anti-Doping Code came into force in 2004 and aimed to harmonise anti-doping policies, rules and regulations. In order for sports to be included in the Olympic and Paralympic Games programmes, international federations must comply with the World Anti-Doping Code. In the UK, NGBs must comply with the National Anti-Doping Policy to be eligible for public funding.
- Standards for Safeguarding and Protecting Children in Sport were published by the Child Protection Sports Unit in 2002. The Standards aim to help create a safe sporting environment for children and young people, and protect them from harm. Sports bodies across the UK must comply with the Standards in order to receive funding from any of the five Sports Councils.
- Each sport is governed at the global level by an IF. These are non-governmental organisations that lead and given their support with members, usually national federations, affiliating to the international body. IFs are an integral part of the Olympic Movement and must comply with the Olympic Charter for the sport to be considered for inclusion in the Olympics.
- UK NGBs will seek to influence at international levels as this may assist in securing the rights to host major events and effect changes to competition rules that benefit British athletes.

4

Governance structures

▩ Introduction

This chapter outlines the different governance structures adopted by sports organisations and the impact these structures can have on the composition of the board and its effectiveness. Also covered are the divisions of responsibility between different organs of a sports body, and the need for clarity in setting out their respective responsibilities. The governing document, along with a clearly communicated organisational purpose, will help ensure decisions meet constitutional requirements and strategic ambitions.

▩ Governance structures in sports organisations

The governance structures of any organisation will significantly influence its ability to make decisions. These have tended to evolve from structures established when many sports were formed as unincorporated associations. Even with incorporation, sports bodies have not necessarily adjusted their governance structures to accommodate their additional duties and responsibilities. For example, the Football Association of Wales has a council made up of 36 non-executive directors elected by the membership. To enable more agile decision making, an executive committee has been formed that includes council members and independent non-executive directors.

In October 2017, British Rowing members voted to replace their ruling council with an elected body of regional representatives. These representatives hold all the powers of the members of a company as defined by the Companies Act (such as power to call general meetings and the power to vote on resolutions). In addition, the regional representatives have the power to elect four directors to the board. It is the board, however, that is the ultimate decision-making body as required by the Code for Sports Governance.

Articles and the memorandum of association

The Articles of Association set out how the company is run, governed and owned. They include the responsibilities and powers of the directors and the means by which the members exert control over the board. The Memorandum of Association is a simple statement that the initial subscriber wishes to form a company and agrees to become a member by taking at least one share.

Up until 2009, a company was restricted to whatever the objects clause of the memorandum said it could do. Now a company can do anything lawful unless its articles say otherwise. A company formed before 2009 will have had the objects clause from its memorandum automatically transferred to the articles.

Companies House templates
There are model articles for the three most common types of company: private company limited by shares, private company limited by guarantee and public limited company. These are set out in the Companies (Model Articles) Regulations 2008 and are available on the Companies House website: www.gov.uk/guidance/model-articles-of-association-for-limited-companies.

In addition, for charitable companies the Charity Commission has a set of model articles: www.gov.uk/government/publications/setting-up-a-charity-model-governing-documents.

The Community Interest Companies Regulator provides model articles for community interest companies: www.gov.uk/government/publications/community-interest-companies-constitutions.

Constraints and limitations
The powers and rights of shareholders or members are also enshrined in the articles and cannot exceed those set out in the Companies Act. For example, members have the right to remove directors by passing an ordinary resolution.

The articles will include details of the ways in which certain decisions can be taken by members – for example, by ordinary resolution, special resolution as well as the voting rights associated with such decisions. Some NGBs award greater numbers of votes to clubs with greater numbers of individual members. Others will have full, associate and affiliate members, which might be organisations or individuals, who may or may not be able to vote at general meetings.

While model articles are available, sports bodies must take time to prepare a governing document that is relevant to the purpose, size, structure, complexity and capacity of the organisation.

The differences between Articles of Association, rules, standing orders and constitutions
The Articles of Association set out how the company is run, governed and owned. They include the responsibilities and powers of the directors and the means by which the members exert control over the board. This is the governing document and the board must operate within its limitations. As well as the duties and powers of the directors, the articles may also set out how board members are appointed, how meetings will be conducted (including the AGM) and the establishment of governance structures across the organisation.

Rules may be included in a company's Articles of Association. These will relate to decision-making processes, participation in meetings and the records to be kept. These are formal rules that directors must abide by, and some will reflect statutory duties to the organisation. Rules can also be applied to employees under their contract of employment. Such rules might include office dress codes or requirements to adhere to equality, safeguarding and other policies.

Smaller organisations, such as sports clubs, may establish rules for members beyond those applied on the field of play. Clubs may have rules around attire in the clubhouse or access to parts of the club, such as gym or offices. On joining a club, new members will usually have to acknowledge the rules and their commitment to adherence as part of the membership agreement.

Standing orders relate to procedures for meetings of the board and, in so far as they are applicable, committees. Standing orders can include:

- the number of times a board or committee that shall meet each year;
- notice period for each meeting and the method of communication to members (electronic format, hard copy and so on);
- dates and times of meetings;
- remote attendance and record of attendance;
- quorum – the number of board or committee members required to be in attendance for decisions to be made;
- order of business – who shall determine this and how it might be altered;
- voting, for example, decisions by a majority of votes, by show of hands or secret ballot;
- the role of the chair and, in their absence, chairing of the meeting;
- rules of debate including the roles of proposers and seconders of motions or resolutions;
- minutes – their inclusion as an agenda item from a previous meeting and who signs them as a true record (the publication of minutes might also be contained in the standing orders); and
- conflicts of interest – declarations in accordance with the organisation's conflict of interest policy.

Some sports bodies, including clubs, will separate standing orders from articles so that they can be changed without requiring a general meeting and member vote.

Lastly, the constitution of a company is formed by a company's Articles of Association together with the Memorandum of Association.

Formal and informal rules

Informal rules are also sometimes employed, especially in smaller organisations. For example, in a club environment the club captain may accept responsibility for chairing the executive committee while also being expected to lead all aspects of the playing activities. The former is not always contained in role descriptions but does require large amounts of time, while the latter is perceived as the main responsibility.

Boards, councils and executive committees

The Code for Sports Governance is explicit in its requirements in respect of boards, stating that organisations must be led by a board which is collectively responsible for the long-term success of the organisation and exclusively vested with the power to lead it. In practice this will mean that while funded organisations may retain councils, such groups will not be the primary decision-making body.

As most NGBs are registered as companies, the need to meet legal and funding requirements has driven changes in board appointments. If the board is exclusively responsible for decisions about the long-term future of an organisation, it must be prepared to appoint people with a range of skills and knowledge. Appointments made entirely from within the organisation may limit the diversity and skills needed by the board.

In some sports, an executive committee is appointed with delegated authority from the council to make certain decisions. Examples include the Football Association of Wales (FAW). The FAW Council of 36 is elected by members on a geographical basis and can overrule the executive board established to lead and manage the day-to-day running of the NGB. The council members have the full backing of the wider NGB membership through the election process and in its current form is the primary decision-making body within the sport. As it is a large council, appointing an executive committee (which includes council members) facilitates more efficient decision making.

Smaller organisations, such as clubs, will also have an executive committee as, even though they may be directors of a company, the committee members may be asked to undertake executive functions due to the size and capacity of the organisation. Even if committee members are actively involved at an operational level, they are still bound by their legal duties as directors when acting in that role, for example, at committee meetings.

Role and contribution of sub-committees

The governance structure of an organisation must facilitate the effective flow of information in order to make decisions that will promote the long-term success of the organisation. Given the breadth of sporting, business, stakeholder and ethical matters that boards are expected to deal with, additional expertise and capacity can be created by delegating aspects of the business to sub-committees. Such structures do not relieve boards of their overarching duties and responsibilities, but they can provide high-quality management information that supports effective board decision making.

How sub-committees provide scrutiny and support

The board can only create a sub-committee structure if it has the power do so under the articles. Sub-committees can engage experts in areas of strategic importance to the organisation – for example, an NGB may establish sub-committees for the range of sporting disciplines. In snowsports, this might be alpine skiing or snowboarding. Creating sub-committees means that the board itself does not necessarily have to discuss the details of each discipline's rules or competition schedule; this allows the directors to focus on strategic and business matters.

Sub-committees also offer a scrutiny function in key business areas as the delivery of sporting goals can be monitored more closely than at board level. The Sport Wales Elite Sport Strategy was approved by the board and implementation delegated to Welsh Institute staff. The formation of an Elite Sport Sub-Group (ESSG) included four board members (one of whom was the chair), executive staff from the Institute and independent members with expertise in elite sport. The inclusion of board members ensured there was effective oversight of a key strategy and flow of management information to the board; independent members provided essential expertise; and staff members received support and advice at the highest levels for delivery of elite sport goals.

The audit committee should review the organisation's internal financial controls (that is, the systems established to identify, assess, manage and monitor financial risks) and, unless there is a separate risk committee, the organisation's internal control and risk management systems.

Table 4.1: NCVO Good Trustee Guide: board and committee structures

Who they are	What they do	Special features
Board sub-committee	• Small group assigned by the board to focus on a particular task or area (such as finance, remuneration, nominations, governance) • Committees can be a permanent part of the charity's governance (standing committees) or set up to fulfil a time-limited task (working group) • Remit and any decision-making powers are set by the board of trustees and the governing document in its terms of reference	• Can include non-board members • Cannot make decision unless authorised • Reports to the board • Can add value to governance
Advisory groups	• Group of non-board members that advises the board	• No official role • No voting power • Can provide valuable information and expertise

Advisory and working groups

Advisory groups can be established to provide new perspectives, explore different sporting formats or undertake research. Advisory groups may have few board members, if any at all, and will be made up of predominantly independent individuals sharing their expertise in a designated area. Terms of reference are still important for these groups even if they do not have a scrutiny function, as ultimately they too must demonstrate added value.

The National Council for Voluntary Organisations' (NCVO) Good Trustee Guide (Section 4 – board and committee structures) presents simple guidelines for committees and advisory groups, as shown in Table 4.1.

Divisions of responsibility

Responsibility

While directors and trustees have clearly defined duties to the organisation, the board must also be clear about its responsibilities.

The Code for Sports Governance states under Principle 1 that organisations shall have a clear and appropriate governance structure, led by a board which is collectively responsible for the long-term success of the organisation. The board is the ultimate decision-making body, responsible for setting the strategy, although the council can constructively challenge its decisions and strategy.

These responsibilities cannot be delegated even if an individual, such as the CEO or a sub-committee, is tasked with producing proposals (such as on the organisation's structure) for the board to consider. The final decision rests with the board, and directors/trustees must assume full responsibility for such decisions.

Powers

The powers of the board are set out in an organisation's Articles of Association.

To assist companies in developing their articles, Companies House has created model articles which are available on the Companies House website. Article 5 of the model articles states that the:

> ... Directors may delegate any of the powers conferred on them under the articles to any person (e.g. the CEO) or committee (e.g. to an audit committee), by such means (including by power of attorney), to such an extent, in relation to such matters or territories, and on such terms and conditions as they think fit. If the Directors so specify, any such delegation may authorise further delegation of the Directors' powers by any person to whom they are delegated.

For example, the CEO may delegate some powers to other managers.

Shareholders or members can also exert significant influence by exercising their rights and powers. These include:

- passing resolutions at general meetings;
- voting directors onto the board; and

- requesting the company in writing to provide information held by the company (with a right to appeal to the court if the company refuses).

The Code for Sports Governance's requirement that the board has ultimate authority does not override or supersede the powers of members under law.

Authority

To ensure the board maintains a strategic overview and avoids becoming involved in operational detail, effective delegation is essential. Under Principle 2, the Governance and Leadership Framework for Wales sets a minimum expectation that the board must:

- create appropriate committees which will be given delegated authority; and
- delegate operational issues to individuals with a remit to deliver the operational function (CEO or finance officer, for example).

Boards cannot delegate responsibility but, in delegating authority, they must do so with clarity and transparency. When delegating functions to a committee (such as a communications committee), terms of reference should be produced that set out:

- *the purpose of the committee* – assist the board in its stakeholder management and communication responsibilities;
- *membership* – a minimum number of board members, one of whom may be the committee chair, along with independent experts in the field of communications, digital and social media, etc;
- *limits of authority* – making decisions, for example, on the development of web and media platforms. Significant projects beyond the stated budget would require board approval; and
- *reporting framework* – reporting to the board that enables appropriate oversight.

For instance, there are critical business areas for which the board is responsible regardless of the organisation's size and purpose, such as finance and risk management. The board may delegate aspects of internal control and risk to the audit committee and CEO who could, in turn, delegate to managers for risks appropriate to their departments.

Table 4.2 demonstrates how the board, audit committee and CEO work together to build a robust process through which risk is managed in the organisation.

Table 4.2: Delegation of decision-making authority

Subject	Reserved for the board	Delegated to the audit committee	Delegated to the CEO
Risk strategy and management	Board to approve risk strategy and appetite Audit committee to oversee effectiveness of risk management arrangements	Consider the effectiveness of internal control processes for risk, control and governance Review the corporate risk register Require assurances relating to corporate governance requirements Agree and review the internal audit strategy and programme	Maintain the system of internal control and assurance framework within the organisation Provide the board via the audit committee with assurance on its ongoing effectiveness and appropriateness

The Financial Reporting Council (FRC) updated its Guidance on Audit Committees in 2016, which provides useful advice for the setting up any committee of the board. This is available on the FRC website (www.frc.org.uk/document-library/corporate-governance/2016/guidance-on-audit-committees-april-2016).

Boards can also delegate to external organisations, including affiliate bodies and contractors. In all cases, terms of reference, agreements and contracts should set out the scope, objectives or outputs, reporting processes, time frames and other key elements that will create a robust framework.

Accountability

Having delegated authority, it is important to hold individuals and committees to account. There are practical steps that can be taken and, in the case of individuals such as the CEO, the following could be put in place:

- Job descriptions.
- *Annual work plans* – objectives and outcomes to be achieved over a designated period.
- *Performance management* – effective performance management is both systematic and personalised. While most performance management processes will include annual, bi-annual or quarterly appraisal meetings, management is about people. The CEO is usually line managed by the chair, who should strive to support and constructively challenge them. Formal appraisal meetings can be supplemented with informal conversations so the CEO does not feel isolated, as can often happen in such a role.

■ *Review and plan* – each appraisal meeting should review the previous period and consider the successes as well as any issues that may have hindered progress. Discussing the period ahead will also ensure both parties are clear about the expectations and what must be achieved in that time.
■ *Reporting processes* – there should be a systematic process of reporting from any individual in the organisation that contributes to the operational planning review.

By setting outcomes and objectives, agreeing limits of authority, monitoring progress and measuring performance, the board can delegate with confidence and hold individuals, committees and contractors to account.

Understanding the internal decision-making environment

An organisation that intends its meetings to be efficient, well run and effective will need to establish appropriate procedures. The process by which board and general meetings are called and run should be contained in the articles. Alternatively, beyond statutory duties, more detailed procedures and rules can be drawn up separately.

How structures affect governance in sports organisations

Developing clearly defined structures enables each level of the organisation to focus on its role, including the decisions it is required to make. Structures that enable delegation to staff and committees do not diminish the board's overarching responsibility, and there will always be matters reserved to the board.

According to Slack and Parent (2006), the complexity of an organisation's structure relates to the various ways in which units are differentiated. This includes the vertical, horizontal and spatial (geographical location) differentiation. The greater the various types of differentiation, the greater the complexity of the organisation. A sports organisation may build a flat hierarchical structure while also having to operate across many locations – this is especially true of NGBs where performance operations take place overseas for much of the year.

Mechanisms such as rules, job descriptions, policies and procedures help govern the operations of the organisation and can be referred to as formalisation. These mechanisms exemplify whether authority to make critical decisions is centralised or distributed to lower levels. Bureaucracies tend to be high on both formalisation and centralisation; given the voluntary nature of sports boards, this can create tension with other decision-making units within the governance structure, affecting agility and perceptions of empowerment.

Sub-committees, advisory groups and paid staff will usually form the most senior levels of a sport's governance structure. These can be supported by regional or county committees led by volunteers. Each component part should have terms of reference (board and committees), role descriptions (senior volunteers) and job descriptions (paid staff). These help establish responsibility, delegation of powers and authority, and create efficient flows of information through each function.

Publishing an organisational chart with brief details of the board, committee structures and staff, and how these relate to each other will help new board members, staff, volunteers and stakeholders understand the structure of the organisation and how it operates.

Facilitating good decision making

The ICSA has issued a code for directors and company secretaries on good boardroom practice, which includes the following provisions:

- There should be written procedures for the conduct of board business. Compliance should be monitored, preferably by an audit committee.
- Each director, on first appointment, should be given sufficient information to enable them to carry out their duties properly. This should include details of procedures for obtaining information about the company and requisitioning a board meeting.
- Two fundamental concepts in the conduct of board business are that (1) all directors should be given the same information, and (2) they should be given sufficient time to consider it.
- The board should identify those matters that require its prior approval. As a basic principle, all material contracts should be referred to the board for approval before the company is legally committed to them.
- Decisions about the agenda for a board meeting should be taken by the company chair in consultation with the company secretary.
- The company secretary should be responsible to the chair for the proper administration of board meetings, the meetings of board committees and general meetings of the company. To carry out these responsibilities, the company secretary should be entitled to be present at and prepare the minutes for all such meetings. The minutes of meetings should record all decisions that were taken, and procedures should be established for the approval and circulation of minutes.
- The board should give its prior approval for the membership, terms of reference and powers of any committee of the board that is established. Minutes of board committees should be circulated to all board directors prior to the next board meeting, to give them an opportunity to raise questions at that meeting.

Boards can minimise the risk of poor decisions by investing time in the design of their decision making processes. The FRC published its Guidance on Board Effectiveness in 2011; this includes simple steps to effective decision making as well as the factors that limit it, such as:

- a dominant personality or group of directors, which can inhibit contributions from other directors;

- insufficient attention to risk, and treating risk as a compliance issue rather than as part of the decision-making process;
- a reluctance to involve non-executive directors, or of matters being brought to the board for sign-off rather than debate;
- complacent or intransigent attitudes;
- a weak organisational culture; and
- inadequate information or analysis.

For the most significant decisions, boards may wish to consider extra steps. The FRC guidance suggests that organisations can put in place additional safeguards to reduce the risk of distorted judgements by, for example, commissioning an independent report, seeking advice from an expert, establishing a sole purpose sub-committee or convening additional meetings.

Some organisations opt to have large boards in order to manage high workloads. While enlarging the board might reduce the pressures on volunteers, it can affect the decision-making process. Large boards can be unwieldy, making discussions and meetings excessively long with too much focus on operational detail. Bigger boards also undermine ownership of group decisions, as there may not be time for everyone to be heard.

The chair is key to the decision-making process, and the FRC's Guidance on Board Effectiveness sets out the duties and responsibilities of the role. They should demonstrate the highest standards of integrity and probity, and set the style and tone of board discussions. The role also includes:

- setting a board agenda which is primarily focused on strategy, performance, value creation and accountability, and ensuring that issues relevant to these areas are reserved for board decision;
- ensuring a timely flow of high-quality supporting information;
- making certain that the board determines the nature, and extent, of the significant risks the company is willing to embrace in the implementation of its strategy; and
- making certain that the board has effective decision-making processes and applies sufficient challenge to major proposals.

The full guidance is available at www.frc.org.uk/Our-Work/Publications/Corporate-Governance/Guidance-on-Board-Effectiveness.pdf.

Consequences of poor decision making

The consequences of poor decision making can be financial or reputational. For example, in 2014, the Board of English Lacrosse decided to bid for both the women's and men's World Lacrosse Championships to be held in 2017 and 2018, respectively. There was an ambition to host at least one event in England and the Federation of International Lacrosse (FIL) might not have been expected to award both to the same country. English Lacrosse, therefore, did not expect to have to plan and host two world championships in the space of 12 months.

When FIL awarded both events to England, there was understandable elation and the NGB worked tirelessly to ensure they would be a success. However, FIL contractual demands and commitments placed too great a financial burden on the organisation and, despite regular communication with all stakeholders, the NGB faced a difficult decision – to continue preparing to host both events or to withdraw from one. In April 2017, English Lacrosse issued a press release announcing its withdrawal from hosting the men's 2018 world cup. It stated the decision had been taken with the utmost consideration for the financial sustainability of lacrosse in England. The board found that the event placed the governing body and sport at unacceptable financial risk.

While questions were asked about the risks of bidding for both events, ultimately the board made the decision to protect the long-term future of the NGB even though it faced criticism both nationally and internationally. While this example might be perceived as an example of good decision making (withdrawing in order to protect the organisation), it is worth remembering that the original decision lacked a robust risk assessment to avoid placing the NGB in a difficult situation by the time they reached the decision to withdraw.

Purpose of a sports organisation

If a sports body wants to create impact, it must first understand why it exists and what it is striving to achieve. Setting strategic direction is one of the legal duties of the board, and time must be given to the process of building the organisation's long-term future.

Establishing organisational core purpose

Board members of even the smallest bodies benefit from assessing whether their organisation is doing what it set out to do. Taking time to build an aspirational future can be energising for the board and also ensures it is taking its leadership role seriously.

In the first instance, the organisation should be able to answer the question 'Why do we exist?' Once this is agreed, the strategic direction can be developed. The board is responsible for leading this process, and engagement with stakeholders is vital to reflect their views and gain buy-in across the organisation.

Vision

A vision statement describes an aspirational view of the future. It articulates the hopes for the sport and it reminds stakeholders of what the organisation is trying to build. In its 2013–20 Strategic Plan, British Shooting set out the following vision:

> Target shooting to be recognised as a successful, credible and progressive sport in the UK.

The vision is not necessarily for one organisation to achieve, as it aims to inspire others to work towards the same desired future. In the case of British Shooting, stakeholders such as shooting ranges, coaches and shooting media and funders can help achieve the vision.

Mission

The way in which British Shooting will contribute to the achievement of the vision is through its mission:

> To inspire and enable all those who wish to enjoy and develop their abilities as a target shooter.

Purpose

Some organisations will also develop a purpose statement as a means of explaining their practical activities – what they do that is unique to them.

British Shooting's core purposes are:

- to be a single contact for IF;
- to be a single shooting body in receipt of public funding from UK Sport and Sport England;
- to be the member body of the National Olympic Committee;
- to oversee the development and preparation of world-class shooters for success on the international stage;
- to support the development of grass-roots shooting in England; and
- to promote quality and professional governance for target shooting sports.

Not all organisations will develop a vision, mission and purpose. In fact, many have only one answer to the question 'Why do we exist?' For example:

- LOCOG vision – to use the power of the Games to inspire change.
- Sporting Equals mission – Sporting Equals exists to promote ethnic diversity across sport and physical activity.
- Tenby Golf Club mission – Tenby Golf Club will provide an exceptional and enjoyable experience to members and visitors of all abilities.

Setting an aspirational vision or mission statement can also motivate staff, volunteers and board members, directing their skills and energy. This is important regardless of size or capacity, and can have even greater impact on smaller organisations reliant on voluntary effort by focusing volunteers' time and skills more effectively.

Developing a vision, mission or purpose statement

The process by which a vision or mission is developed is just as important as the final product. Members of a sports body often have a deeper relationship with the organisation than shareholders might with a company. For example, members are also participants or volunteers who help deliver the services.

Focusing on impact

Following the decision to invest National Lottery funds, investment for sport increased significantly and NGBs were required to develop strategic plans that set out how they would achieve high-level goals, especially those supported by public funds. During the funding periods from 1997 to 2009, the strategic priorities were relatively straightforward – increase participation and win medals at European or world levels. Since then, this has shifted towards a focus on impact. For example, Swim England's 2017–21 mission is to create a happier, healthier and more successful nation through swimming.

Such ambitions reflect the increased understanding of the way in the sport and recreation sector can positively influence many other sectors, including health, education and community cohesion. The concept of societal impact is also of greater importance in the private sector: the FRC report *Corporate Culture and the Role of Boards*, published in 2016, states that companies are recognising the value in defining and communicating a broader purpose, beyond profit, which delivers benefits to society as a whole.

Engaging stakeholders in the process of establishing a vision, mission or purpose

The involvement of members is listed in various governance codes. For example, Principle 6 of the Governance and Leadership Framework states that:

> The Board needs to be open and accountable to its athletes, participants and members, and its actions should stand up to scrutiny.

To achieve this, the board should meet certain minimum expectations, including:

- fully engaging with members and participants;
- running consultations with different stakeholders;
- having appropriate mechanisms in place for participants to feed in their thoughts; and
- being able to manage formal communication, engagement with members and social media activity appropriately.

This is reinforced in the Code for Sports Governance, under Principle 3: Communication, which states that transparency about why the organisation exists, what it is trying to do, how and with what results empowers stakeholders by giving them information about the organisation that they need to know.

Theory in action

In 2016, Tenby Golf Club applied to join a pilot initiative under the Wales Golf Business Support Scheme. Using the Governance and Leadership Framework for Wales (GLFW), Wales Golf aimed to build the capacity and competence of clubs to implement good governance.

As part of the scheme, Tenby's Management Committee participated in an independently facilitated consultation meeting, at which the Management Committee created a governance improvement plan. Some of the priorities were as follows:

- Create a mission statement that reflects the club's ambition for the future.
- Develop high-level goals in order to achieve the mission that will focus the club's resources – financial, staff and volunteers.
- Review and revise the governance structure to ensure the club has the right skills appropriately deployed to deliver the strategy.

The Management Committee created a series of newsletter and website features, as well as short presentations for each section of the club, and arranged a consultation meeting for all members. The consultation meeting was independently facilitated and gave members the opportunity not only to provide feedback on the draft mission statement and strategic goals, but also to offer ideas on how these could be best achieved. Following the meeting, a further two-week consultation period was offered, along with a dedicated email address for members to provide input, feedback and ideas.

By July 2016, the mission and strategic goals had been formally adopted and the club was fully engaged in the long-term planning process. The club also witnessed a significant increase in the number of members seeking positions on the new management board and sub-committees.

The benefits of developing a vision or mission for your organisation
Providing board, staff and volunteers with strategic and aspirational direction

The FRC's Guidance on Board Effectiveness states that an effective board develops and promotes its collective vision of the company's purpose, its culture, its values and the behaviours it wishes to promote in conducting its business.

NGBs seek to develop and publish strategies that will inspire internal and external stakeholders. For example, Welsh Cycling reviewed its strategy after the 2015 Commonwealth Games and, to achieve its vision – to inspire Wales to cycle – agreed four high-level aims, as Figure 4.1 shows.

Figure 4.1: Welsh Cycling vision and strategic aims

To Inspire Wales to Cycle
Every child able to cycle
More people having the opportunity to cycle safely and achieve their personal goals
Welsh cyclists achieving international success
To become an effective and sustainable organisation that provides leadership and advice to those with an interest in cycling

The vision and strategic aims are simply worded, and the organisation's structure reflects these priorities. Each person, whether paid or volunteering, understands how he or she contributes to the strategic aims.

Ensuring decision making remains focused on the vision, mission or purpose

The Code for Sports Governance under Principle 1: Structure requires that boards maintain and demonstrate a clear division between the board's management and oversight role and the executive's operational role. Explicit role descriptions along with an effective induction should ensure that all board members, regardless of their appointment process, maintain a strategic outlook as befits their role.

One way to maintain a focus on the vision, mission and strategy is to plan focused agendas for board meetings. Other processes include the following:

■ *Meeting protocols* – these should be documented and disseminated to board and staff members involved in board meetings. These can include when papers are issued and how items under any other business can be raised.

■ *Allocating approximate times to agenda items* – these might only be an indication based on the known complexity or risk to the organisation, and the amount of time that would be deemed reasonable. Suggested times should not be used to close useful or important debates, but can guide board members' input.

■ *Items can be labelled as information, discussion or decision* – the labels do not necessarily equate to the level of risk or opportunity, as some items may only be updates on strategic issues.

■ *Executive report* – some organisations ask the CEO to prepare a brief written or verbal executive report highlighting significant activities, decisions or changes led by the executive. This can be treated as an information item, with questions from board members only needed for clarification.

■ *Consent agenda* – NGBs are more frequently adopting consent agendas. These include concise, written reports from sub-committees and updates on board-level items that do not need decisions.

■ *Time for important, strategic level discussions directly related to the mission* – without doubt, these need the greatest planning, thought and input from board members. Matters such as significant new public funding requirements or organisational restructures would fall into this category. The agenda should allow sufficient time for these items.

Protocols and processes guide and protect board members as they fulfil their duties, but board culture and behaviour are also key factors. Everyone should show discipline and seek to be constructive and concise. The chair must exercise discipline when moving through the agenda, enabling open discussion and reaching decisions on the most critical business areas.

Chapter summary

■ The board is responsible for ensuring the success of the organisation. Powers and authority may be delegated according to the articles, but the board must hold those to whom it is delegated to account.

■ The Articles of Association set out how an organisation is run and governed, and they include the responsibilities and powers of directors. The Memorandum of Association is a statement that the subscriber wishes to form a company and agrees to become a member of taking at least one share. Since 2009, a company's activities can be unlimited, provided they are lawful, unless its articles say otherwise.

■ The board is responsible for creating an appropriate governance structure. Sub-committees can provide both support and scrutiny in key business areas. All sub-committee terms of reference should set out their purpose, membership, required outputs, limits of authority, timelines and resources.

■ Good decision making is facilitated by sound board procedures and the FRC's Guidance on Board Effectiveness advises investing time in the design of decision-making processes and board procedures.

■ By establishing a vision, mission and purpose, a board can plan for the future with clarity. Engagement with stakeholders in the development process will help secure support and ownership by those tasked with delivering the mission. Principle 3 of the Code For Sports Governance requires funded organisations to engage effectively with stakeholders and nurture internal democracy.

5
Roles and responsibilities

Introduction

This chapter explores the role of the board and governance structures with a particular focus on board appointments. It looks at the ways in which board members are appointed and how to ensure the board has access to the skills, knowledge and experience needed to lead the organisation. The chapter also address the roles and responsibilities of different stakeholders.

Role and duties of the board

Separation of powers

Executive powers

A board may contain non-executive and executive directors, all of whom will share the duties of directors as enshrined in the Companies Act 2006. Executive directors will also very likely be employed by the organisation, and these roles include executive powers which the board can delegate, enabling decision-making agility.

Alternatively, the organisation may choose to establish an executive committee (sometimes called a management board or committee) that contains executive directors and a small number of non-executive directors (NEDs). There are distinct advantages for the CEO and the organisation in having an executive committee. CEOs can rely on the executive committee to vet matters that are highly confidential or are not ready for formal, full board deliberations. It is often easier for smaller executive committees to get together in an emergency than to gather a larger board. Executive committees can also handle routine matters that would otherwise take up the full board's limited time.

Clarity on the executive committee's role is important to avoid situations where it becomes too powerful or where board members who are not members feel all the decisions are being made before they reach the full board.

Supervisory responsibility

Large corporate organisations will sometimes put in place a management board or executive committee that is led by the CEO and consists of executive directors but no non-executive directors. This management board is responsible for the day-to-day running of the business, and the articles and terms of reference set out clearly its role, limits of authority and relationship to the supervisory board.

The supervisory or corporate board will have a wider membership, is responsible for the strategic oversight of the organisation and is led by the chair.

Setting strategic direction and objectives

What is the difference between values, objectives and strategy?

Values are a fundamental part of an organisation's strategic framework that includes its vision, mission and strategy. Values are not selling messages or business goals; they are intrinsic elements that underpin the behaviour of an organisation.

Values can be integrated into codes of conduct, role descriptions, appraisal processes and customer care policies. Organisations can place values at the heart of their decisions and operations, thereby providing stakeholders with a high quality service and generating confidence.

Example of sports organisational values include:

- International Paralympic Committee – determination, courage, equality, inspiration; and
- British Triathlon Federation – fair play, respect, consistency and transparency, embrace change, encourage high aspirations, recognise success, environmentally conscious.

Objectives are a way to break down a strategy into a set of achievable targets for purposes such as performance management. An objective might be a target used to measure progress towards a strategic goal – for example, annual membership objectives that move the organisation towards a long-term membership goal.

A strategy is a long-term plan that sets high-level goals or aims. The Governance and Leadership Framework for Wales, under Principle 3, provides a useful success measure: vision, mission and strategy unite staff and stakeholders, and are used to drive everyday delivery.

Consequences of not having a strategy

Financial impact

Whether it is a community club or NGB, there are limited resources available to fulfil the invariably high expectations of stakeholders. Without a strategy that sets out what is to be achieved, how and with what resources, financial resources can too easily be wasted due to lack of direction and oversight. Maintaining discipline in implementing a long-term strategy through annual business plans will ensure that the available funding is dedicated to the agreed activities that are most likely to deliver the strategic goals.

Reputational damage

An organisation that lacks direction, wastes valuable resources (people and financial) and fails to oversee its activities may lose the confidence of its stakeholders. While members may have the opportunity to raise concerns via an AGM and funders will expect to see tangible improvements at regular partner meetings, potential commercial partners that undertake due diligence are unlikely to engage with an organisation that appears to be poorly led and managed.

Employee de-motivation

In 2015, *Harvard Business Review* reported that 95% of employees did not understand the business plans of their organisations. Without a clear and ambitious plan, staff and volunteers can easily lack direction and become disheartened. Creating an aspirational future and defining each person's contribution to this not only unites the organisation; it can maintain high levels of motivation among the workforce.

Matters reserved for the board

In the ICSA's guidance notes Matters Reserved for the Board (2013) and Matters Reserved for the Board of Trustees (2011), specimen schedules for companies and charities set out the areas on which only the board should make decisions. Examples of matters reserved for the board include:

- overall leadership of the organisation;
- setting and reviewing the organisation's structure;
- setting budgets and maintaining proper financial oversight;
- maintaining effective board performance;
- ensuring a sound system of internal control and risk management;
- board appointments/removal as required under the organisation's articles;
- approval of major contracts;
- establishing board committees and setting terms of reference;
- approving remuneration; and
- approving policies, for example, code of conduct, whistleblowing, equality and bribery.

Creating clear board terms of reference, committee terms of reference, job descriptions for senior executives and a delegated authority policy will all help ensure the division of responsibility is maintained, as is the internal control system.

Roles and responsibilities of directors

The duties of directors are covered in Chapter 2 (pages 42 to 44), as are their legal duties.

The Corporate Code sets out its own view of the role of the board, summarised as:

- providing entrepreneurial leadership;
- setting strategy;
- ensuring the human and financial resources are available to achieve objectives;
- reviewing management performance;
- setting the company's values and standards; and
- ensuring that obligations to shareholders and other stakeholders are understood and met.

The FRC's Guidance on Board Effectiveness expands on this list stating that in particular, a board:

- provides direction for management;
- demonstrates ethical leadership, displaying (and promoting throughout the company) behaviours consistent with the culture and values it has defined for the organisation;
- creates a performance culture that drives value creation without exposing the company to excessive risk of value destruction;
- makes well-informed and high-quality decisions based on a clear line of sight into the business;
- creates the right framework for helping directors meet their statutory duties under CA 2006, and/or other relevant statutory and regulatory regimes;
- is accountable, particularly to those that provide the company's capital; and
- thinks carefully about its governance arrangements and embraces evaluation of their effectiveness.

Liabilities of directors
As well as the duties owed to the organisation, directors may be personally liable:

- to a fine if the company does not comply with any of the requirements in the Companies (Trading Disclosures) Regulations 2008 and fails to make the trading disclosures required under those Regulations;
- for contracts signed by them purportedly on behalf of the company before its incorporation (s. 51 of the Act);
- if they act in the management of the company while disqualified;
- for damages if they make a fraudulent or negligent misrepresentation in the course of negotiating a contract between the company and the third party;
- under the criminal offence of making a false statement as to the affairs of the company with the intent of deceiving shareholders or creditors of a company (s. 19 of the Theft Act 1968);
- for imprisonment (up to ten years) or a fine if they are knowingly party to the company carrying on its business with intent to defraud creditors of the company or of another person or for any fraudulent purpose;
- under a contract if they fail to make it clear that they are contracting as an agent of the company and not personally;

- to a third party for damages for breach of an implied warranty of authority if they conclude a contract on behalf of the company but exceeds their authority in so doing and the company is therefore able to set the contract aside; and
- for negligence manslaughter, which carries a maximum sentence of life imprisonment.

Legal responsibilities

The Companies Act 2006 is explicit in setting out the seven duties of directors. As explained in Chapter 2 (pages 42 to 44), the duties of directors are to the company itself, not to its shareholders, its employees or any person external to the company. However, a director's duty to promote the success of the company will mean they have to have due regard for the interests of stakeholders, including employees, suppliers and customers.

Directors must be able to demonstrate the means by which a decision is taken in the event that a key stakeholder is negatively affected. In a sporting context, decisions to meet funding requirements that affect members will need robust evidence and effective communication that demonstrate how the needs of members were considered in the decision-making process.

Possible legal sanctions both individually and collectively

A number of statutes contain provisions stating that if a company commits a criminal offence, a director is also guilty of the offence if it is proved to have been committed with the consent or connivance of, or to have been attributable to, any neglect on the part of the director. In this context, 'consent' means being aware of what is going on and agreeing to it, and 'connivance' means knowledge together with a negligent failure to prevent. 'Neglect' implies that there is no need for knowledge of the matters amounting to the offence; instead, there merely is a failure to act when under a duty to do so.

Legal obligations

Directors are not generally personally liable to third parties, unless they have given a personal guarantee for the company's liabilities. However, various statutes have imposed personal liability on directors in a wide range of situations, including health and safety, environmental, competition and securities matters.

A commitment to continuous improvement and board training will assist in maintaining a focus on the board's legal duties and obligations, reducing risks to the organisation and individual directors or trustees.

Evaluating board effectiveness

In 2013, UK Sport and Sport England placed a requirement on all funded organisations to undertake an annual board effectiveness review. The Code for Sports Governance has since set out more detailed requirements that reflect those of the UK Corporate Governance Code. Principle 4: Standards and Conduct states the following:

- The board, led by the chair, shall undertake, and maintain in writing a record of, an annual evaluation of its own skills and performance and of individual directors, and that of its committees (committee evaluation need not be undertaken annually).
- External evaluation of the board shall be facilitated at least every four years or at the request of UK Sport/Sport England.
- The board shall agree and implement a plan to take forward any actions resulting from the evaluations.

Internal measures

The benefits of undertaking a review internally include speed and relatively low costs. A skills audit and performance review of the board and individual board members can be led by the chair and supported by the company secretary/CEO, enabling a comprehensive review leading to recommendations on process, culture and development. It can give an organisation a sense of being in control of the process.

The disadvantage of internally led reviews are that they may lack objectivity, with any aspects that are rated or scored not subject to moderation, leading to inconsistent or even inaccurate outcomes. There is also greater pressure on the chair, whose relationship with each board member may influence any face-to-face meetings with board colleagues.

External audit

An external audit of the board can be carried out through a multi-phased process that will most likely involve more board time (collectively and individually), greater cost, and may even create tensions or difficult discussions, if the outcomes are challenging.

Some of the ways in which an independent audit could be undertaken include:

- a review of board papers – up to a year to understand how the organisation makes decisions;
- interviews with each board member and senior staff;
- online surveys;
- observation of board meetings and potentially committee meetings; and
- facilitated discussion with the board on initial findings to review the board's strengths and agree priority development areas.

It is also useful for independent auditor to return after an agreed period to reassess progress including behaviours.

Appointing board members

Many sports organisations are run as micro and small businesses with finance, ethical, commercial and legal responsibilities borne by the board. Accessing essential skills and knowledge to fulfil these responsibilities will enhance decision-making processes, help identify and maximise opportunities, and effectively manage risks, while ensuring the organisation stays focused on its purpose.

Code requirements in respect of appointing board members

In any organisation, the mission or core purpose provides the basis on which it is structured. Put simply, form follows function. If a sports body exists to deliver participation opportunities and also win medals at major events while developing an ambitious business model and commercialising its assets, then the structure and, in particular, board composition will reflect these aims. Recruiting staff and appointing board members who have the necessary skills, knowledge and experience will ensure the organisation is accessing expertise and views that are relevant.

The Code for Sports Governance requires that organisations recruit and engage people with appropriate diversity, independence, skills, experience and knowledge to take effective decisions that further the organisation's goals. This reinforces the principles laid out in the UK Corporate Governance Code, the Principles of Good Governance for Sport and Recreation, and the Governance and Leadership Framework for Wales.

Diversity – developing inclusive sport

According to Sport England's Active Lives Survey, sporting communities are still predominantly of white British ethnic origin and male. Governance codes and related funding requirements have therefore established expectations around diversity that sports organisations must actively pursue. The Active Lives survey is available on the Sport England website: www.sportengland.org/media/11498/active-lives-survey-yr-1-report.pdf.

There is significant research from the commercial sector that indicates greater board diversity correlates to improved organisational performance. Business in the Community (BITC) is a charity that seeks to support businesses on issues including the environment, education and employee accessibility. Opportunity Now is a BITC programme that aims to encourage gender-balanced leadership in companies. BITC research cited the following impact of inclusive leadership (Business Impact of inclusive Leadership 2014):

- 81% improved performance;
- 81% greater engagement and loyalty;
- 86% increased innovation and creativity;
- 70% new likely to capture a new market;

- 84% increased motivation; and
- 79% improved collaboration.

Consequently, the Code for Sports Governance includes a requirement of 30% female or male representation on boards and, while there are no specific targets for other under-represented groups, the expectation is clear – sports bodies must demonstrate they are actively seeking to diversify.

Quotas remain a contentious issue in the UK, and the Code for Sports Governance requirement is a more direct approach. There is, however, evidence of progress in respect of gender balance on boards, with Women in Sport reporting that women make up 30% of Sport England-funded boards and 29% of Sport Wales-funded boards (*Beyond 30%*, 2017).

The business case for diversity now appears to be even greater than the moral case, with the achievement of organisational outcomes linked to board composition. Since 2013, when Sport England and UK Sport first set an expectation of 25% female representation on the boards of funded organisations, anecdotal evidence suggests the move towards gender balance has had a positive impact on board performance. Sports bodies report better board behaviour and adherence to codes of conduct, that discussions stayed on track, and that the breadth of insight and expertise has improved the quality of decisions.

Women in Sport have produced a Checklist for Change; this is a practical tool to help organisations attract and recruit women into senior positions. The checklist recommends practical actions under the following six headings:

1. transparency across the board;
2. flexibility in working practices;
3. mentoring and role models at all levels;
4. fit for future structures, terms and conditions;
5. proactive recruitment; and
6. inclusive culture.

This can be downloaded from the Women in Sport website: www.womeninsport. org/resources/trophy-women-2015-checklist-for-change.

Unitary and two-tier board systems

Under a unitary board structure there is a single board of directors, comprising executive and NEDs. By comparison, there are two separate boards under the two-tier structure:

- the management (operating) board which is responsible for the day-to-day running of the business, consisting of executives only and led by the CEO; and
- the supervisory (corporate) board with a wider membership, responsible for the strategic oversight of the organisation and led by the chair.

Companies in most countries have unitary boards, consisting of both executive and non-executive directors under the leadership of the chair. A unitary board makes collective decisions and is accountable to the shareholders. The advantages of the unitary system are the superior flow of information due to more frequent meetings, the requirement to make and monitor decisions, and better understanding and involvement in the organisation by the board. If directors, especially NEDs, are making important decisions, they are incentivised to supply themselves with all the relevant information as they are ultimately responsible under CA 2006 and, if it is a registered charity, under the Charities Act 2011.

This is often replicated at club levels, with a president or chair leading the executive committee and a club or general manager managing operational matters. Even if executive committee members undertake operational tasks, there still needs to be a range of skills on the committee to meet the business demands of the club.

Size and composition of the board

Size matters – the number of board members will correlate to the complexity of an organisation's function as well as its capacity. The UK Corporate Governance Code states that 'the Board should be of sufficient size that the requirements of the business can be met and that changes to the Board's composition and that of its committees can be managed without disruption, and should not be so large as to be unwieldy'.

The Principles of Good Governance for Sport and Recreation set a range of 8 to 12 members, while the Code for Sports Governance requires that funded sports' boards are no larger than 12. In all cases, the organisation must be able to establish an optimum size that meets its purpose and enables effective decision making.

A board that is too small may not have the necessary skills or knowledge to make informed decisions, and will face further risks if one or two individuals leave. In addition, it may be difficult to build a sub-committee structure if there are too few board members to lead and serve on the sub-committees.

A board that is too large can create an environment where debate is difficult to manage, leading to decisions that have not been fully discussed and all the best options explored. This can be due to the sheer number of people engaged in the discussion, dominant personalities who limit the opportunities of others to contribute, a vast range of disparate views that cannot be focused into a single or coherent decision, or quite simply a lack of time available for everyone to offer a view. One of the most common reasons for large boards is a desire to ensure the voice of the participant or member is heard. This would, in theory, assist in meeting the principle of accountability and transparency with democratic representation being a key factor.

Larger boards may be composed of individuals who have been elected on a geographical or technical basis – for example, those voted into position by members from a designated area of the country or because they are experts in a discipline such as coaching or officiating. This is visible in the Olympic and Paralympic Movements with Medical and Athlete Commissions, among others, as well as in community sports clubs where individuals will be elected by their women, junior or senior sections. This concept of representation is a fundamental, democratic component of current and historical approaches to board appointments in sport. However, appointing solely from within the sport, especially when such appointments are designated as representative, can also bring risks to decision making.

The UK Corporate Governance Code is very clear on the duties of directors who 'must act in the way s/he considers, in good faith, would be most likely to promote the success of the company for the benefit of its members as a whole'.

By seeking a blend of skills, knowledge and experience from within and beyond the sport, an organisation is most likely to be able to create dynamic and informed debate with diverse views providing objectivity, balance and also deterring factions. Looking beyond the membership allows a sports body to access vital expertise from different talent pools.

Guiding any board appointment process will be the core function of the organisation. GB Taekwondo and British Hockey are examples of national sports bodies that have only one function – to identify, develop and support potential medal-winning athletes. It is the role of other organisations to widen access to their sports and increase participation – for example, home country hockey associations. With this in mind, the skill set required to lead the organisation can focus on high-performance sport and business skills – both bodies have developed visible brands and secured significant commercial partnerships.

In contrast, British Cycling leads the development of cycling from schools through recreational cycling to Olympic and Paralympic performance programmes. The board would be expected to have an understanding of sports development, diversity, business development, finance and marketing, and high-performance cycling. In short, form (board composition) follows function (core purpose and strategy).

The UK Corporate Governance Code sets out different requirements for large listed companies and for smaller companies (smaller companies are defined as companies outside the FTSE 350 for the whole of the year immediately prior to the reporting year).

- Except for smaller companies, at least one half of the board, excluding the chair, should be independent NEDs.
- For smaller companies, there should be at least two independent NEDs.

For sports bodies in receipt of public funding from Sport England and UK Sport and that are categorised as Tier 3, 25% of the board must be independent NEDs, one of whom will be the senior independent director (SID).

In terms of board roles, the following should be considered to ensure clear leadership, informed discussion, appropriate challenge and effective scrutiny from a range of perspectives:

- chair;
- vice chair;

- senior independent director (who might be the vice chair);
- non-executive directors, of whom 25% must be independent to meet Sport England and UK Sport requirements;
- CEO (may or may not be a director); and
- executive directors.

Some sports bodies also include the CEO as a director with voting rights. There are benefits to such an approach, including shared responsibility or greater credibility within the community. Risks include potential conflicts of interest in respect of executive remuneration or the division of responsibility becoming blurred between chair, board and CEO.

Conducting a skills audit

An effective board needs a range of competencies, skills, knowledge and experience to enable it to work towards the aims and objectives of the organisation. Carrying out a skills audit is a simple but effective way of keeping a register of your organisation's board skills and knowledge.

Establishing the competencies, skills and knowledge

Even if an organisation is not imminently planning an appointment process, building a picture of the skills of the current directors or trustees is still invaluable. It gives the organisation the information it needs to assess the degree to which the board's collective strengths are aligned with its strategy. A skills matrix will also help organisations respond more quickly when new board members are needed.

The matrix should be created with the present and future in mind. For example, if a sports body has aspirations to increase its commercial income streams over 4 to 12 years, the necessary skills will be needed sooner to assist in the development of appropriate strategies. Undertaking an audit of the current board can fulfil many helpful and important functions:

- It creates a documentary record of the ways in which current board members add value to the organisation.
- The auditing process will identify the strengths of the current board as well as gaps in skills or knowledge that are needed to lead the organisation in the future.
- Individual audit responses will highlight development areas for each board member.
- If a large proportion of the board reports limited knowledge or understanding of one aspect of core business, for example, high-performance sport, this will inform development options for the board as a whole.

Once competencies, skills and knowledge have been prioritised, each board member is asked to rate themselves against each one. If resources and capacity are limited, this can be done via an online survey to reduce costs and administrative burdens.

Organisations may choose to use an external facilitator who includes one-to-one interviews as well as online surveys and observations. The benefits of this approach include:

- a fuller understanding of each competency or area of expertise;
- the possibility that individuals will rate themselves more accurately as they respond to an interviewer who is independent;
- a moderation process that guides the board members on the relative level of their expertise; and
- an independently produced set of recommendations.

Finding board members with appropriate skills and knowledge

The first step to finding the right person for your board is to set out the duties, expectations and requirements of the role itself. These should reflect your legal status and the duties that apply to board members. It is also reasonable to include expectations in terms of time commitment and the contribution that might be anticipated beyond board meetings, including sub-committee roles or attendance at events. The role description should be accompanied by a person specification listing the competencies, skills, behaviours and experience required.

Examples of board role descriptions are freely available on the UK Sport, Sport and Recreation and the Sport Wales Club solutions websites.

To assist golf clubs in developing good governance, the golf unions of Wales, England, Scotland and Ireland jointly developed the Governance Guide for Golf Clubs resource. Contained within the guide are exemplars for the range of golf club committee positions. These models are useful as a starting point for any voluntary club role, regardless of the sport, and clubs can tailor these role descriptions and person specifications to their own unique needs.

The ways in which individuals can be appointed to the board

Most sports organisations were originally formed as associations, meaning that people would quite literally associate on the basis of a shared interest, such as archery or judo. As membership bodies, they offered structure and governance by way of organised competition and leagues, setting the rules of the sport and selecting national teams. Serving members is paramount for most sports bodies, and the democratic nature of leadership and decision making is reflected in their structures.

Effective appointment processes

Once a role description and person specification have been developed and a skills audit has been completed, the organisation can embark on an appointment process.

In the first instance, the organisation should develop a recruitment policy that sets the overarching aims, for example:

- to reach potential candidates who have the skills and knowledge required for the position;
- to actively encourage applications from diverse backgrounds;
- to select the most suitable candidate to carry out the duties of the post;
- to make selection decisions which do not discriminate unfairly against any group or individual and enable an increase in the diversity of the organisation; or
- to give a good impression of the NGB as a professional and progressive organisation.

Once in place, the policy is most likely to be implemented transparently and methodically by a nominations committee or selection panel. This will be a sub-group of the board and should have terms of reference that establish clarity of purpose, role and tasks.

Its activities should reflect the recruitment policy and process, including the tasks associated with the advertising, application and interview process. Specifically, the panel should agree:

- selection criteria;
- advertising and notification of the vacancy;
- method(s) for short listing or pre-selection;
- method(s) of assessment of shortlisted candidates, where candidates are asked to complete a task or presentation;
- competency-based questions which will be asked of all candidates;
- a scoring system that measures the candidates' responses against the competencies;
- interview process including the questions allocated to each interviewer;
- formal note taker; and
- reference check (written or telephone, at an agreed point in the process).

It is the responsibility of the lead recruiter, who might be the panel chair or HR lead, to ensure that all selection panel members are fully aware of their legal and procedural obligations.

Best practice suggests that interview panels contain both men and women, and consist of at least three people. NGBs are also increasingly inviting independent members onto their selection panels, often from other sports. This provides a greater degree of objectivity from a peer organisation as well as a high level of professional insight.

The process for the appointment of elected board members need not be significantly different. It is still good practice to appoint a nominations committee to lead and implement the appointment process, and information circulated to members should outline aims and details of the process. This will include publication of the role description and person specification, as it is more likely to attract candidates with the skills and knowledge to fill the vacancy. Subject to the organisation's articles, the nominations committee may also be able to filter nominated candidates, with individuals best matching the requirements shortlisted for the members' final vote.

It is worth checking the governing document to see if such a system is allowed. If not, the board might consider adjusting the articles to enable the nominations committee to shortlist on a competency basis.

Theory in action

Hockey Wales changed its articles of association to ensure a balanced board of elected and appointed directors. Hockey Wales signed up to the GLFW and to ensure the board was equipped to lead the sport into the future, a number of governance changes were implemented:

- Board competency and skills framework – to meet recruitment, training and behavioural expectations.
- Board skills analysis – competency-based interviews, psychometric tools and a skills and experience chart.
- Recruitment policy and process – resulting in the recruitment of four new directors who work in industries other than sport.
- Independent chair appointed.
- A board evaluation and review.

The board now has a full complement of elected and appointed directors, and the quality of discussion and challenge has increased significantly, as has the quality of support and guidance offered to the executive team and organisation.

The improved clarity of roles for the CEO, chair and board has improved the ability to engage, challenge and support at the right level. Confidence in the board has increased, especially from a staff perspective.

Induction process

FRC guidance states 'on first appointment, a NED should devote time to a comprehensive, formal and tailored induction'. Furthermore, Institute of Directors guidance reinforces the value of an effective induction as 'there is not much scope to learn on the job, and liability and accountability exist from day one'.

The board is a living entity defined not just by its skills and knowledge but also by the quality of its relationships and interactions. By changing one member of the board, the dynamics and skills base can all change. Therefore, taking time to establish relationships as soon as a new board member arrives is time well spent. In sport, most board members are volunteers, some of whom will have had limited experience but may still have preconceptions about their role and duties.

FRC's Guidance on Board Effectiveness (2011) states at 1.18 that a NED should, on appointment, devote time to a comprehensive, formal and tailored induction which should extend beyond the boardroom. An induction should be strategic, practical and personal, enabling an individual to understand fully the organisation, its people, its culture and their role in supporting these. On appointment, new board members should receive a letter of appointment setting out their responsibilities included the time commitment and expectations in respect of conduct. This should be supplemented by a range of documents which provide the new board member with sufficient information to understand the current status of the organisation as well as its long-term aspirations. This could include:

- organisational strategy, current operational plan and risk register;
- current financial status and relevant financial reports;
- organisational structures and profiles of board members and senior staff;
- sub-committee structures and terms of reference (plus any information on expectations placed on board members in respect of sub-committee leadership or membership;
- board terms of reference;
- code of conduct and/or handbook with relevant policies;
- minutes from recent meetings;
- dates of board meetings and other key events; and
- a summary of funding agreements or similar contracts with strategic partners.

This may seem like a long list; however, the information can be provided in several parts so as not to overburden, or deter, new board members. Information on practical matters such as venues for meetings and events, management of expenses or people to contact for further information should also be provided.

New board members will be more comfortable and confident in contributing if they feel welcome, valued and well supported. Rather than presuming relationships will form and settle of their own accord, sports bodies can put in place mechanisms to bring people together for the purpose of introductions, learning about different roles, and the ways in which the organisation functions. This is particularly important when introducing a new member who has not served on a board before or comes from a different background.

Soon after appointment, the new member should meet with the chair and CEO. If a board meeting has taken place, additional time for existing members to meet their new colleagues can be incorporated into the schedule. A new director might also be partnered with a board colleague and a senior member of staff to understand how the organisation's culture and strategy are applied on a day-to-day basis.

In the first six months, the chair or the vice chair could make contact with the new board member on a regular basis. This creates a useful means by which new directors or trustees can ask questions, seek clarification or offer ideas in an informal environment. It also creates an opportunity for them to receive feedback on their contribution and the ways in which they can continue to develop.

A comprehensive induction should mean new board members are informed, confident and motivated. The process is a crucial first step not just for the board members, but also for the organisation which depends on their contribution from the moment they are appointed.

Succession planning

Earlier in this chapter, the skills matrix was presented and explained. A key benefit of a skills matrix – the breakdown of competencies, skills, knowledge and experience needed on the board – is the ability to plan for the future. This includes occasions when key people leave the organisation.

Many sports bodies will have among their leaders individuals who are 'walking archives'. These people hold vast amounts of knowledge of the sport, the organisation, its past and its people. While such individuals can offer invaluable insight, they present a risk if the organisation depends on their knowledge. Similarly, individuals with professional qualifications or unique experience in areas such as finance, legal or high-performance sport will be especially valuable, and their loss could be a strategic risk.

In all cases, sports bodies should use the results from their skills audit to identify the priority skills and knowledge, who in the organisation currently offers these, and how the organisation will respond to the loss of such skills and knowledge. Producing a succession plan for planned and unplanned changes will reduce risks and costs. This process should apply to senior staff as well as board members.

Known changes will include a refreshing of the board – for example, when board members reach the end of their term of office. With a current skills matrix, sports bodies can create a person specification to ensure they attract individuals with the skills and knowledge to maintain an effective balance.

Unforeseen changes, which may occur due to illness, resignations or removal from office, can be managed in different ways. If a board is facing an immediate and significant skills gap, individuals may be co-opted on the board to fulfil this function until a permanent replacement can be appointed. Such a decision would depend on whether the body's articles of association allow individuals to be co-opted; it is worth checking your articles to see what flexibility the board has to co-opt. Alternatively, advisory, non-voting roles can be created to avoid conflict with the governing document, while temporarily accessing essential expertise. However, these roles would be short term until a permanent replacement is appointed.

In respect of a senior staff member leaving abruptly, especially the CEO, consideration can be given to the ongoing development of executive directors. This would include training in key areas that would enable at least one person to fill the role on an interim basis. Many sports bodies now appoint chief operating officers who generally deputise for the CEO and would automatically step into the role if required.

In all cases, knowing which skills and knowledge are needed to lead the organisation, be they non-executive or executive roles, will enable a sports body to anticipate and respond smoothly to changes.

Role of the company secretary

Company secretary's role in assisting in the governance and administration of the organisation's affairs

The company secretary acts as the chief administrative officer of the company, and shares various responsibilities with the directors under CA 2006. Private companies are no longer obliged to appoint a company secretary, although most companies continue to do so. The UK Corporate Code states that:

> Under the direction of the chairman, the company secretary's responsibilities include ensuring good information flows within the Board and its committees and between senior management and Non-Executive Directors, as well as facilitating induction and assisting with professional development as required.

> The company secretary should be responsible for advising the Board through the chairman on all governance matters.

Legal duties of the company secretary

The law does not state explicitly what the company secretary should do. In practice, however, the company secretary plays a central role in the governance and administration of an organisation's affairs, with particular responsibilities in three main areas:

- **The board:** The company secretary provides essential practical support to the chair and other directors, both as a group and individually, ensuring that statutory and regulatory requirements are met for the conduct and running of board meetings, and that the board has access to the information it requires.
- **The company:** The company secretary is responsible for ensuring that the statutory and regulatory requirements are met, particularly in relation to CA 2006 and related legislation governing the reporting of the activities of the company (such as filing statutory returns).
- **The shareholders (members):** The company secretary is the primary point of contact for all shareholders and is principally responsible for the maintenance and management of shareholder records, such as the register of members, and organising shareholder-related events, such as paying dividends, producing and issuing the annual report and accounts, and coordinating general meetings.

Other duties of the company secretary

The company secretary should be present at all board meetings and general meetings, and will be responsible for coordinating these. This includes drafting the agenda and agreeing it with the chair and CEO, as well as collecting, organising and circulating the papers required at the meetings. They will also be responsible for the minutes of board meetings and circulating these according to the organisation's articles and standing order or rules.

As well as servicing the board, the company secretary is likely to be responsible for organising sub-committees and acting as a channel of communication for non-executive directors.

The duties of a company secretary are diverse, and one of the most important functions is the advisory nature of the role. They will stay abreast of all relevant legal, statutory and regulatory requirements and best practice, and must also be able to give impartial advice and support to the directors. This includes advising the board if it appears to be acting in breach of legal requirements or the organisation's articles.

In the private sector, the company secretary is the focal point for all shareholder communication. In a sports organisation, this will be same in relation to general meetings including the AGM. However, the organisation may also use a variety of communication tools to engage and consult with members on a less formal basis – for example, in developing new formats or programmes. While the company secretary may not be the focal point on these occasions, it is still valuable to maintain their involvement to be sure of meeting regulatory duties, such as data protection and information management.

Sports Councils' assurance frameworks

UK Sport and the four Home Country Sports Councils have developed assurance frameworks that enable the monitoring and measurement of governance performance by those organisations in receipt of public and National Lottery funds. What is measured and the volume of information required will vary according the size of award and the outcomes sought. For example, Sport Wales offers small grants up to £1,500 under its Community Chest scheme, which is administered by local authorities, who also gather monitoring data on behalf of Sport Wales. NGBs, such as British Athletics, receive multi-million pound awards from UK Sport and are subject to rigorous assurance processes including:

- submission of financial information to UK Sport on a quarterly basis;
- independent audit carried out by a UK Sport commissioned auditor at least once every four years; and
- completion of an evidence-based assurance statement which addresses governance, strategic planning, finance, HR, organisational policy and risk management.

The launch of the Code for Sports Governance has reframed the Sport England and UK Sport assurance process and recipients of funding now have to demonstrate consistently and at least annually, with evidence, how they meet the funding requirements set out in the Code.

Procurement policies

Sports bodies that seek to live by a strong set of values aimed at promoting ethical sport may stumble if their suppliers adopt policies contrary to these values. A procurement policy therefore has to be consistent with the organisation's own values, with expectations clearly set out in any contracts and agreements. For example, an NGB equality policy statement and expectations of potential bidders in respect of inclusion and equality can be displayed in any tender information. Thereafter a contractual clause can be included that reaffirms the requirement for suppliers and contractors to adhere to the NGB equality policy or provide a copy of the supplier's own equality policy statement.

Role of the board in ensuring effective stakeholder relations

Board members should not routinely take over the role of engagement – apart from engagement with those to whom they have a direct accountability, for example, at the AGM or chairs and board members may meet with ministers or senior personnel of a funding Sports Council. In the broader arena of stakeholder engagement, their responsibility is to ensure that appropriate engagement takes place, and that they and others are properly directed and supported when engaged with shareholders.

Identification of key stakeholders

One of the board's roles is to identify key stakeholders; it is worthwhile spending board time on this activity. This will not only create a prioritised stakeholder engagement strategy, but will also ensure greater efficiency in terms of time, people and resources dedicated to those relationships.

Broadly, boards with their senior executives should identify stakeholders in terms of their influence over the organisation and their interest (how much time and energy they expend learning, observing and seeking a relationship with the organisation). Figure 5.1 (see page 102) provides a useful starting point for stakeholder identification on the basis of interest and influence.

Developing a stakeholder strategy

The board and senior staff need to discuss and agree the position of each stakeholder including the organisation's relationships with members, funders, sponsors, the media, other sports organisations, international federations and local or national government, along with any other partners or interested parties the organisation deems important. Once the level of influence and interest has been agreed, a plan can be developed that targets resources appropriately at communications and activity that engages, informs, encourages and enhances the priority relationships.

Providing assurance to investors

The annual report should contain details of the governance improvements that have been undertaken, as well as any future governance challenges. The ICSA guidance note Contents List for the Annual Report of a UK Company provides helpful advice on the information that can be included in the annual report in order that members can assess the organisation's position. This includes the chair's report, governance statement, financial report and reports on sustainability, ethics, values and/or corporate social responsibility.

The creation of a robust control system overseen by a skilled audit committee will provide assurance to stakeholders. Internal and (where appropriate) external audit will provide independent scrutiny and require management responses to governance challenges.

Assurance to investors, such as Sports Councils, local government, commercial partners or (in the case of charities) donors, can be provided by visibly implementing good governance. Principle 4 of the Code for Sports Governance states that having the right values embedded in the culture of the organisation helps protect public investment and also enhances the reputation of the organisation, earning stakeholder trust. Signing up to a recognised code, undertaking a governance review and creating a governance improvement plan with dedicated resources all combine to reassure stakeholders, especially investors, that the organisation is striving to be well led and well governed.

Overview of other key stakeholders in sports organisations

Sports organisations do not exist in isolation. They need to maintain relationships with a range of stakeholders, stakeholders being people, groups, or organisations that have a direct or indirect stake in an organisation because it can affect or be affected by the organization's actions, objectives, and policies. Indeed, in sport, the diversity of stakeholders is particularly large. In this section we will cover those found within the majority of sports organisations, whatever the level. We will then expand on stakeholder engagement in Chapter 13.

The board and stakeholders

Board members should not routinely take over the role of engagement – apart from engagement with those to whom they have a direct accountability, for example, at the AGM or chairs and board members may meet with ministers or senior personnel of a funding Sports Council. In the broader arena of stakeholder engagement, their responsibility is to ensure that appropriate engagement takes place, and that they and others are properly directed and supported when engaged with shareholders.

Identifcation of key stakeholders

One of the board's roles is to identify key stakeholders; it is worthwhile spending board time on this activity. This will not only create a prioritised stakeholder engagement strategy, but will also ensure greater efficiency in terms of time, people and resources dedicated to those relationships.

Broadly, boards with their senior executives should identify stakeholders in terms of their infuence over the organisation and their interest (how much time and energy they expend learning, observing and seeking a relationship with the organisation). Figure 5.1 provides a useful starting point for stakeholder identifcation on the basis of interest and infuence.

Developing a stakeholder strategy

The board and senior staff need to discuss and agree the position of each stakeholder including the organisation's relationships with members, funders, sponsors, the media, other sports organisations, international federations and local or national government, along with any other partners or interested parties the organisation deems important. Once the level of infuence and interest has been agreed, a plan can be developed that targets resources appropriately at communications and activity that engages, informs, encourages and enhances the priority relationships.

Figure 5.1: Influence and interest of stakeholders

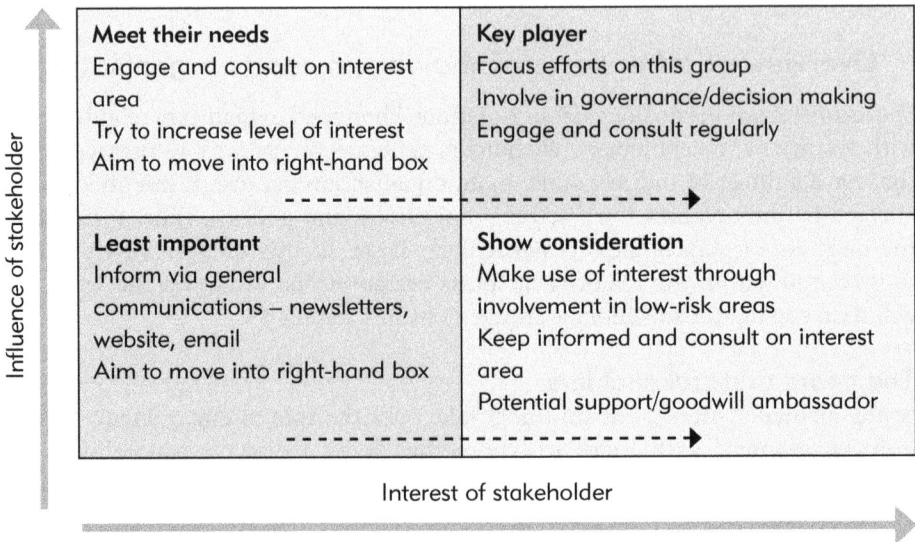

Meet their needs	Key player
Engage and consult on interest area	Focus efforts on this group
Try to increase level of interest	Involve in governance/decision making
Aim to move into right-hand box	Engage and consult regularly
Least important	**Show consideration**
Inform via general communications – newsletters, website, email	Make use of interest through involvement in low-risk areas
Aim to move into right-hand box	Keep informed and consult on interest area
	Potential support/goodwill ambassador

Influence of stakeholder (vertical axis)

Interest of stakeholder (horizontal axis)

Providing assurance to investors

The annual report should contain details of the governance improvements that have been undertaken, as well as any future governance challenges. The ICSA guidance note Contents list for the annual report of a UK company provides helpful advice on the information that can be included in the annual report in order that members can assess the organisation's position. This includes the chair's report, governance statement, financial report and reports on sustainability, ethics, values and/or corporate social responsibility.

The creation of a robust control system overseen by a skilled audit committee will provide assurance to stakeholders. Internal and (where appropriate) external audit will provide independent scrutiny and require management responses to governance challenges.

Assurance to investors, such as Sports Councils, local government, commercial partners or (in the case of charities) donors, can be provided by visibly implementing good governance. Principle 4 of the Code for Sports Governance states that having the right values embedded in the culture of the organisation helps protect public investment and also enhances the reputation of the organisation, earning stakeholder trust. Signing up to a recognised code, undertaking a governance review and creating a governance improvement plan with dedicated resources all combine to reassure stakeholders, especially investors, that the organisation is striving to be well led and well governed.

Trustees, guardians and governors

Sports clubs may appoint trustees once they have registered as a company. This is particularly the case where the company owns land. The trustees will be named directors but will not always serve on the management committee/executive committee, leaving the day-to-day running of the club to elected volunteers. This may represent a risk to clubs, as the individuals named as directors are bound by legislation to fulfil their duties to the club. Trustees whose role has been reduced to occasional attendance at general meetings would be well advised to ensure they have suffcient information and decision making authority to execute their duties appropriately.

Some sports place great value on the traditions, ethos and philosophy of their sports. The sport of parkour (freerunning or art du deplacement) and its NGB, Parkour UK, were recognised in 2016. Its board is composed of elected and independent members and governors. The distinctions between these three are described as follows:

- *President* – an individual who is the ceremonial figurehead of Parkour UK, appointed by the voting members of Parkour UK.
- *Governors* – appointed by the board as custodians of the philosophy of the sport/discipline.

- *CEO and elected directors* – appointed by the voting members of Parkour UK to oversee and direct the work of the NGB.
- *Independent directors* – appointed by the board and external to Parkour UK. At least one appointed independent director will hold the position of independent chair.
- *Elected directors – home nations* – appointed by the voting members of Parkour UK, in each home country of England, Wales, Scotland and Northern Ireland to oversee and direct the work of the NGB.

The philosophy of Parkour is important to its founders and participants, so the position of governors helps ensure the NGB does not stray from its original ethos.

Members/shareholders

In companies limited by guarantee, the rights of members attach solely to the members, as no shares exist. The rights and powers of members are set out in the organisation's articles including voting rights. Legislation in respect of shareholders and their additional rights (for example, the rights to a dividend) does not apply to sports bodies where there are no shareholders.

Relationship between the organisation and its members

In this area sport can claim a sense of uniqueness as, for a membership NGB, members can also be defned by many other roles including volunteers (clubs and regions), directors of the board, coaches and offcials, tutors and participants. In all cases they are also customers who are in receipt of products and services developed by the NGB including competition opportunities, leadership development and coach development. The nature of the relationship is much more than a transactional one – whereby an individual pays a fee and receives a service, as so many members contribute to the delivery of said services in their different capacities. As a result, the organisation seeks to maintain a much deeper connected relationship with its members, as they are much more than customers or investors. This is most visible in consultation and decision-making systems, where members are engaged from grass roots to board level via committees and other structures.

Relationship between the board and members

Both the Principles of Good Governance in Sport and Governance and Leadership Framework highlight the benefts of engaging directly with stakeholders, especially members many of whom are volunteers. The Principles of Good Governance, under Principle 7: Engaging with the Wider Sport and Recreation Sector, lists the following practical steps organisations can take:

- The board should understand the unique role of volunteers and must strive to appreciate and encourage appropriate ways to involve them.

- The board should ensure that the views and opinions of stakeholders are considered and discussed at board meetings where relevant.
- The board should use their annual general meeting or general meetings as a useful means to develop dialogue with members and other stakeholders.

Rights of members

The principal rights of members to information about a company are:

- to inspect and request copies of various statutory books and records;
- to inspect directors' service contracts or request a copy of a service contract (where these exist);
- to inspect written memoranda of the terms and conditions of a director's contract of service for the company and any of its subsidiaries;
- to be provided with a copy of the company's Memorandum and Articles of Association;
- to receive a copy of the annual accounts at least 14 days before the general meeting at which they are to be laid;
- to be provided with a copy of the latest accounts of the company;
- to receive notice of all general meetings;
- to inspect minutes of general meetings and to request copies; and
- to attend general meetings and to ask questions of the directors.

Powers of members

Companies limited by guarantee are normally incorporated for non-profit making functions. Although they share some of the same characteristics as a private company limited by shares, they are formed without share capital. Members are liable, to the extent of their guarantees (that is, the amount they undertake to contribute to the assets of the company, usually a nominal sum), only if the company is wound up and a contribution is needed to enable its debts to be paid.

Under CA 2006 members have distinct powers, including the right to:

- bring an action on behalf of the company against a director or a third party for an act or omission if the company has suffered loss; and
- attend general meetings and to vote on any resolution. In addition, a member can requisition a general meeting or require that a resolution be added to the business of the AGM. A member can also appoint a proxy to attend and vote at a general meeting on his or her behalf.

The articles of association will set out specifc rights of members for each organisation but in all cases, under CA 2006, resolutions at AGMs can only be passed with defned voting majorities. The voting requirements for passing resolutions at general meetings are as follows:

- 50% (a simple majority) of those attending and voting (in person or by proxy) for ordinary resolutions; and
- 75% of those attending and voting for special resolutions.

While sports bodies will rarely have shareholders owning different classes of shares, it is common for them to create classes of membership, some having lesser rights. One example, Parkour UK offers three membership classes:

1. Associate (individual) – rights include attendance at Congress, access to Parkour-specific insurance and discounts on qualifcations. Associate members cannot vote at Congress.
2. Affliate (organisations) – rights include one vote at Congress, enhanced discounts on Parkour qualifcations and personalisation in the Parkour app for the organisation.
3. Affliate+ (organisations) – rights include one vote at Congress, Parkour-specifc insurance for events and activities, and free use of the Parkour app with personalised branding.

Voting rights may be more important to some groups than others even though no shares are attached. Annual general meetings do not always attract large numbers of members but some sports, such as the British Parachute Association, have built events around the AGM to engage members in the wider development of the sport. Ultimately, where members have concerns about the strategic direction, leadership or fnances of the organisation, they can effect changes at the AGM by presenting special resolutions or voting on board appointments.

Volunteers

Volunteers are the lifeblood of sport and without their effort, time, energy and expertise, the whole sector would founder. From Boccia clubs to NGBs of professional sports, volunteers contribute at every level including coaching, offciating, maintaining facilities and sitting on boards.

In recent years, most NGBs have created workforce development plans that seek to attract, develop and retain paid and unpaid workers in the wide range of roles. The main benefts of a workforce development plan include:

- improved skills and knowledge, motivation, attitudes and career options;
- smarter and more effcient working;
- reduced paid-staff turnover;
- improved relations between paid staff and unpaid volunteers;
- increased diversity of the workforce;
- reduced business costs;
- good publicity and marketing for the organisation;
- improved attitudes towards staff and volunteers;

- more people wanting to be involved with the organisation; and
- achieving organisational targets.

While volunteering is often perceived as a way for individuals, especially young people, to develop new skills and competencies, sports bodies should not take their effort for granted. At board level, this would mean providing directors and trustees with role descriptions that set out the requirements and expectations associated with the role, a comprehensive induction programme, and ongoing development while in post.

Partners and suppliers' responsibilities

The Institute of Business Ethics in its 2016 report *Stakeholder Engagement – Values, Business Culture and Society* states that a company that seeks to build a positive relationship with a wide range of external stakeholders must be clear what its values are, and its own behaviour must be consistent with the message it gives to stakeholders. A company claiming values that it does not adhere to will be found out and exposed quickly.

Chapter summary

- The board's unique duties and responsibilities are set out in the Companies Act 2006. These include the responsibility for setting the vision, values, culture and strategy for the organisation.
- Matters reserved for the board are usually enshrined in the articles and include setting and reviewing the organisation's structure, systems of internal control and approving remuneration.
- The Code for Sports Governance requires that organisations appoint board members based on diversity, independence, skills and knowledge in order to take effective decisions. Organisations funded by Sport England and UK Sport are required to have at least 30% female or male representation on their boards.
- A skills matrix provides a sound basis on which to recruit to the board. A skills audit helps identify strengths, gaps in skills and knowledge, and potential development areas for individuals and the board collectively.
- Board appointments should reflect the core purpose of the organisation, as well as the outcomes of the skills audit and the ongoing drive to create a balanced and inclusive board.
- Directors and trustees bear responsibility from the day of their appointment, so an induction must give them sufficient information on the organisation's purpose, culture, objectives, structures and systems for them to fulfil their role.
- Although it is not a legal requirement for private companies to appoint a company secretary, this role can bring essential knowledge, guidance and

skills to the board and the organisation that will enhance the implementation of good governance.

- One of the board's roles is to identify key stakeholders and design information with appropriate communication tools for each. These will range from government departments to members, and from commercial sponsors to elite athletes.

6
Conflicts of interest

Introduction

This chapter outlines the definition and the nature of conflicts of interests in sports bodies. We shall explore the practical steps organisations can take to manage potential conflicts and encourage independent judgement. Independence will be defined and the benefits of appointing independent board members outlined in terms of the relationship of independent board members to the sport and its constituent groups.

Conflicts of interest

In any organisation, whether sporting, non-sporting, commercial or not-for-profit, board members and senior staff may face conflicts of interest. This section seeks to define conflicts of interest and provide practical guidance on how these can be managed at board level.

Definition of a conflict of interest

The Companies Act 2006 and Charities Act 2011 place explicit duties on directors and trustees in respect of conflicts of interest.

Section 173 of CA 2006 states that directors have a duty to exercise independent judgment. Directors' obligations to the organisation must not clash with other interests or with obligations they owe to others.

Under the Charities Act, trustees have a legal duty to act in the interests of beneficiaries and avoid conflicts of interest. They must not put themselves in any position where their duties as a trustee may conflict with any personal interest they may have, including conflicts of loyalty.

The Charity Commission guide, the Essential Trustee, states that a conflict of interest is any situation where a trustee's personal interests could, or could appear to, prevent them from making a decision only in the charity's best interests. For example, if a trustee (or a person connected to them, such as a close relative, business partner or company):

- receives payment from the charity for goods or services, or as an employee;
- makes a loan to or receive a loan from the charity;

- owns a business that enters into a contract with the charity;
- uses the charity's services; and
- enters into some other financial transaction with the charity.

Under Principle 4: Integrity, requirement 4.6 of the Code for Sports Governance defines how conflicts can occur.

Conflicts of interest can arise where there is a conflict between the interests of the organisation and director's staff or other volunteer personal interests or those of another body with which the individual is involved.

Sports bodies, in particular membership organisations, often face situations that could be described as conflicts of loyalty. These conflicts arise because, although the affected board member does not stand to gain any personal benefit, their other interests could influence their decision making. For example, a board member's loyalty to the organisation could conflict with:

- loyalty to the club, region or constituent group that voted them onto the board;
- their membership of a section of the sport, for example, being a member of the women's section of a club;
- an associated organisation, which may have nominated them;
- another sports body of which they are a board member or employee; and
- a member of their family or another connected person or organisation.

To manage conflicts of interest in a transparent and systematic way, organisations should develop a policy that sets out how potential conflicts will be identified and resolved.

It is important to note that users of the organisation's services can add value to the decision-making process. The Charity Commission guidance on users as trustees states that they can contribute their direct experience to the development of services and help other trustees develop a greater knowledge of the user perspective. Taking on a trusteeship can restore a sense of ownership and empowerment to users. The same point is made under Principle 6 of the Principles of Good Governance for Sport and Recreation – Accountability and Transparency, which encourages the involvement of internal stakeholders such as members, coaches and volunteers, in a sports organisation's structures.

Preventing conflicts of interest from affecting decision making is a legal requirement and, having identified a conflict of interest, board members must consider the issue so that any potential effect on decision making is eliminated. It is also a matter of ethical leadership as would be expected by stakeholders. How a board prevents the conflict from affecting decision making will depend on the circumstances. The Charity Commission Essential Trustee Guide explains that:

- individual trustees should always declare any conflicts of interest which affect them;
- any failure to declare a conflict of interest is a serious issue;

- the trustee body should consider whether serious conflicts of interest should be removed or require authority;
- affected trustees should not participate in any decisions where they stand to gain, whether directly or indirectly, through a connected person;
- where there is a conflict of loyalty, trustees should carefully handle any participation by a conflicted trustee; and
- irrespective of the approach trustees take to prevent a conflict of interest from affecting their decision making, they should be able to demonstrate that their decision was made only in the best interests of the charity.

Establishing a register of interests

The critical step in managing conflicts of interest is to identify and record them. It is not unusual for an organisation to require board members, all staff and senior volunteers to register interests. This has the benefit of reinforcing the importance of related conflicts of interest policies and reminding staff and volunteers of their duties and responsibilities.

The declaration should be updated annually or whenever the circumstances of an individual change. Remember, it is a legal duty to declare any conflicts of interest, so updating the register of interests is the responsibility of the individual. The board members' register of interests can be made available to members and stakeholders as evidence of transparency in decision making. The conflicts of interest policy and requirement for declaration will often be referenced in the Articles of Association but even if not, there should still be a policy and process in place to manage conflicts of interest.

The ICSA guidance note and specimen conflict of interest policy, declaration form and register of interests for charity trustees provide useful advice and templates for voluntary organisations. There is no definitive list of possible connections that could be interpreted as potential conflicts of interest for board members; however, the following influences, drawn from the ICSA guidance, are commonly listed in declaration forms:

- current employment and any previous employment in which the individual might continue to have a financial interest;
- appointments (voluntary or otherwise), including trusteeships, directorships, sports body roles, local authority membership or tribunals;
- membership of any professional bodies, special interest groups or mutual support organisations;
- investments in unlisted companies, partnerships and other forms of business, major shareholdings;
- gifts or hospitality offered by external bodies in the last 12 months; and whether this was declined or accepted;

- using, are related to or have a close connection with a user of the organisation's services (this could include spouses/partners, siblings, parents or grandparents, business associates, etc); and
- any contractual relationship with the organisation or its subsidiaries.

Board members' and senior staff declarations of interest

Although the register of interests enables full declaration of board member and senior staff interests, this alone does not prevent close connections and conflicts from potentially influencing decisions. How you prevent a conflict of interest from affecting a decision will depend on the circumstances and the seriousness of the conflict of interest.

At board and committee meetings, the agenda should include an item that allows participants to declare conflicts of interest. The chair may highlight the need to do so as relevant to the agenda, and participants are expected to use their judgment based on the content of the meeting, likely discussions and impact of decisions when deciding whether to declare a conflict. The most effective means of managing conflicts is to ask the conflicted board member to leave the room while discussions take place and decisions are made. Although chairs may use discretion when asking individual board members to leave the room for the relevant item, it is important to avoid a situation where a conflicted board member is still able to influence discussions and decisions through non-verbal behaviour.

Even with a conflict of interest policy, a register of interests and an item on all agendas, it is still beholden on directors and trustees to fulfil their legal duties in declaring any conflicts of interest in meetings. If the non-conflicted board members can demonstrate that a conflict involves no material benefit and poses a low risk to decision making in the best interests of the organisation, they may permit the affected board member to participate. For the most serious conflicts of interest – for example, the potential awarding of lucrative contracts to a company in which a board member has an interest and will benefit personally – it may mean obtaining permission from the Charity Commission, deciding not to proceed with a proposal or even resigning as a trustee.

In circumstances where a conflict of loyalty may exist, it is still appropriate for board members to be open with each other about the potential influence on decisions. For example, a board member elected by a regional constituent group might not declare their affiliation as a conflict of interest but, as discussions unfold, reminders from the chair about such associations can help keep the debate focused on board members' duties to the organisation as a whole. The organisation might also choose to include these situations in its conflict of interest policy to highlight board members' duties and maintain transparency in decision making.

Maintaining a gifts and hospitality log

The significant profits that can be generated and the often conflicting interests associated with a sport require governing bodies to be particularly vigilant and to put in place effective mechanisms to prevent corrupt practices.

As the organisers of international events, sports governing bodies are required to make decisions that have significant financial implications and affect a wide range of stakeholders. They are responsible for the selection of the host country and venue, the awarding of broadcasting rights to TV networks and the negotiation of sponsorship deals with multinational organisations.

In 2014, FIFA declared profits of £91 million and, annually, the organisation generates billions in revenue from TV rights and sponsorship. It describes itself as an 'association of associations with a non-commercial, not-for-profit purpose'. Investigations revealed that despite the unprecedented interests involved, a relatively small group of people made all the key decisions, with very limited transparency requirements and no controls over the contracts they signed. This resulted in widespread corruption, with businesses paying bribes to FIFA officials in exchange for exclusive deals or being awarded the opportunity to host the World Cup.

At any level in sport there will always be a risk that an individual may be induced by a gift, hospitality or bribe. To mitigate this reputational and strategic risk, all senior staff and board members should declare any association with relevant organisations, such as sponsors, funders or internal stakeholders. A gifts and hospitality log does not prevent an individual being the guest of a partner at a sporting event or awards ceremony, but by being open and transparent about the exchange, stakeholders are able to identify if such a connection has any material influence on decisions. The log can be presented at each board meeting and should be available to stakeholders.

Independence

The Higgs review of the role and effectiveness of non-executive directors emphasised the value of independence as follows:

> A board is strengthened significantly by having a strong group of non-executive directors with no other connection with the company. These individuals bring a dispassionate objectivity that directors with a closer relationship to the company cannot provide.

In a sporting context, the same principles of dispassionate objectivity are equally important.

Definition of independence – Code for Sports Governance requirements

All board members, regardless of how they are appointed, must demonstrate independent judgement. Whether conflicts of interest have been declared or conflicts of loyalty exist, each person must demonstrate objectivity and transparency in the way they approach discussions and decisions. Elected board members from within the sport will bring vital knowledge and insight, for example, of clubs, coaching or talent development. By blending sporting insight with essential business skills, sports can build balanced boards that provide diversity of opinion and ideas.

The Code for Sports Governance defines independence as follows:

A person is independent if they are free from any close connection to the organisation and if, from the perspective of an objective outsider, they would be viewed as independent. A person may still be deemed to be 'independent' even if they are a member of the organisation and/or play the sport. Examples of a 'close connection' include:

(A) they are or have within the last four years been actively involved in the organisation's affairs: for example, as a representative of a specific interest group within the organisation such as a sporting discipline, a region or a home country;

(B) they are or have within the last four years been an employee of the organisation; or

(C) they have close family ties with any of the organisation's directors or senior employees.

The same definition appears in the Principles of Good Governance for Sport and Recreation, which ensures sports organisations can define, with consistency, the nature of independence when recruiting to their boards.

The role of independent non-executive directors in sports organisations

The Higgs review states that non-executive directors are the custodians of the governance process. As they do not report to the chief executive and are not involved in the day-to-day running of the business, they can bring a fresh perspective and contribute more objectively in supporting, as well as constructively challenging and monitoring, the management team.

In practice, smaller voluntary sports organisations with few staff may need non-executive directors to get more involved in operational matters via committees and, provided there is absolute clarity of role in each situation, this should not impair their performance at board level.

The need for high standards and professional behaviours is also highlighted in the Higgs review, which states that non-executive directors should question intelligently, debate constructively, challenge rigorously and decide dispassionately. They should also listen sensitively to the views of others, inside and outside the board. Such attention on board behaviours is reinforced in the Governance and Leadership Framework for Wales, which lists behaviours that would be deemed acceptable and unacceptable in the boardroom. Table 6.1 shows an example.

Table 6.1: Governance and Leadership Framework for Wales – Principle 7 behaviours

Principle 7: Understanding and engaging with the sporting landscape	Minimum expectation	Effective behaviour	Ineffective behaviour
The board needs to be aware of the international and domestic sporting environment and position its organisation appropriately.	Establishing strategic relationships and working with other organisations to maximise the mutual benefits of partnership.	Demonstrates a professional demeanour and speaks with impact to instil confidence with stakeholders.	Publicly disagrees with decisions that the board takes as a group with which they personally do not agree.

Anecdotal evidence from NGBs suggests the introduction of independent board members has generated a significant and positive impact on the operation of sports boards. Appointing individuals with no connection to the sport, especially constituent groups expecting representation at board level, has brought greater levels of objectivity. In addition, sports report higher-quality debate on key business areas, including governance, commercial strategies and digital communications, than would have been likely without the injection of business skills through open appointments.

Other stakeholder groups

In Chapter 5 (pages 102 to 107), the role of stakeholders was covered in depth. If asked to identify wider groups of stakeholders, board members might also add the following.

Regulators

These might include the Charity Commission or sector-specific bodies such as the Civil Aviation Authority for air sports. Maintaining an open and productive relationship with regulators assists in building their confidence and ensures the organisation accesses governance information, resources and guidance.

Commercial partners and sponsors

Many sports bodies are seeking to reduce their dependence on public funds; however, activating commercial partnerships can be complex and time-consuming. Good governance contributes to the building of productive strategic relationships, but poor governance will deter potential partners. McDonald's is one of FIFA's top-tier sponsors. Following the revelations of corruption involving senior FIFA officials, in July 2017 McDonald's issued a public statement which insisted that it will continue to hold FIFA accountable for meaningful reform. Sponsors do not like to be associated with poorly run sports bodies.

Funders

These include sports councils, local government and the National Lottery. While sports councils will insert specific requirements into funding agreements with sports bodies, their role is not as a regulator. Sports organisations in receipt of public and National Lottery funds will often seek to engage as much as possible with their respective funder to provide assurance.

The media

Although many sports do not receive the same level of interest as professional sports, too often bad news and scandals can attract media attention whatever the sport. Almost all sports organisations, from club and community bodies to international federations, will operate on a range of social media platforms in order to communicate with stakeholders; however, generating broadcast and press coverage remains an aspiration for them and, where relevant, their commercial partners.

Creating a communications plan that incorporates local and/or national media will help ensure the organisation's key messages about participation, membership, performance or governance, are understood and visible. A plan will also help allocate scarce resources on the most important media outlets. Social media is covered in Chapter 8 (pages 160 and 161).

The effect of conflicts of interest on the long-term interests of sports organisations

The sport sector is relatively small compared to the finance, charity or retail sectors and, as a result, individuals with experience and knowledge will often fulfil multiple executive and non-executive roles. Consequently, an individual in a position of authority and power may find themselves operating on behalf of more than one entity. This can have serious consequences if not managed at an early stage.

In 2016, former British Judo Association (BJA) Chair Kerrith Brown was blamed for Glasgow being stripped of the 2015 European Championships following an independent investigation. The report claimed Brown personally strove for a contract signed in 2014 between the BJA and the Combat Sports Federation (CSF), of which he was a director, which represented a clear conflict of interest. It stated that Brown 'stood financially to benefit' from the deal with the CSF, which was brokering an agreement with the Ultimate Fighting Championship (UFC). The sponsorship agreement was not agreed by the European Judo Union (EJU) and Brown had misled both the CSF and his own board.

In a statement published on its website, the EJU said that the BJA did not meet hosting criteria as it 'had entered into a sponsorship agreement which did not meet the EJU values. BJA persisted in this, notwithstanding that it had been warned on a number of occasions that this arrangement was unacceptable to the EJU.'

Brown was forced to step down from his role with the BJA and the NGB received criticism for its failure in respect of oversight and the ultimate loss of medal, economic and development opportunities associated with hosting a major event.

Other issues in sports governance where conflicts of interest can arise

Budgeting and forecasting

Budgeting is a subject area which takes its roots from the field of management accounting. This, in essence, is about the collection, collation, analysis and reporting of financial information for planning, decision making and control purposes. Budgeting can be shown to be part of the overall planning process for a business by defining it as the overall plan of a business expressed in financial terms. These plans might involve trying to achieve a predetermined level of financial performance such as a profit of £x over the year, or having sufficient cash resources to be able to replace equipment relevant to an organisation's needs. To that end, organisational business planning can be summarised as an analysis of four key questions:

1. Where are we now?
2. How did we get here?
3. Where are we going?
4. How are we going to get there?

To illustrate the link between general business planning and budgeting, the question 'Where are we now?' can be modified to 'Where are we now in financial terms?' Similarly the question 'Where are we going?' can be modified to 'Where are we going in financial terms?' To diagnose where a business currently is in financial terms requires the ability to be able to 'read' a statement of comprehensive income (profit and loss account), a statement of financial position (balance sheet) and a cash flow statement. To predict where a business is going is difficult (as is any attempt to predict the future), but techniques such as compiling an expected statement of comprehensive income, statement of financial position and cash flow statement can help to focus attention on the business essentials. Furthermore, the very process of planning ahead using budgets can help to test whether what you wish to achieve and the accompanying financial consequences are compatible or 'internally consistent'.

Once an acceptable match has been achieved between an organisation's business objectives and the financial consequences of those objectives, a line needs to be drawn under the 'preparation of budgets' stage. The point at which this line is drawn is at the 'approval of budgets' stage, which effectively puts an end to the various iterations of the budget and leads to the formal adoption of the budget the organisation wishes to pursue. It is recognised good practice for the approval of a budget to be formalised in the minutes of a board or committee meeting. Furthermore, budgets should be approved in advance of the financial period to which they relate. The wider significance of a budget being approved formally is that those who have compiled it, and those whose performance will in part be judged by it, know exactly what their responsibilities are. This has two benefits. First, if you know what is expected of you, then evaluation of performance can be objective rather than subjective. Second, expectation generates accountability, which in turn gives managers the focus to concentrate on those things which are important in terms of meeting the organisation's objectives.

Conflicts of interest can arise in budgeting at different stakeholder levels throughout an organisation. As suggested above, it is recognised good practice that a budget is approved in the minutes of a board meeting, but what if not everybody approves of the budget and the perceived direction of travel? This conflict is perfectly underlined with a political link. Every year a budget is put together by the chancellor that outlines what the country will spend its money on and where it can make savings or profits to benefit the country as a whole. Naturally, the whole of the UK population is never going to agree a consensus on the budget; likewise organisations often struggle to achieve consensus on their budgets and where they want to be in financial terms. Budgets require everyone within an organisation to pull in the same direction at all times.

Financial reporting and auditing

Each and every sports organisation has a responsibility to produce financial statements: the legal requirements will be determined by the nature of the company (for example, whether they are a sole trader or a public company). Two main financial statements need to be drawn up by financial accountants: the statement of financial position and statement of comprehensive income. In simple terms, these documents help define a company's operations against the following key financial equation:

$$Assets - Liabilities = Capital$$

It is worth mentioning here that 'assets' are resources that the business owns, for example, buildings, machinery and vehicles. Such resources will be used by the business in its operations. There may also be bank balances and cash. These will hold the funds that the business needs to operate. However, the business may also owe money to its owners, other people or organisations – these are liabilities. A limited company will produce an income and expenditure statement for the period of one year. However, it is not uncommon for internal users to produce statements of comprehensive income on a quarterly or even monthly basis. Statements of comprehensive income that you come across are likely to be in annual reports and will therefore be for a 12-month period. Organisations that are 'not-for-profit' such as charities and many volunteer-led sport clubs will produce a similar statement called an income and expenditure account; this will show any surplus of income over expenditure (or a deficit if expenditure exceeds income).

All limited companies in the UK have to produce the above documentation on an annual basis and this information has to be consistent with the accounting standards in place in that particular country. In the UK, for example, most companies adhere to Financial Reporting Standards (FRS), of which there are currently 31. In addition, there is also something called UK GAAP (Generally Accepted Accounting Principles) which also has an international version – there is also a set of International Financial Reporting Standards (IFRS) as well as different accounting practices in different countries. This differentiation in approach needs to be recognised as a potential conflict of interest. Be mindful of which standards are the most effective to follow.

It is evident that many business entities may be still be reporting financial performance in different ways, and while this is still acceptable under the regulatory framework, it has the potential to create huge conflicts of interest at governance level. For this reason, as part of any objective setting, you should ensure that you pre-determine some performance measure (such as profitability, liquidity and debt) and benchmarks to ensure that conflicts do not arise.

Directors' remuneration

Subject to the company's Articles of Association, the remuneration of directors is set by the board. Remuneration of private company directors is decided by the board unless there is a shareholder or investment agreement in place with other requirements. The UK Corporate Governance Code states that the boards of listed companies should establish a remuneration committee, which should follow formal and transparent terms of reference for developing policy on executive remuneration and for fixing the remuneration packages of individual directors. Directors of listed companies should not be involved in deciding their own remuneration.

Disclosure

The annual accounts of all companies (other than very small companies) must include details of directors' remuneration and benefits. A small company is defined as having two or more of the following: a turnover of £10.2 million or less, £5.1 million or less on the statement of financial position or 50 employees or less. Other quoted companies are required, under the Listing Rules and the Large and

Medium-sized Companies and Groups (Accounts and Reports) Regulations 2008, to provide shareholders annually with a detailed remuneration report. Annual accounts are required by the government to make sure that the company tax return is being followed as part of guidelines set by HM Revenue & Customs and to make sure that accounts are being prepared in relation to IFRS and/or UK GAAP.

Shareholder approval

The Companies Act 2006 gives shareholders of quoted companies an advisory vote on the directors' remuneration report, meaning a director's remuneration is not conditional on shareholders' approval. In addition to an advisory vote on the directors' remuneration in the relevant financial year, shareholders must pass a binding vote on the directors' remuneration policy every three years.

In its March 2013 FAQ guidance on the directors' remuneration reforms, the Department for Business, Energy and Industrial Strategy (BEIS) stated that a company had three options should shareholders fail to approve the remuneration policy:

1. Continue to operate according to the last remuneration policy to have been approved by shareholders.
2. Continue to operate according to the last remuneration policy to have been approved by shareholders and seek separate shareholder approval for any specific remuneration or loss-of-office payments that are not consistent with that policy.
3. Call a general meeting and put a (further) remuneration policy to shareholders for approval.

The Companies Act 2006 indicates that remuneration payments made without shareholder approval are unauthorised and any underlying contractual obligation is deemed unenforceable. In addition, any non-compliant payments made will be held on trust by the recipient on behalf of the company. Clearly, ensuring transparency and accountability in the setting of director remuneration is critical here to avoid any conflict.

Most people would agree that, in business, it is only right that directors get paid for the work that they do. Of course, in some cases, there are those who will often think that directors get paid too much. The nature of sport and sports organisations does sometimes blur the lines here.

Such conflict of interest (when directors think that they should be paid more than other stakeholders) could also occur internally in respect of different directors having different views on what they think the remuneration should be – much like the practical problem with budgeting that was alluded to earlier in this chapter. Obviously, there is a conflict resolution process in place as mentioned above, but it could create a practical problem for sports organisations if directors cannot agree on what the remuneration should be. It could lead to lengthy negotiations that could either harm or disrupt day-to-day business operations.

Organisation–stakeholder relations

It is widely accepted that a stakeholder will affect or be affected by an organisation. A slightly different perspective defines stakeholders as individuals/groups who have placed something at risk in their relationship with the firm, voluntary or not. Furthermore, there is also a notable distinction between primary and secondary stakeholders. Primary stakeholders are those whose continued participation is necessary to the survival of the firm – for example, stockholders, investors, employees, customers and suppliers – whereas secondary stakeholders influence or are affected by the firm but do not make any transaction with it and are not essential for its survival – for example, the media and associated public relations bodies.

Understanding relationships

The relationship between stakeholders is complex in any industry. However, it can become increasingly complex in the context of sports organisations where there are a number of different primary and secondary stakeholders to consider.

Theory in action

In professional football there might be two main models: the shareholder model, which emphasises the shareholder versus manager relationship, and the stakeholder model, which takes into account the different stakeholders of the organisation. Stakeholders deemed relevant to football clubs include shareholders, players, leagues and federations, local authorities, support associations, spectators, supporters, television and other sponsors. Each different group will have its own objectives, which are often sporting and financial, although political values cannot be ruled out. Parallels are naturally drawn here to two main business objectives present in professional team sports. Historically, these two objectives have been polarised across two main continents and a variety of professional team sports.

The two objectives are profit maximisation (whereby the ultimate aim of the team is to make a profit for its owners) and utility maximisation (whereby the ultimate aim of the team is to maximise sporting performance by primarily reinvesting in playing talent to improve sporting performance). Historically, profit maximisation has been the primary aim in North American team sports such as the NBA, NFL, NHL and MLB. However, utility maximisation has been more prevalent in European team sports, in particular football in countries such as England, France, Spain, Italy and Germany. Indeed, there is evidence to suggest that French clubs in particular follow a utility maximisation and a stakeholder approach to governance.

There has been a blurring of the lines in recent years, with American investors increasingly becoming the majority shareholders in English football clubs. The Glazer takeover of Manchester United in 2005 was perhaps the first takeover in English football with profit maximisation at the heart of the decision, while the Roman Abramovich takeover of Chelsea FC in 2003 followed a more utility maximisation approach. Recent regulations mean that the utility maximisation approach is not as easy to do on a short-term basis, but the traits of objectives like this one still fit closely with a stakeholder approach to football club governance where the whole is greater than the sum of its parts.

In a professional sports organisation, numerous stakeholders with varied goals are present with power games being significant and visible, especially in the European sporting model. They are equally prominent in public and voluntary sectors too, though often less visible. The difficult part is outlining which stakeholders really count and to whom managers should pay attention. For a professional football team, it can be argued that, among these stakeholders, players were probably those whose individual interests are best taken into account under the assumption that better players that are at the top of the game will equate to better sporting performance on the pitch, which will ultimately satisfy primary stakeholders. Nevertheless, the overly high attention paid to players is often at the expense of other stakeholders who are quite significant though less visible. For example, stakeholders such as supporters obviously have an interest in how the team is performing, which may determine whether they go to watch a game and pay money to the club through tickets and merchandise, etc. It must be noted, however, that this is also heavily reliant on player performance.

A further challenge for professional sports teams is to appease the supporters (whose views are often at odds with primary stakeholders). This also has inherent links to financial performance and strategic objectives. Any strategic objective taken by the organisation at boardroom level will ultimately affect the financial performance and competitive position of the organisation. This relationship is further strained in professional football given the delicate balance between maximising both playing performance and financial performance. Naturally, supporters would want to see any spare funds or income reinvested into the playing squad to drive on-pitch performance. However, this is not always the decision taken at boardroom level. Often, funds and income are reinvested into players or other areas of perceived growth within the organisation (such as stadium development or youth infrastructure), but sometimes income is retained by the board of directors to pay dividends to the main shareholders – a decision which often upsets a number of both primary and secondary stakeholders.

The numerous actors at play in professional sports organisations make managing organisation–stakeholder relations a difficult challenge. Different organisations understandably operate under different strategic business objectives, often in relation to their governance and ownership structure. Appreciating the multitude of different stakeholders is the first step in helping us understand how they interact with each other and how this has a direct impact on performance in the modern-day sports industry.

Risk-taking and the management of risk

Under the UK Corporate Governance Code, the board of a listed company should maintain sound risk management and internal control systems to ensure that its decisions are effective and in alignment with strategy. It should monitor the company's risk management and internal control systems and, at least annually, carry out a review of their effectiveness and report on that review in the annual report. The monitoring and review should cover all material controls, including financial, operational and compliance.

The UK Corporate Governance Code also states that the audit committee should review the company's internal financial controls and, unless expressly addressed by a separate board risk committee composed of independent directors or by the board itself, review the company's internal control and risk management systems. The Disclosure and Transparency Rules (DTRs) require listed companies to provide a description of their internal control and risk management systems in their corporate governance statements. Further guidance is given in the FRC's Guidance on Risk Management, Internal Control and Related Financial and Business Reporting and its Guidance on Audit Committees.

Under common law, board members are required to exercise reasonable skill and diligence when undertaking their duties. Common law calls for a fiduciary relationship which exists whenever there is a situation where one person undertakes duties or obligations with powers that may be exercised for the benefit of someone else. Board members must operate in their positions remembering that they exist for the good of the organisation and should only exercise power when it benefits the organisation. Conflicts of interest can arise in these situations where board members have the power to make decisions that influence other people and the organisation. For example, a company's CEO orchestrates a deal to acquire a struggling company owned by his best friend. Assuming the acquisition was not in the best interests of the acquirer and actually hurts its bottom line (and share price), the shareholders may pursue a breach of fiduciary duty lawsuit to recover losses. The main difficulty with understanding statutory requirements is that they will differ in terms of governance behaviour between different country, state/provincial boundaries and on the basis of organisational structure.

Responsibility of board members

Board members have a relationship of trust with the organisation and the fundamental responsibility of a member is to represent the interest of the members in directing the business of the organisation and within the law. This representative role requires board members to fulfil three basic duties:

1. *The duty of diligence*: this is the duty to act reasonably, in good faith, prudently and with an eye on the best interests of the organisation and its members.
2. *The duty of loyalty*: this duty puts the interest of the organisation first and determines that one should not use one's position as a director to further private interests.
3. *The duty of obedience*: this is the duty to act within the scope of the governing policies of the organisation and within the law, rules and regulations that apply to the organisation in the territory in which it resides.

Any board member failing to fulfil these duties can be found liable, with this liability generally occurring in one of three different circumstances:

1. when the law is broken, this could result in a fine or imprisonment;
2. when a contract is breached and potentially results in financial compensation or some other form of remedial action, being owed to correct the breach; or
3. by an act or failure to act which leads to injury or damage to another person again leading to financial penalty.

Board members of sports organisations, be they large or small, listed companies or not-for-profit incorporated associations, must fulfil their obligations under common law and the specific requirements of any legislation applied to the territory where the organisation operates. That said, any statutory requirements are only intended to provide a framework for the minimum standards of behaviour.

Communication (including e-communication) and information transfer between directors and stakeholders

The Companies Act 2006 provides information to suggest that directors have a statutory duty to avoid situations in which their personal interests (actual or potential) conflict (directly or indirectly) with the company's interests. Such conflicts can ordinarily be authorised by the rest of the board, provided that:

- the other board members who authorise the conflict are independent of that conflict; or
- the conflicted director (or any other interested director) does not vote on the authorisation.

Either the company's articles permit the directors to authorise the conflict (in the case of a public company) or they contain nothing that would prevent such authorisation (in the case of a private company). CA 2006 also imposes a duty on directors to declare the nature and extent of their interest in a proposed (or an existing) transaction or arrangement with the company. The company's articles may provide that a director who has disclosed an interest will not be counted for quorum and voting purposes.

The Companies Act 2006 imposes restrictions on the following transactions between a company and its directors:

- directors' service contracts with a guaranteed term of more than two years;
- substantial property transactions involving the acquisition of non-cash assets by the director from the company (and vice versa);
- loans, and giving a guarantee or providing security in connection with loans, to directors;
- quasi-loans or other credit transactions (this applies only to public companies or companies associated with public companies); and
- payments for loss of office in connection with a share or business transfer.

In terms of communication to a wider field, CA 2006 also requires directors of private and public limited companies to disclose to the public certain information about the company (such as the identity of the shareholders, names of directors and accounts). Some of this information is held on the public record at Companies House and shareholders are also entitled to inspect records of general meetings, including all passed resolutions.

Extensive information has to be disclosed to shareholders and, in many instances is made public through the financial reporting requirements of CA 2006. Regulated entities also have to disclose certain information to the relevant regulatory body or bodies.

Ethical conduct and corporate social responsibility

The essence of sporting competition forces sports organisations to balance multiple objectives in order to satisfy a variety of different stakeholders. Sports organisations nowadays operate under a concept of multiple institutional logics, more simply defined in relation to the fact that sports organisations have to satisfy a number of different groups of people who all have a vested interest in the operations of the team. By way of an example, consider a publicly funded swimming facility. There will be a number of people who are interested in how the facility is operating, including (but not limited to) the service provider, local authority leaders, the manager, the staff, the users, a governing body overseeing the sports that use the facility, and the general public itself. Keeping all of these people happy is a difficult task. Furthermore, sports organisations exist and operate in a competitive and changing environment, which in today's modern world involves much more than maximising performance in the facility itself.

A fundamental aspect of sport is that it has a profound social impact. Consequently, one aspect of managing sports organisations that has attracted considerable interest in recent years has been the concept of 'corporate social responsibility' (CSR). The concept of CSR has become significant for modern sports organisations. In general terms, it refers to a duty of the organisation to maximise the long-term positive impact on society while simultaneously minimising the negative impact. There are several reasons why sports organisations should deploy a CSR strategy:

- The popularity and global reach of sport can ensure that these practices have mass media distribution and communication power.
- Sport has youth appeal, thus children's engagement in programmes designed to tackle or contribute towards the above-mentioned issues becomes easier if such programmes are associated with a sports organisation or a well-known athlete.
- By its very nature, sport offers the perfect platform to encourage activity, including health awareness and anti-obesity campaigns as well as disease prevention. Thus, social interaction can be facilitated by group participation in sports activities. Environmental and sustainability awareness and consciousness can be further reinforced, especially with the hosting of mega-sporting events, such as the Olympic Games or the football World Cup.
- Sport may also lead to enhanced cultural understanding and integration.
- Both active and passive participation in sport offer immediate gratification benefits with unclear social advantages, albeit important.

CSR in sport is also a relatively new concept and professional sports organisations are now entering into socially responsible initiatives at a rapid pace. The majority of literature on CSR notes the benefits of corporate initiatives to the organisations. The importance of CSR to sports organisations is evidenced by the increasing number of teams that have set up charitable foundations as part of their business operations during the last 20 years or so.

Chapter summary

- The Companies Act 2006 under section 173 states that directors have a duty to exercise independent judgement. Their obligations to the organisation must not clash with other interests or with obligations they owe to others.
- Organisations should create a register of interests for board members and staff to help meet requirements of CA 2006 and the Charities Act. The register of interests should be updated annually.
- The Code for Sports Governance defines a person as independent if they are free from any close connection to the organisation and if, from the perspective of an objective outsider, they would be viewed as independent.
- Independent non-executive directors have made a positive impact on the balance of skills and the quality of debate in sports organisations funded by Sporting England and UK Sport must appoint at least 25% independent directors to the board.
- The Companies Act 2006 requires that a director must act in the way that they consider would be most likely to promote the success of the company for the benefit of its members as a whole, and in doing so have regard to stakeholders. Sports organisations now deal with a range of internal and external stakeholders including members, athletes, funders, commercial partners and the media.

■ A conflict of interest can arise in any situation where an individual's personal interests could, or could appear to, prevent them from making a decision only in the organisation's best interests.

■ Considering how other issues in sports governance can represent conflicts of interest can help organisations manage risk.

■ To prevent and limit unnecessary risk, it is important to understand the importance of sound financial reporting and auditing.

■ Conflict of interest arising from the perception of how much directors should be paid can be reduced by using organisational objectives to determine directors' remuneration.

■ Maintaining good lines of communication within a sports organisation, both electronic and face-to-face is critical.

■ Spending an appropriate amount of time to consider risk management processes in an organisation can help prevent conflict.

■ It is important for an organisation to promote good practice in relation to ethical conduct and maintain a strong public image through the incorporation of CSR programmes.

7
Managing risk

▨ Introduction

This chapter outlines the nature of risk and how boards should approach risk management. We shall explore the types of risk faced by sports bodies and the way risk can be managed through the organisation. In addition, we shall consider the specific risks all sports face, including illegal gambling and doping.

▨ Overview of risk

The Cadbury Report (1992) described risk management as 'the process by which executive management, under Board supervision, identifies the risk arising from business ... and establishes the priorities for control and particular objectives'. With the board bearing ultimate responsibility for risk and control, board members must prioritise risk strategy, appetite and management.

The most common risks facing sports organisation include the following:

- *Finance* – loss of funding, such as sports council funding or from commercial partnerships, or diminishing funds due to declining membership.
- *Health and safety* – many sports carry a degree of physical risk. In the case of adventure sports such as parachuting or mountaineering, these are significant, requiring specialist knowledge and risk management procedures.
- *Safeguarding* – the high volume of people involved in sport coupled with large numbers of volunteers may facilitate abuse. Some of the safeguarding legal, policy and process issues are covered in Chapter 3 and, in light of the rising number of cases of abuse reported in sport, remain under constant review.
- *Declining membership and participation* – with so many alternative activity, leisure and social interests available to people, especially young people, sports bodies now find themselves in a marketplace, having to develop new ways to attract and retain participants.

The nature of risk

In everyday life, there is a risk of being involved in a road accident or having a house burgled. This can be described as downside risk, because it is a risk that something negative or damaging will happen that would not normally be expected.

There is also upside risk. This is the possibility that actual events might turn out better than expected. Risk management involves making decisions about upside risks as well as downside risks. For example, businesses make investment decisions and every investment is risky. Actual returns could be lower or higher than expected. In deciding whether or not to undertake an investment, the risks as well as the potential returns should be taken into consideration. In a sporting context, this might mean a club board discussing whether to invest in building accommodation to encourage participants to stay and play. This would require investment on which the club would hope to receive a return. The returns may be more or less than forecast, and critically, more or less than the original investment. The board would have to discuss all the possible risks of such a venture before approving implementation.

A distinction can be made between strategic risk and internal operating risks.

- *Strategic risks* include external factors such significant shifts public policy on sport leading to changes in funding and access to public or Lottery funds. The risks faced may well be determined by the strategies that the organisation pursues – for example, an NGB may choose to focus on grass-roots development, reducing its potential access to elite sport funding.
- *Operating risks* are risks of losses that arise through ineffective controls within the processes and systems of an organisation's operations. One example is the risk of cybercrime. According to the Government's Office of Cyber Security and Information Assurance, cybercrime costs UK businesses £21 billion a year. Sports organisations of all sizes are vulnerable to this type of crime. The introduction of the General Data Protection Regulation from May 2018 places clear and unequivocal responsibility on organisations for the protection of personal data.

Categories of business risk

Most organisations will face risks that relate to their core business, for example, maintaining membership, while others affect corporate operations such as facilities. Most of these would be considered business as usual risks that can be foreseen, assessed and managed even if they cannot be eliminated.

Professional sport faces exceptional risks, as its economic sustainability is often dependent on the availability of marketable assets. The £197 million paid by football club Paris Saint-Germain for Brazilian footballer Neymar would not have been solely for his footballing skills. As one of the world's best male footballers, Neymar would make a significant contribution to marketing, merchandising and other business strategies at the club. His value also meant there were risks (of injury, for example) which needed to be assessed, mitigated and managed.

The most common categories of business risk include the following:

- *Reputation risk* – there may be a loss in member or stakeholder support following an event that damages the organisation's reputation. This is often associated with risks arising from unethical behaviour, for example, a person who is found to have taken bribes.
- *Competition risk* – performance may differ from expected performance because of actions taken (or not taken) by rivals. The sports sector does not often openly talk of commercial rivals, yet sports bodies all seek to attract and retain users as members, talented athletes and volunteers. Understanding the potential market better than others is now a critical factor as sports organisations compete in a marketplace.
- *Business environment risks* – significant changes may occur in the business environment from political, regulatory, economic, social and technology factors. For example, the Code for Sports Governance seeks to create a shift in the way sports bodies are led and governed, and in 2017 the Table Tennis England resolution to restructure the board to meet Code requirements was rejected by members. This led to a loss of £9 million per year in Sport England funding. The proposal was approved at the second attempt.
- *Financial risks* – financial conditions may change, for example, sports that engage in international influence may be affected by changes to the exchange rate.
- *Liquidity risk* – the company may have insufficient cash to settle all its liabilities on time, and so may be forced out of business. The board should monitor this risk at least annually when they prepare their going concern statement for the annual report and accounts.

How each risk applies to individual sports bodies will vary; however, the board is responsible for giving due consideration to the likelihood and impact.

Risk appetite and risk tolerance

Responsibility for the management of risk is delegated to executive management, but the board must decide the risk appetite of the organisation.

The Institute of Risk Management (IRM) defines risk appetite as 'the amount and type of risk that an organisation is willing to take in order to meet its strategic objectives'. It is the organisation's, specifically the board's, desire to take on risk in order to obtain a return.

Risk tolerance is the amount of risk that an organisation is prepared to accept in order to achieve its objectives, expressed as a quantitative measure, such as a permitted range of deviation from a specified target. Risk tolerance could be expressed in numerical terms, such as the maximum loss that the board would be willing to accept on a particular venture if events turn out adversely. Risk tolerance is therefore a quantitative expression of the risk appetite.

The 2011 IRM guidelines on risk appetite and risk tolerance provide some useful insights:

■ Risk appetite should be formulated within the context of the company's risk management capability. There are two aspects to risk management: one is taking on risks and the other is exercising control over them. A company should not have a high risk appetite if its ability to control risk is weak.

■ The UK Corporate Governance Code focuses on risk at a strategic level, whereas in practice there has to be coordination at strategic, tactical and operational levels for risk management to make sense.

To avoid 'risk blindness', the boardroom should be a place where the most critical issues are discussed, where everybody feels they can ask the necessary questions and get fair and appropriate answers. If a senior staff member proposes a new membership initiative or talent programme, the proposal itself should include the risks and mitigating actions for the board to consider. This does not preclude board members from raising other risks not previously defined or suggesting mitigating actions to ensure these are sufficient and proportionate.

The differences between risks and hazards

A hazard is something that can cause harm while the risk is the chance, high or low, that a hazard can actually cause harm. In sport, hazards are usually associated with dangers on or around the field of play such as damage to the playing surface or issues with the structural integrity of the stadium.

The likelihood and impact of an accident or injury would have to be assessed and mitigated at a strategic level as part of a facility management plan.

Risk management policies, systems and procedures

The Institute of Directors guidance note on risk states that it is important for directors to recognise that most risk management activities should not be directly undertaken by the board. The CEO, individual line managers and specialist units, such as compliance or internal audit, will often lead operational risk management. Most sports bodies do not have the capacity to establish separate risk and compliance teams, but should be clear about accountability for risk management below the board.

Developing a risk strategy

The Turnbull Report, *Internal Control: Guidance for Directors on the Combined Code*, was first published in 1999 and set out best practice on internal control for UK listed companies. In October 2005, the FRC issued an updated version of the guidance with the title Internal Control: Guidance for Directors on the Combined Code.

With reference to the Combined Code (now the Corporate Governance Code), the Turnbull Report states that the board of directors should set appropriate policies on internal control and seek regular assurance that will enable it to satisfy itself that the system is functioning effectively. In determining its policies with regard to internal control, the board's deliberations should include consideration of:

- the nature and extent of the risks facing the company;
- the extent and categories of risk which it regards as acceptable for the company to bear;
- the likelihood of the risks concerned materialising;
- the company's ability to reduce the incidence and impact on the business of risks that do materialise; and
- the costs of operating particular controls relative to the benefit thereby obtained in managing the related risks.

The importance of risk assessment

The assessment of risks calls for procedures to assess the potential size of the risk. The expected losses that could occur from adverse events or developments depend on the:

- probability that an adverse outcome will occur; and
- size of the loss in the event of an adverse outcome.

Where a risk is unlikely to materialise into an adverse outcome, and the loss would be small, no management action might be necessary. Where the risk is higher, measures should be taken to protect the organisation so that the remaining exposure to risk is within tolerance levels and consistent with risk appetite. It is possible to apply a quantitative or Red/Amber/Green (RAG) rating to each risk in order to establish the necessary responses. Table 7.1 is a commonly used tool to rate the likelihood and impact of a risk.

Table 7.1: Risk assessment matrix

		A	B	C	D	E
		Negligible	Minor	Moderate	Significant	Severe
E	Very likely	Low Med	Medium	Med Hi	High	High
D	Likely	Low	Low Med	Medium	Med Hi	High
C	Possible	Low	Low Med	Medium	Med Hi	Med Hi
B	Unlikely	Low	Low Med	Low Med	Medium	Med Hi
A	Very unlikely	Low	Low	Low Med	Medium	Medium

Having assessed the risks facing the organisation, the resultant rating can be plotted on a graph. For reporting purposes, this helps focus discussions on the principal strategic risks. Table 7.2 provides a simple template on which to plot each risk.

Table 7.2: Risk heat map

Heat map of results

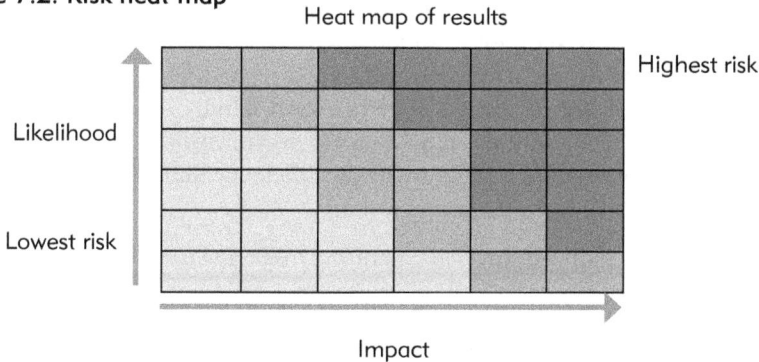

Highest risk

Likelihood

Lowest risk

Impact

Responsibility for risk at operational levels

Responsibility for reviewing the effectiveness of the risk management system may be delegated by the board to the audit committee, where one exists, which is also likely to have responsibility for reviewing the internal control system. The advantages of this delegated role may include the ability to appoint independent specialists in governance and risk.

At management level, there may be a risk committee consisting of senior executives. This committee would manage risks at an operational level and should report (through the CEO) to the board. The board need then only focus on the strategic risks and therefore will not need to review every operational risk identified.

Risk management

Risk management is the discipline of:

- identifying and assessing all the risks to which you are exposed;
- setting risk appetite for those risks aligned to strategic objectives;
- deploying the resources needed to control and monitor the risks; and
- reporting and re-assessing those risks in a documented and evidenced framework.

All employees are accountable for implementing internal control systems relevant to their roles. For sports bodies, this would extend to senior volunteers and the same would apply in a club or community environment, as volunteers are also accountable for financial, people and reputational risks.

The system of internal control should:

- be embedded in the operations of an organisation and form part of its culture. For sports organisations, this would mean an integration of risk assessment into all processes, whether led by paid or unpaid personnel;
- be capable of responding quickly to evolving risks arising from factors within the organisation and to changes in the business environment. This might include the loss of key staff, for example, the head coach; and
- include procedures for reporting immediately any significant control failings or weaknesses that are identified, together with details of corrective action being undertaken. For example, how a sports organisation is able to respond to safeguarding concerns is a measure of the efficiency and effectiveness of its internal control and communication system.

Strategic risks may be reduced through any of the following measures (sometimes called the 'Four Ts'):

- *Tolerate* – accept the risk, because it is not a significant threat or because they are external risks (such as regulatory risks and funding risks) over which the organisation has no control.
- *Transfer* – move some or all of the risk to someone else, for example, by taking out insurance when hosting a sporting event to minimise losses if it has to be cancelled.
- *Trim* – take suitable measures to reduce the risks, for example, developing an equality policy and educating staff and volunteers, thereby reducing the likelihood of discriminatory behaviour.
- *Terminate* – avoid the risk entirely, by withdrawing from the area of business operations where the risk exists. The board of a club may choose not to approve investment in building accommodation if the risks cannot be mitigated and managed.

Measures to manage risk may reduce the risk without eliminating it entirely. When this happens, there is some residual risk, but this should be within the level or limit that the board is prepared to tolerate. In the example of the club planning to build accommodation, the board could agree that financial losses that would be tolerated for two years after completion, with a view to reducing the losses and achieving a profitable return in year three.

Risk registers and other risk management processes
Risk registers can be separated into corporate and operational risk registers. The former details the strategic risks facing an organisation which the board must keep under review. The latter helps engage all levels of the organisation below the board in identifying, managing and monitoring risks.

The risk register should incorporate the quantitative or RAG rating and also account for the risk profile after mitigating actions have been taken. For example, if there is a risk that the long-term strategic goals will not be met, the organisation can develop annual business plans to ensure objectives, resources and key performance indicators are in place and monitored regularly. Any deviation from the business plans can be overseen by the board and appropriate action taken to keep the organisation on track against the strategic goals.

The risk register should also include:

- risk category – reputation, compliance, finance, etc;
- risk appetite – categorised as Low (1–3), for example, safeguarding children, Medium (4–7), for example, disruption to IT systems and High (8–10), for example, investing in a new format for the sport;
- RAG rating – this compares the risk profile (post controls) against its appetite and gives a RAG rating accordingly; and
- risk ownership – the person accountable for managing the risk.

Creating departmental risk registers ensures that those with knowledge and understanding of technical business areas, such as coaching, can contribute to the risk management process. It also assists in building shared accountability for risk across the organisation, rather than assuming the compliance, legal or other function will assume responsibility.

Risk training

A requirement of the UK Corporate Governance Code is that directors should have a programme for continuing professional development, and this should include, where necessary, suitable training in risk management. Training is particularly important for members of the audit or other committee with responsibility for reviewing the risk management system.

Principle 5 of the Principles of Good Governance for Sport and Recreation – Controls and Compliance, states the following:

- Board meetings should include strategic priorities and risk as standard agenda items.
- The board must make sure that there are appropriate internal controls and risk management procedures in place and that organisational risks are regularly reviewed.

To perform adequately, board members should feel confident when contributing to such discussions, and training in risk management should be central to the board's ongoing development.

Risks specific to sports organisations

Maintaining integrity

Most sports organisations will not have the resources to appoint an integrity officer, although they should have a suite of integrity-related policies including anti-bribery, match fixing and whistleblowing.

Illegal gambling and betting

A core function of all sports governing bodies is to maintain, and be seen to maintain, the integrity of their sport. This helps to preserve public confidence and protect their reputation and financial viability. The board has a duty to assess the risks of illegal gambling and betting and can take steps to mitigate these. This includes the development of anti-bribery and whistleblowing policies, and, subject to risk assessment, dedicated resources for prevention.

The SRA has established a Sports Betting Group that has developed a Code of Practice setting out seven key actions sports bodies should take to protect their sport. These are as follows:

- *Action 1*: establish rules, regulations and sanctions – rules must make it clear what is and what is not acceptable in relation to betting.
- *Action 2*: designate a contact person – this person should be responsible for ensuring that basic rules and sanctions are in place and should liaise with participants, the Gambling Commission, betting operators, international federations and law enforcement.
- *Action 3*: establish an integrity function, especially where the volume of betting on a sport is substantial.
- *Action 4*: introduce an education programme. This will ensure participants are fully aware of the rules and sanctions in relation to betting.
- *Action 5*: check competition contracts. In most cases participants will be bound by the NGB rules; however, it is good practice to ensure event contractual arrangements set out betting integrity obligations.
- *Action 6*: establish information sharing arrangements, as the Gambling Commission and betting operators should know who to contact in the event of suspicious betting patterns. In addition, sports might consider putting in place information sharing agreements with betting operators which set out the terms under which information can be exchanged.
- *Action 7*: undertake a regular review – integrity arrangements should be reviewed at least annually.

Doping in sport

In 2017 the CEO of UKAD, the UK's national anti-doping agency, stated that drug use at every level of sport was 'fast becoming a crisis'. UKAD research found more than a third (35%) of amateur sports people personally knew someone who has doped, and 8% said they had actually taken steroids.

Against this backdrop, sports bodies in the UK must take steps to address possible doping as it is a strategic risk that can cause sporting, reputational and financial damage. In the first instance, the likelihood of the risk needs to be assessed and this varies from sport to sport. For example, Polish weightlifter Tomasz Zielinski received the 2012 Olympic bronze medal despite finishing ninth, as six other athletes from the men's under kg final tested positive for performance-enhancing drugs when their 2012 samples were retested. Weightlifting is a sport categorised as high risk, so doping policies and testing processes are prioritised for competitive weightlifting athletes.

Not all doping issues involve professional sportspeople. There is a range of enhancement substances known as image and performance-enhancing drugs (IPEDs) which includes anabolic steroids and growth hormones to increase muscularity and modify appearance. A 2016 study by Liverpool John Moores University found that 89% of survey respondents used IPEDS primarily to gain muscle.

Clubs are unlikely to create testing programmes; however, there is a responsibility to raise concerns if any participant shows signs of substance abuse. Having a clear process in place to deal with such situations will protect the athlete and the club. Depending on the sport or environment, the club may want to run educational sessions so their participants, coaches and volunteers all have a better understanding of the dangers of drug use. Athlete welfare should feature in a club's risk register and, consequently, mitigating actions in respect of substance abuse would be expected.

The board's responsibility is to identify and mitigate the threat. It must ensure that the organisation has a robust anti-doping policy that has been widely communicated and is underpinned by effective procedures. Adopting the national anti-doping policy and drawing on UKAD resources and guidance is a good start; however, the sport must be vigilant and ensure athletes at all levels have access to information, education and support. The same applies to coaches, managers and other support personnel.

Paralympic classification

Athletes competing in paralympic sports have an impairment that leads to a competitive disadvantage. Consequently, a system has been put in place to minimise the impact of impairments on performance and to ensure the success of an athlete is determined by skill, fitness, power, endurance, tactical ability and mental focus. This system is called classification, and determines who is eligible to compete in a paralympic sport. It groups athletes into classes according to their limitation.

The *Layman's Guide to Paralympic Classification*, a resource that explains the classification system, is available on the IPC website: www.paralympic.org/sites/default/files/document/120716152047682_ClassificationGuide_1.pdf. The guide lists eligible impairment types which include physical, visual and intellectual impairment. Examples of sport classes are:

- Athletics: T/F11–13 (T = track or F = field): 11, 12 and 13 are allocated to athletes with carrying degrees of visual impairment with 11 applying to those with the least vision.
- Judo: B1, B2 and B3: Judoka in this sport are diagnosed with visual impairment and B1 athletes are either blind or have very low visual acuity. B2 and B3 athletes will increasingly higher visual acuity.

Classification is a complex field and there have been examples of athletes seeking a performance advantage by claiming their impairment has greater impact than is actually the case. Throughout 2016 and 2017, athletes and administrators raised concerns about the integrity of the paralympic classification system. As a result, the UK Athletics (UKA) Board commissioned an independent review into its domestic classification processes. The findings were released in February 2017 and, although UKA found classification procedures to be robust, there were recommendations to increase access to independent expertise to support the system, appoint an independent oversight committee and increase communications around classifications processes to ensure athletes are fully briefed on their rationale.

Sports bodies that offer competition opportunities to people with disabilities should ensure classification processes are transparent and in line with NGB and international federation standards.

Duty of care

In 2017, British sports faced a series of allegations of misconduct, bullying, harassment and grooming by coaches and other support personnel. The revelations came at the same time as an independent review into athlete welfare and sport's duty of care was being completed.

Some of the sports facing high-profile issues included the following:

- British Cycling – in 2016, sprint cyclist Jess Varnish made public allegations of sexism within the British Cycling World Class Programme. Although the allegations were investigated internally, the Independent Inquiry into the Culture and Climate of British Cycling established by UK Sport and British Cycling accused the board of 'sanitising' the internal investigation findings. As a result, the Performance Director, Shane Sutton, was removed and several other female athletes publicly declared their own experiences of the sport's sexist culture.
- British Canoeing – in 2017, a criminal investigation was launched into allegations of grooming and sexual assault. There was an internal investigation; however, once the allegations became public, UK Sport and British Canoeing set up a joint investigation into the abuse claims. A GB coach was suspended and a police investigation initiated.

Duty of Care in Sport Review

The review, commissioned by the Department for Digital, Culture, Media and Sport and led by Baroness Tanni Grey-Thompson, found that much more needed to be done to ensure athletes at all levels, but especially those on world class performance programmes, were protected from abuse and harassment. The final *Duty of Care in Sport* report, published in April 2017, made seven recommendations:

1. *A Sports Ombudsman* – the government should create a Sports Ombudsman with powers to hold NGBs to account for the duty of care they provide to all athletes, coaching staff and support staff.
2. *Measurement* – the government should measure duty of care via an independent benchmark survey giving equal voice to all stakeholders in the system.
3. *Named board member responsible for duty of care* – all NGB boards should have a named Duty of Care Guardian.
4. *Induction process* – an induction process should be carried out for all participants entering elite levels of sport. It could also include topics such as financial and pension advice, the role of agents, first aid training and information about medical issues.
5. *Exit survey for elite athletes* – as participants leave formal programmes, an independent exit interview should be conducted, the results of which would be taken account of in future funding discussions.
6. *Duty of Care Charter* – this Charter should be established by government, explicitly setting out how participants, coaches and support staff can expect to be treated and where to go if they need advice, support and guidance.
7. *The British Athletes Commission (BAC)* – government should independently fund the BAC to enable it to provide the best support to participants on talent pathways in Olympic and Paralympic sports.

While most sports organisations do not cater for elite athletes, the need to ensure the welfare of all participants is paramount. A failure to do so could affect participant numbers, as people join but do not stay if the experience is poor. Leadership conduct is a key factor in any participant's enjoyment and the organisation needs to ensure the behaviour of coaches, managers and other volunteers meets minimum standards. Developing organisational values and the publication of a code of conduct are practical steps that can be taken to provide assurance to participants (at all levels), parents, staff and volunteers.

Athlete selection

In 2012 there were 19 formal appeals against Team GB and Paralympics GB athlete selections. This may not be entirely surprising as the desire for British athletes to be selected was heightened by the opportunity to perform on the world stage in front of a home crowd.

Appeals were heard by independent panels convened by Sports Resolutions UK (SRUK), the organisation established to provide a dispute resolution service for sport. Following the 2012 Olympic and Paralympic Games, a number of lessons were learned as a result of panels, not least that athlete selection policies needed to be more robust, objective and transparent.

The guidance is comprehensive and includes information on:

- the legislative context;
- accommodating sports chairs;
- fire evacuation;
- changing areas;
- induction loops and signs;
- visual requirements; and
- pool design.

There is also a checklist which facility managers can use to audit their current provision.

While not all facilities are large, complex centres with multiple users, even community spaces can give consideration to the factors that affect access by disadvantaged groups. Making reasonable adjustments is a legal requirement and should be considered a risk if, for example, a disabled user is unable to access a facility or service. An inclusive approach using the available guidance will mitigate any possible legal challenges or reputational damage.

Facility ownership

With local government budgets being cut year on year, local authorities have to find ways to ensure there is some provision while reducing the financial risk of managing sports facilities. The awarding of contracts to specialist leisure providers has become commonplace, with agencies such as Greenwich Leisure Limited and Everyone Active invited to run and manage leisure facilities on behalf of local authorities.

In terms of risk, sports clubs will often seek partnerships with schools not only to use their facilities out of school hours, but also to encourage children to participate in their sport and potentially join their club. Reduced access will mean fewer opportunities to engage young people and grow membership.

Other non-financial risks

While school sport is an important element of an active lifestyle for children, there is a decline in the levels of activity outside of school. One study, funded under Persil's Dirt Is Good scheme, reported in 2016 that 74% of children spend less than an hour a day outdoors – less than a prison inmate. The concept of playing on the street or in a local park is diminishing due to parental fears around potential road accidents and strangers, and the number of community spaces where ball games are allowed is in decline.

Physical education and organised sport

In 2010, Michael Gove, then Education Secretary, revised the education budget and scrapped £162 million of funding for the School Sports Partnership programme which had been established to ensure every pupil had access to two hours' physical education and school sport per week. The announcement created a significant response from both the education and sports sectors, and the decision was partially reversed, with £65 million awarded for schools and £7 million for school games. In 2015, the Youth Sport Trust's National PE, School Sport and Physical Activity Survey Report suggested that there had been a significant drop in the number of children achieving the two hours per week activity level.

School physical education and sport programmes have adapted with the introduction of new activities such as Zumba and taekwondo, and girls are now much more likely to play cricket and football in school. The natural pathway to local clubs via district teams is not as clear, so building relationships with schools can bring great benefits in terms of engagement with young people who may form an interest in a particular sport.

Obesity and children dropping out of sport

The government launched Childhood Obesity: A Plan for Action strategy in January 2017, stating that nearly a third of children in the UK aged between two and 15 are overweight or obese. Some of the key aims of the plan include:

- *Soft drinks industry levy* – revenue from the levy will be invested in programmes to reduce obesity and encourage physical activity.
- *Helping all children to enjoy an hour of physical activity every day* – every primary school child should get at least 60 minutes of moderate to vigorous physical activity a day.
- *Improving the coordination of quality sport and physical activity programmes for schools* – from September 2017, every primary school in England has access to a coordinated offer of high-quality sport and physical activity programmes. NGBs will offer high-quality sport programmes to every primary school.

Sports bodies recognise obesity and inactivity as risks to young people's engagement in sport; however, the introduction of additional investment represents a means of addressing this. For local clubs, there may be additional opportunities to create partnerships with schools while, for NGBs, there will be a need to consider resources and capacity to provide programmes in primary schools.

Chapter summary

- The Cadbury Report (1992) described risk management as 'the process by which executive management, under Board supervision, identifies the risk arising from business ... and establishes the priorities for control and particular objectives'.
- How each risk applies to individual sports bodies will vary; however, the board is responsible for giving due consideration to their likelihood and impact.
- The Institute of Risk Management defines risk appetite as 'the amount and type of risk that an organisation is willing to take in order to meet its strategic

objectives'. It is the organisation's, specifically the board's, desire to take on risk in order to obtain a return.

■ Risk assessment considers the probability that an adverse outcome will occur and the size of the loss in the event of an adverse outcome.

■ Paralympic classification determines who is eligible to compete in a paralympic sport and groups athletes into classes according to their limitation.

■ All organisations are required under the Equality Act 2010 and Disability Discrimination Act 1995 to make reasonable adjustments that enable access to goods, facilities and services that would be offered to nondisabled people. Sport England's Accessible Sports Facilities Design Guidance assists in the planning, design and maintenance of accessible facilities.

■ A third of children in the UK aged 2–15 are overweight or obese so, in 2017, the government launched its Childhood Obesity: A Plan for Action. One key aim of the plan is investing in programmes to encourage physical activity.

8
Integrity, ethics and culture

Introduction

At its simplest, ethics is a system of moral principles. Ethics affect how people and organisations make decisions and behave.

The authors of the *Final Report for the FIFA Governance Reform Project* had this to say in 2014:

> There should however, be little doubt, that the reason for inappropriate conduct can usually be determined. It is almost always a combination of personal greed, a breakdown in systems and controls and a lack of ethical and moral culture within an organization.

All three reasons in the quote relate to ethics and behaviours. In this chapter, we shall look at a broad range of areas of ethical concern within modern sport that you need to know and manage. We shall first look at participant welfare and the concept of ethics, then corruption issues, and how to collect and manage information relating to all of these.

Integrity

Integrity is the quality of being honest and having strong moral principles. There are many threats to the integrity of the sector that have seen individuals, and indeed entire organisations, succumb and compromise the integrity of their sport. Some of these were outlined in Chapter 3 (pages 49 to 55). This chapter will go into some of those in more detail as well as introducing other areas of concern for the sector going into the future.

Anti-doping movement
International
Since the Russia doping scandal, an overview of which is provided in Chapter 3 (pages 49 to 51), WADA and the global anti-doping movement has been under sustained pressure to become more accountable and reform.

As a result of this, WADA published a paper, *Progress of the Anti-Doping System in Light of the Russian Doping Crisis*, which was last updated on 22 January 2019.

WADA's views of the main issues were:

1. The cheating in Russia was encouraged, organised, and protected, and thus not detected.
2. The Moscow and Sochi Laboratories were institutionally controlled, protected and thus the cheating was not detected.
3. There were no proper channels for whistleblowers to provide information regarding alleged Anti-Doping Rule Violations (ADRVs) under the World Anti-Doping Code; non-compliance violations under the Code; or any act or omission that could undermine the fight against doping in sport.
4. Upon receipt of such information, WADA had no power to investigate until it was accorded those powers within the 2015 Code (which came into force on 1 January 2015).
5. Following WADA's independent investigations, there were no defined sanctions agreed by all stakeholders that could be applied and there was no clear delineation as to which organisations were accountable for applying consequences in relation to outcomes of the investigations.
6. There was no clear dispute resolution mechanism in place that could have led to a decision being accepted and applied by all anti-doping organizations. (ADOs).

Measures WADA has taken to address these issues include:

■ In 2016, WADA shifted its focus to ensuring that signatories to the WADA Code have quality anti-doping programs in place and, in keeping with strong demand from stakeholders, that their compliance be monitored rigorously. To do so, in 2016, WADA initiated development of an ISO9001:2015 certified Code compliance monitoring program that was expanded in 2017. The programme, which represents the most thorough review of anti-doping rules and programmes that has ever taken place, aims to reinforce athlete and public confidence in the standard of ADOs worldwide.

■ In 2017, WADA put in place a laboratory working group to review the accreditation process and the quality control of laboratories. The group's conclusions were adopted by WADA's executive committee and board in May 2018, with a clear recommendation for more laboratory audits and proficiency testing to take place.

■ With the launch of Speak Up! in March 2017, and the implementation of a whistleblower policy and program, WADA now has a secure, digital platform through which athletes and others can report alleged ADRVs under the Code; non-compliance violations under the Code or any act or omission that could undermine the fight against doping in sport.

- In June 2016, WADA appointed Gunter Younger, a former Interpol officer and Head of Cyber Security with the Munich police, to set up and head its Intelligence & Investigations (I&I) Department. Since then, the WADA I&I Department has grown to seven staff, Speak Up! has been put in place and, via a new policy that was approved in May 2017, independence has been given to the I&I Department from the WADA executive committee board and management to ensure that there would be no political interference whatsoever with their investigations. The policy dictates that the I&I Department is independently audited annually to ensure full compliance of the work conducted. Since its establishment, the I&I Department has conducted numerous investigations and continues to be active on the Russian file. In addition to managing the day-to-day flow of new information, at the end of 2017, the I&I Department had run one long-term project; 10 sophisticated cases; one global operation with Interpol; and had 214 registered cases with the majority having been sent to ADOs for follow up.
- As a result of the disjointed responses to the Russian Doping Crisis, as well as calls from many in the anti-doping community – in particular athletes – to hold ADOs to a higher degree of accountability, the WADA board approved the development of the new International Standard for Code Compliance by Signatories (ISCCS), which came into force on 1 April 2018.
- Implementation of the ISCCS is one of the key legal tools that will avoid the issue where no clear dispute resolution mechanism was in place that could have led to a decision being accepted and applied by all ADOs. The ISCCS creates significantly more legal certainty around roles and responsibilities, sanctions, and mechanisms to get an independent decision on these questions. Unless all parties agree, CAS is the ultimate authority that decides on the appropriate sanctions, thus taking away any political component to these decisions.

United Kingdom

In parallel, the UK Anti-Doping Agency (UKAD) has been subject to a 'tailored review' by the Department for Digital, Culture, Media and Sport (DCMS), the report of which was published in January 2018. In doing so, the DCMS looked at three broad areas:

1. effectiveness
2. efficiency
3. corporate governance.

Key recommendations from the Review included:

- Sport England/UK Sport to release supplementary guidance on clean sport to the Code for Sports Governance, which has been agreed with government and UKAD.

- UKAD to prepare an evidence and risk-based proposal in order for government to assess the case for funding an increase in testing across sports by 50%.
- UKAD should consider proactively publishing information on its investigatory function (strategic trends, statistics and successful cases) quarterly, as well as via an annual state of the nation report, and use this to support the case for improved internal practices in sports, to encourage collaboration from law enforcement agencies, and to give more confidence to potential and existing whistleblowers.
- Data protection legislation should provide a processing condition for special categories of data for the purposes of anti-doping. Such processing should also be exempt from the notification requirements (to avoid 'tipping off' the person being investigated).
- UKAD to start a dialogue with sports and membership bodies to look at gaining access to athlete data (membership, phone and email records) with a view to producing UKAD guidance on data sharing.
- To improve resilience and expertise and to reduce expenditure on outside counsel, UKAD should consider bolstering its in-house legal team.
- UKAD to consider reframing its education function into an assurance programme to support NGBs who have varying levels of capacity.
- Sports in receipt of public funding should report annually on their anti-doping education compliance to UKAD and publish this information on their websites.
- Home Country Sports Councils to work with UKAD to deliver clean sport education to the 'talent pathway'.
- A values-based training programme focusing on 'healthy training' (nutrition, sleep, good training practice) is developed to reach young people via the curriculum and early sports pathways.
- Health harms associated with the abuse of IPEDs should be integrated into drug information and education.
- UKAD should work with the Chartered Institute for the Management of Sport and Physical Activity (CIMPSA), UK Coaching and SRA to insert compulsory clean sport education into all coaching/trainer qualification levels.
- UKAD should establish an Innovations Committee in the first quarter of 2018 with a remit to signpost new trends in doping and to focus on coordinated opportunities for research funding.
- DCMS and UKAD should continue to actively seek to improve black, Asian and minority ethic (BAME) representation among staff and at board level in line with the principle laid out in the Code for Sports Governance.
- UKAD continue to review its cyber security and to report on this at its quarterly updates with DCMS.
- UKAD develops a trust and empowerment culture, with clear and inclusive direction from the chair and CEO.
- Recommend regular communications with NGBs.

■ UKAD to review annually the most appropriate channels for young elite sports people to receive anti-doping messaging and use that intelligence to shape future social media activity.

■ Government to explore whether flexibility can be given to UKAD to enable it to use its earned income to support a more sustainable operating model.

■ UKAD should hold an open annual general meeting, exploring how to do so in a digital forum.

Gene doping

An emerging threat to the integrity of sport in respect of doping is gene doping.

The possibility of gene doping, defined as the transfer of nucleic acid sequences and/or the use of normal or genetically modified cells to enhance sport performance, is a real concern in sports medicine. The abuse of knowledge and techniques gained in the area of gene therapy is prohibited for competitive athletes.

Currently gene therapy is an experimental medical treatment where, typically, an individual with a malfunctioning gene has that gene replaced by a working copy of the same gene. As yet there is no conclusive evidence that that gene doping has been practiced in sport.

However, given that gene therapy techniques improve continuously, the likelihood of abuse will increase.

Gene doping was placed on the WADA banned list in 2003. A year later, it created the Gene and Cell Doping Expert Group, tasked with studying advances in the field, methods of detecting gene doping and overseeing WADA research on the topic. At the 2016 Rio Olympics, athletes' blood was tested for added copies of a gene coding for EPO, a hormone that increases red blood cell levels.

As regards detection, looking further into the future, WADA have discussed undertaking genetic sequencing of athletes, which would be an extension of an idea of the athlete biological passport (ABP).

Betting integrity and match-fixing

When it comes to match-fixing, the Council of Europe's definition in its Convention on the Manipulation of Sports Competitions (the Macolin Convention), for the 'manipulation of sports competitions' (a broader term which also encompasses match-fixing) is:

> 'an intentional arrangement, act or omission aimed at an improper alteration of the result or the course of a sports competition in order to remove all or part of the unpredictable nature of the aforementioned sports competition with a view to obtaining an undue advantage for oneself or for others'.

As a result of technological advances, particularly the emergence and growth of the online gambling market, sports betting opportunities have increased dramatically, both in terms of the number of sport events and the number of betting markets available. Today, sports betting is used by 'professionals', including traders to make legitimate profits, but also by criminals for money laundering.

Athletes and officials in certain sports are already, and will further become, targets of criminals in order to manipulate a competition for betting purposes.

Sports betting, particularly online betting websites based in unregulated or lightly regulated jurisdictions, has dramatically increased in recent years and is used as a mechanism for profit for organised crime.

Understanding the threat from match-fixing

The usual process for match-fixers to make money from the global betting markets is illustrated in Figure 8.1:

Figure 8.1: Match-fixing

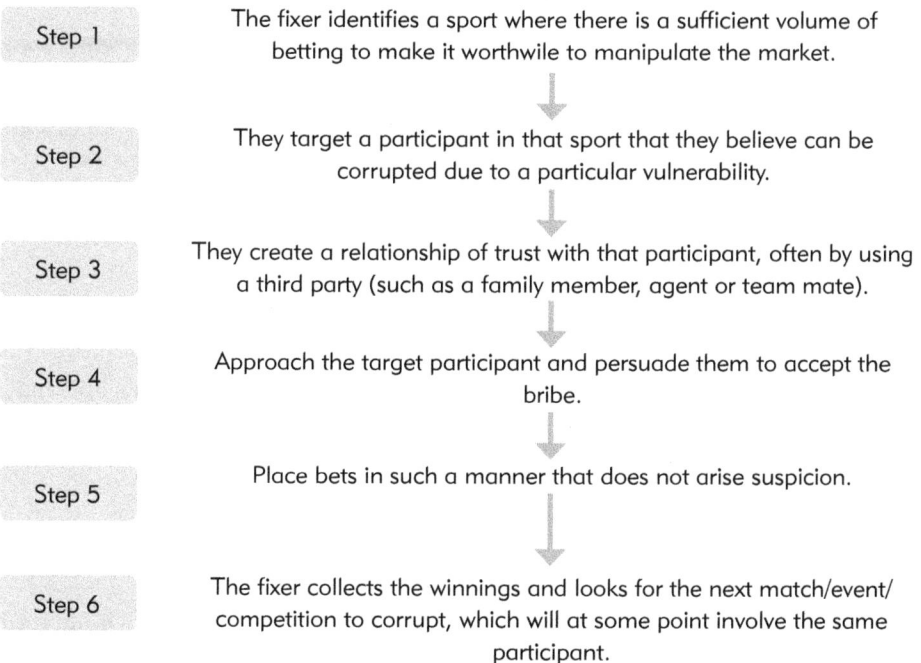

Step 1	The fixer identifies a sport where there is a sufficient volume of betting to make it worthwile to manipulate the market.
Step 2	They target a participant in that sport that they believe can be corrupted due to a particular vulnerability.
Step 3	They create a relationship of trust with that participant, often by using a third party (such as a family member, agent or team mate).
Step 4	Approach the target participant and persuade them to accept the bribe.
Step 5	Place bets in such a manner that does not arise suspicion.
Step 6	The fixer collects the winnings and looks for the next match/event/competition to corrupt, which will at some point involve the same participant.

There are a number of reasons why a particular participant may be seen as a potential target by a fixer:

- whether their salary has been paid;
- addiction – drugs, sex, alcohol, gambling and so on;
- living beyond personal income and high personal debt;
- greed; and/or
- naivety.

The 'grooming' of a participant takes place over a period of time whereby, typically, the following steps are undertaken by a 'corruptor' (see Figure 8.2).

Figure 8.2: Grooming

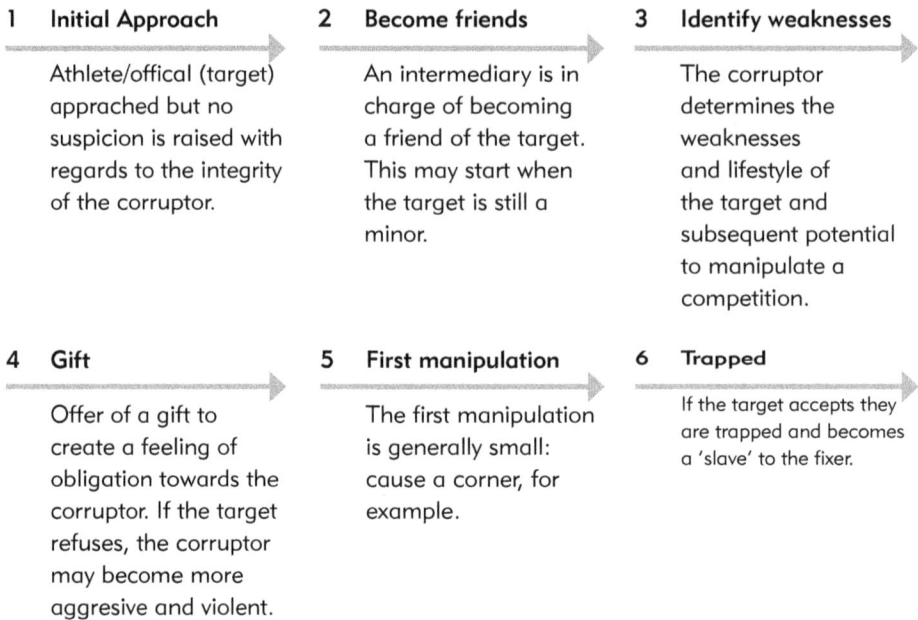

1 Initial Approach	2 Become friends	3 Identify weaknesses
Athlete/offical (target) apprached but no suspicion is raised with regards to the integrity of the corruptor.	An intermediary is in charge of becoming a friend of the target. This may start when the target is still a minor.	The corruptor determines the weaknesses and lifestyle of the target and subsequent potential to manipulate a competition.

4 Gift	5 First manipulation	6 Trapped
Offer of a gift to create a feeling of obligation towards the corruptor. If the target refuses, the corruptor may become more aggresive and violent.	The first manipulation is generally small: cause a corner, for example.	If the target accepts they are trapped and becomes a 'slave' to the fixer.

If the participant engages with the match-fixers via the above modus operandi, the likely consequences are:

- the fixers are not friends.
- the participant takes the risks, the fixer takes the money; and
- when the participant gets caught, the fixer disappears and the participant takes the blame.

Inside information is one particular area of risk. Inside information can be defined as information relating to the participation in, or likely or actual outcome of, an event which is known by an individual as a result of their role in connection with that event and which is not in the public domain. Common types of inside information include:

- injury news;
- team line-ups;
- a participant's personal situation; and
- a club's financial situation.

Betting integrity offences

A set of betting integrity regulations should contain:

1. betting on the sport in question;
2. misuse of inside information;
3. match-fixing and competition manipulation;
4. failure to report a corrupt approach; and
5. failure to co-operate with an investigation.

Attempts at match-fixing, or any of the other unethical conduct stated above, should be prohibited and may be sanctioned.

Tools to protect a sport from competition manipulation

Specialist companies have developed a sophisticated bet monitoring system which monitors worldwide sports betting markets 24/7 to identify unusual and/ or suspicious betting activity and provide real-time alerts. Once such an alert has been made, human analysts in the field of sports betting use this information (together with information from third-party sources) to thoroughly investigate the event and produce detailed reports for the sport.

There are a wide variety of intelligence sources that can help combat and address integrity concerns (and rule breaches). A sport should look to utilise as many of these as possible, including:

- betting monitoring reports;
- referrals, reports or inquiries from other jurisdictions, including from law enforcement, other sports organisations, the media and so on;
- physical surveillance at competition venues for suspicious behaviour; and
- hotlines or other reporting mechanisms.

Consequences of engaging in match-fixing activity

By engaging in match-fixing activity and any related conduct, a participant committing an offence faces three possible consequences:

a. *Sporting sanctions* – this is usually in the form of a lengthy ban, accompanied by a hefty fine.
b. *Criminal sanctions* – far more serious are the potential riminal sanctions for participants getting embroiled in match-fixing, in particular imprisonment.
c. *Reputational impact* – the final consequence, and one which is often underestimated, is the reputational damage that will be caused should a participant be found to have engaged in match-fixing activities. Even when a sporting ban and/or prison term has been served, the longer-term consequence is that the participant's reputation will be ruined. It is unlikely they will be able to return to their sport in any capacity.

Key messages to participants
Having set out the modus operandi of match-fixers, along with the potential consequences, it is important the message stressed strongly to participants is:

- your reputation
- your responsibility
- your career.

Finally, each participant must have the following 'Three Rs' at the forefront of their minds:

1. *Recognise* when a match-fixing approach is being made or when you receive relevant information;
2. *Resist* any attempt to engage in the match-fixing activity by saying 'no'; and
3. *Report* the incident to the appropriate person or through the relevant channel.

Safeguarding and participant welfare
Sport in the UK has faced a number of difficult and uncomfortable challenges in respect of safeguarding and participant welfare in recent years.

Football has perhaps faced the most troubling allegations regarding historic sexual abuse. In November 2016, disclosures were made in the media relating to child sexual abuse, which is alleged to have been carried out by coach Barry Bennell and others against a number of professional footballers and former academy scholars at various professional clubs. Such has the volume of allegations been that the Football Association (FA) has determined that it is necessary to instruct external leading counsel to conduct a review into what, if anything, the FA and clubs knew about these allegations at the relevant time, what action was taken or should have taken place. The latest from Clive Sheldon QC, who is leading the Independent Review into child sex abuse allegations in football, was that his team's report had been delayed due to concurrent ongoing criminal investigations which are not to be compromised. Indeed, in carrying out the Review, there has been close and constant co-operation with Operation Hydrant and the police forces around the country investigating allegations of abuse.

Independent reviews have been commissioned by other national governing bodies into similar allegations. In January 2019, the Lawn Tennis Association (LTA) published a report produced by a wide-ranging independent review into events at Wrexham Tennis Centre following the conviction and subsequent imprisonment of its former head coach in July 2017. The report concluded that Wrexham Tennis Centre failed to properly address a number of historic complaints made about the behaviour of coaches at the Centre, including the former head coach. The Wrexham Tennis Centre internal investigation, carried out in 2012, was found to be insufficient and serious concerns raised by parents and coaches were not adequately addressed at the time or subsequently. Tennis Wales and the LTA we both found to have failed properly to recognise the safeguarding concerns that should have been evident at the time and to have acted inadequately in failing to initiate proper proceedings against the head coach prior to his arrest in 2017.

Other organisations have heeded the warnings from these investigations and sought to be proactive in safeguarding participants and their welfare. The British Horseracing Authority announced at the end of 2018 the publication of a new, overarching safeguarding policy, regulations and code of conduct for the sport, which came into effect from 1 January 2019. The Safeguarding Policy is applicable to everyone who works in British racing and is designed to complement and underpin the existing safeguarding policies that various racing organisations already have in place. It will enable everyone in racing to manage any safeguarding issues with confidence, efficiency and appropriate support. The BHA policy covers areas such as abuse, inappropriate relationships, reporting safeguarding concerns and safer recruitment practices.

Concussion in contact sports and the mental health of participants continues to be at the forefront of policies and initiatives in this area of integrity. An example of the former was the Rugby Football Union (RFU) trialling a lower tackle height in the second-tier cup competition to try and lower the rate of concussions; however, this been ended prematurely after the number of concussions actually increased. When it comes to mental health, The Mental Health Charter for Sport and Recreation, led by the SRA sets out how sport organisations can adopt good mental health practice to make activities inclusive, positive and open to everyone. The overall vision for the Charter is to embed mental health within sport and recreation to create a culture shift that removes the stigma around mental health. To supplement this, in March 2018, the UK Government launched the Mental Health and Elite Sport Action Plan which sets out some key areas for further work around the clarity of support available, sharing of best practice across the sport sector and improved mental health education and training in sport. The Government wants all elite sports to have a clear mental health strategy by 2024.

Other emerging integrity threats

Sport organisations must remain vigilant, aware and proactive in respect of integrity, as those looking to undermine it are always looking for new ways to do so. A couple of recent examples from around the world being 'technological fraud' in cycling through the use of hidden motors in bicycles to boost their performance, and horse racing trainers being charged for possessing devices used to deliver electric shocks to make horses run faster.

Ethics, behaviours and culture

Participant welfare

The welfare of the participants in sport must be front-and-centre of the governance of all organisations, above all other aims. Participant welfare in sport can mean a multitude of things, including:

- child safeguarding;
- protection from discrimination, bullying and harassment;
- physical health (concussion, for example); and
- mental health (including depression and anxiety).

In addition to active participants, the welfare of coaches, match officials and all employees/volunteers should also receive attention.

Historically, little consideration has been given by sports organisations to the welfare of participants on the assumption that athletes are mentally 'tough' enough naturally and should only be concerned with winning. This is, of course, entirely misplaced, and participant welfare has come under the spotlight in the past couple of years.

Duty of care

The duty of care can be defined as an obligation to safeguard others from harm while they are in your care, using your services or exposed to your activities. This can be a legal, regulatory and/or moral (ethical) duty. The concept of a duty of care is central to the behaviour of those working in sports organisations.

In law, finding the existence of a duty of care is the first stage of the test to bring a successful action for negligence. A duty of care has been recognised to exist in the following situations:

- Coaches have to take reasonable care to ensure they are training the players under their control in a manner that does not cause them reasonably foreseeable harm.
- Referees, and other match officials, will be held liable for their failure to ensure that players are able to play the sport in a reasonably safe environment.
- Sports governing bodies owe a duty to take reasonable care to ensure that the advice they provide to event organisers is sufficient to enable them to provide facilities that are reasonably safe for participation in the sport.
- Additionally, governing bodies need to have protocols in place to ensure that an injured athlete's position is, as a minimum, not made any worse by the actions of those who treat them.

Recent scandals have caused serious concerns regarding the duty of care being taken by governing bodies and their employees, not just in relation to the law but also ethically, including allegations of bullying in elite cycling and historic allegations of child abuse in football. As a result, the UK Government, in its Sporting Future strategy document, ordered an independent report to be produced on the topic, with a view to introduce a new duty of care for all athletes and participants, because sport should be safe for and inclusive of everyone.

The working group for the report was chaired by decorated Paralympian Baroness Tanni Grey-Thompson, and the *Duty of Care in Sport: Independent Report to Government* was published in April 2017. This is an extremely wide-ranging report covering seven themes, with much of great use to improve the ethics and behaviours in sport.

Education

There are sad stories regarding athletes who are ill-equipped for a life outside sport, which can occur for many reasons, including lacking skills to get a job and build a career. Therefore, it is important for organisations to encourage athletes on talent pathways to develop their education alongside their sporting and other interests, to gain qualifications and enjoy a more well-rounded approach to life. This is often referred to as the 'dual career' approach. One way an organisation could do this, as recommended in the report, is to partner with education institutions (including colleges and universities) to put in place a duty of care policy, to support participants following a dual career route.

Transition

Very closely linked to the importance of education is the overall transition of participants, both on entering and leaving top-level sport.

For those entering top-level sport, it is advised you have an induction process to ensure a common understanding of important processes throughout your sport and what support is available, such as independent and confidential support services. Although this induction should be targeted at the athletes themselves, parents and other support people should attend the induction as they are the participant's key support network.

When it comes to a life after sport, which could arise at any time, athletes should be actively encouraged to consider and talk about their future plans, allowed time to do this and given information and support wherever possible about career options and skills development. Organisations can help sportspeople explore and develop their employment skill sets by considering links with sponsors and corporate partners, which may provide work experience or employment opportunities.

An athlete's transition out of sport can arise as a result of deselection from a team or squad. This process has to be managed carefully to avoid too much distress to the athlete. This may require some specific training, as coaches may not have the 'people skills' necessary to handle such difficult conversations.

Upon leaving, to obtain as much information as possible to improve behaviours and processes for the future, organisations should arrange exit interviews with those athletes. The interview should be administered by an independent body, preferably a players' association, to ensure the sportsperson can be open and honest about their experience. The anonymised results can be fed back to the sport and funding body.

Representation of the participant's voice

There is a chronic lack of recognition for the importance of the athlete (and other participants) in sport, which is nonsensical given that without them there would be no sport. Therefore, they should be given a meaningful voice in the running of your organisation.

Theory in action

The UK Athletics Athletes' Commission was formed in 2017, with the aim of ensuring athletes' voices are heard by UK Athletics' Performance Oversight Committee and the UK Athletics Board. It consists of 12 current and former British international athletes.

Meeting twice a year as a minimum, the Commission provides a formal mechanism whereby the perspective and expertise of Great Britain and Northern Ireland's international athletes will be heard by the UKA hierarchy on the many initiatives and programmes operated by the NGB.

Furthermore, the Commission seeks to ensure that athletes possess a meaningful voice on important matters heard at board level, in turn allowing the UKA board to benefit from the perspective and expertise of international athletes in its deliberations and decision making. The commission will also be able to bring matters to the Performance Oversight Committee for discussion and recommendation.

Equality, diversity and inclusion

From a behavioural perspective, equality, diversity and inclusion are very sensitive and important topics. As well as complying with legislation to prevent discrimination, sports organisations must take the moral stance that all forms of discrimination are equally unacceptable to the values of society and their sport. This is a zero-tolerance approach and organisations have a responsibility to stamp out discriminatory behaviours, practices and cultures amongst participants.

When it comes to equality, diversity and inclusion in organisational leadership training on the duty of care should be given to support a new diverse generation of leaders, as there is currently a real lack of diversity at board level in sport. A more diverse board will lead to better decision making.

Safeguarding

Safeguarding is an area of the duty of care and sports governance where there is already a significant amount of legislation and regulation, particularly regarding child welfare. Safeguarding is a complex area, therefore the training given to participants (in particular volunteers) should provide greater clarity about the required standards and good practice so that the organisation can put in place appropriate and comprehensive policies and processes.

In addition to safeguarding children, adults and other vulnerable participants have safeguarding needs regarding those in 'positions of trust' (given the broadest possible meaning). In this regard, there is a need for continual vigilance. It may be advisable to introduce a duty to report in rules and regulations (see pages 179-190).

In addition to Disclosure and Barring Service checks for people working in sport, organisations should consider introducing a licensing scheme for coaches and other athlete support personnel if there are enough resources and operational capability.

Mental welfare

Society in general has become more aware in recent years of the importance of mental health and well-being. This is even more acute in elite sport where the regime is one of continuous training, performance and selection, which brings significant mental resilience challenges for athletes, coaches and other support personnel.

Organisations should foster an environment where people feel able to discuss mental health issues. Participants should be aware of where they can obtain advice and assistance. This should be available within the organisation (a safeguarding officer, for example), but also externally on a confidential basis from mental health professionals.

Coaches should also receive specific professional development training on how to identify and deal appropriately with mental health issues that athletes may face.

To embed this commitment to mental well-being within the governance framework, organisations can also sign up to the Mental Health Charter for Sport and Recreation. This has been created and developed by the SRA, alongside the Professional Players Federation and the mental health charity Mind, setting out how sport can use its collective power to tackle mental ill health and its stigma. The Charter outlines six actions that sport as a whole can take to help make mental health a commonly understood matter and to help those in need. Of those six actions, the following points can be drawn out and adapted to become strategic behaviours:

- Use sport to promote general well-being, focusing on encouraging physical activity and social interaction for their contribution to good mental health.
- Carry out public communication campaigns which promote and adopt good mental health policies and encourage best practice within sport.
- Find people within sport who have suffered from mental health issues, and if they are comfortable to do so, invite them to promote positive messages as role models/ambassadors to reduce the stigma attached to mental health problems.

- As part of a zero-tolerance approach to discrimination in your sport, actively tackle discrimination on the grounds of mental health to ensure that everyone is treated with dignity and respect.
- Ensure organisations regularly monitor their performance in this area and are up-to-date with the latest good practice from other sports and sectors, as this is a constantly developing area of healthcare.

Safety, injury and medical issues

Safety and athlete welfare must be placed above all other concerns. A failure to do so has seen high-profile organisations such as the NFL and World Rugby face significant criticisms in relation to the effects of repeated concussions. Boxing in the UK has been through significant challenges when it comes to safety.

Theory in action

In 1991, Michael Watson fought Chris Eubank in a boxing match sanctioned by the British Boxing Board of Control (BBBofC). Due to failures in the treatment given to Mr Watson at ringside, having been knocked out, he suffered life-changing brain injuries.

Mr Watson successfully argued before the court that the BBBofC had not acted as a reasonable and competent governing body, as it had failed to ensure that it was sufficiently knowledgeable of current emergency treatment protocols for traumatic brain injury.

First, the Court of Appeal held that the safety of the participants in a sport is of paramount concern to the relevant governing body. As a result, each body owes a duty to take all reasonable care in the circumstances to ensure that those competing in the sport it regulates are reasonably safe from foreseeable harm.

Then, on the facts, the court found that the professional expertise of the doctors ringside, and the equipment available to them, had been inadequate to cope appropriately with Mr Watson's condition of intra-cranial bleeding when he was knocked unconscious. Such deficiencies had meant that emergency treatment in the form of intubation, the insertion of an endotracheal tube, the administration of a diuretic to reduce the swelling of the brain and the administration of oxygen had been delayed for about 30 minutes until Mr Watson had reached hospital, by which time it was too late.

The key findings of the court, as regards the failings by the BBBofC, were as follows:

- Failure to provide adequate guidelines regarding medical provision at ringside.
- The BBBofC were in the best position to determine safety protocols.
- The BBBofC were under a duty to minimise the risk admittedly inherent in a dangerous sport.

- The BBBofC had special knowledge about the risks involved when compared to Mr Watson.
- Those advising the BBBofC on medical and safety issues should have been fully aware of current best practice in the treatment of injuries.
- The BBBofC's duty was to take reasonable care to ensure that reasonably foreseeable personal injuries sustained were treated properly.
- The BBBofC owed participants a duty to ensure the advice that it gave event organisers was sufficiently well prepared to enable the organisers to run a contest safely.

When dealing with medical issues relating to participants, organisations must fully respect the duty of confidentiality that medical professionals have when treating those who are injured. For instance, sharing information about someone's medical history within an organisation can be useful in agreeing a course of treatment, but this process needs to be handled sensitively, appropriately and in line with professional guidelines and preferably an internal agreed process. A participant must be fully informed as to how their information is being used, with consideration being given to a separation within a performance team of the medical and safeguarding staff and from the performance coaches. This will provide a clear line of demarcation in the case of potentially conflicting advice.

Disclosure and Barring Service checks

The Disclosure and Barring Service (DBS) is a government service which helps employers to make safer recruitment decisions and prevent unsuitable people from working with vulnerable groups, including children, by checking the backgrounds of certain individuals, and is therefore vital for sports organisations to be aware of. Scotland has its own similar but separate service, Disclosure Scotland.

Individuals who are passionate about sport should have the right skills, knowledge and attitude, and previous history of good conduct, for a particular role. It is therefore essential that there are effective recruitment and selection procedures for both paid staff and volunteers.

Undertaking a DBS check for current and prospective employees and volunteers who are carrying out 'regulated activities' must be central to an organisation's recruitment policy.

The Safeguarding Vulnerable Groups Act 2006 set out the scope and operation of the vetting and barring scheme. Most importantly, an organisation determines which roles are considered 'regulated activity'. This is work that an individual barred from working with vulnerable groups including children must not do. It is an offence for a barred person to seek to work in regulated activity, and for an employer knowingly to employ a barred person in regulated activity. Examples of regulated activity are as follows:

■ Unsupervised activities such as teaching, training, instructing, caring for or supervising children, providing advice/guidance on well-being or driving a vehicle only for children.

■ Carrying out work regularly (at least weekly), frequently (four times a month or more, overnight (between 2.00am and 6.00am) or work in a limited range of establishments ('specified places'), with opportunity for contact (schools, children's homes or childcare premises, for example).

The Child Protection in Sport Unit, which is a partnership between the NSPCC, Sport England, Sport Northern Ireland and Sport Wales, suggests that a safe-recruitment policy should contain, in addition to the DBS check:

■ writing a role and person description;
■ using an application form to gather relevant information about each applicant;
■ requiring written references;
■ interviewing the applicant;
■ undertaking a risk assessment of any concerning information;
■ verifying qualifications and experience;
■ making a record of the recruitment decision;
■ providing an induction to the role which must cover safeguarding policies and procedures and signing up to the Code of Conduct as a minimum.

If relevant information comes back on an individual following the request for a DBS check, then an organisation should consider this alongside all other information gathered and a full risk assessment. This decision must be made in conjunction with someone (either inside or outside the organisation) with appropriate safeguarding knowledge, experience and preferably training.

There is further helpful guidance on this area of high importance on both the CPSU website (https://thecpsu.org.uk) and the DBS website (www.gov.uk/government/organisations/disclosure-and-barring-service).

Use of social media

Social media can be a powerful tool for participants, clubs, governing bodies and other sports organisations to enhance public profiles, improve communication and engagement, and increase value and attractiveness to sponsors. Conversely, if used in the wrong way, through poor behaviours and practices, social media can have far-reaching negative implications.

There is often a delicate ethical balance to strike between honesty and appropriate engagement, especially for participants and employees of sports organisations. They may say things that cause offence, damage their own reputation and/or bring the governing bodies into disrepute. Hugh Morris, the former Managing Director of the England and Wales Cricket Board, summarised the situation as follows regarding players' use of social media: 'When [social media is] done poorly it is a complete and utter nightmare for those of us trying to manage and lead teams. It is like giving a machine gun to a monkey.'

Theory in action

Stephanie Rice was an Australian swimmer who won three gold medals at the 2008 Olympics. In September 2010, following a rugby match in which Australia beat South Africa, she posted 'suck on that faggots!' on her Twitter page. She was criticised in many quarters for what was widely deemed to be a homophobic comment, and lost her lucrative sponsorship deal with Jaguar the following week.

Organisations should be proactive to maximise the benefits of social media through encouraging positive behaviours with its use. Some recommended steps include:

- *Public comment*: the essential message for all participants in your sport, including those working for the governing body, is the public nature of social media. As a simple rule of thumb, they should not post anything on social media they would not be happy to say in a media interview.
- *Education*: educating the participants on the rules, regulations and expectations of a particular sport, along with the positive ways in which channels can be used, is essential. However, this cannot be used in isolation. Any education programme should be complemented by ongoing support and guidance where required.
- *Code of conduct*: The messages in a code of conduct (which is likely to cover more than just social media) should be clear, unequivocal and simple to understand.
- *Contractual provisions*: Many governing bodies and clubs are now putting so-called 'morality clauses' into the contracts with their participants. Such clauses act as a reminder for participants to behave ethically when it comes to their social media activity, and also provides a clear contractual requirement.

Organisations should take a holistic approach to the use of social media by using the above points to formulate a social media policy for participants which encompasses not only regulation and punishment, but also education.

Culture

The simplest way to define any organisation's culture is, 'the way we do things around here'. Culture is a key component in business and has an impact on the strategic direction of business. Culture influences management decisions and all business functions.

The introduction to the UK Corporate Governance Code states, 'a company's culture should promote integrity and openness, value diversity and be responsive to the views of shareholders and wider stakeholders. Principle 4 of the Code for Sport Governance states, 'having the right values embedded in the culture of the organisation helps protect public investment and also enhances the reputation of the organisation, earning stakeholder trust'.

In the corporate world, it is generally accepted that sound governance is essential to promote high ethical standards and foster a value-based culture. Where such sound governance is lacking, and there is poor behaviour and an accompanying poor culture, it is often difficult and takes time to change.

International sports federations have all too often exhibited a culture whereby poor governance practice has been allowed to thrive. One such reason for this is a lack of accountability.

In May 2018, ICSA released one of few reports specifically addressing culture in sports governance, *Organisational Culture in Sport: Assessing and improving attitudes in behaviour*. The key findings and outcome of this report were:

- Organisational culture is taken to mean an agreed set of customs and norms that inform, and are evident in, the behaviour of those who work in and for an organisation.
- Culture should be taken to encompass what an organisation does, why it does the things it does and how it goes about doing those things.
- One major cause of negative behaviour identified was a poorly stated or poorly communicated set of values adopted by the organisation.
- Boards must take the lead in setting and establishing the culture of an organisation and the ethical parameters within which it acts, and retain oversight of the implementation.
- The board should also gain experience of the organisation to see for themselves what it feels like, what processes are in place, what works and what does not.
- A disconnect between the board and the executive can undermine, dilute or confuse the stated culture. The two need to work together to embed and monitor agreed values and standards.
- Important indicators as to culture:
  - board composition;
  - (im)balances of power and dominant personalities;
  - staff and board turnover rates;
  - financial discipline;
  - stakeholder relations;
  - policies.
- A key area both of pressure on culture and of opportunity for change is the issue of diversity.

■ Establishing a coherent culture throughout the organisation can take time, planning and training at all levels in order to ensure that there is acceptance across all departments and teams.

■ A vital step towards establishing an organisation-wide culture is to begin with a clearly articulated mission, vision and set of values.

In addition to the organisational culture issues in sport, there have also been significant revelations and concerns regarding the performance culture and the treatment of participants. Indeed, this is stated as one of the sport-specific challenges to organisational culture in sport in the ICSA report. Such incidents are not entirely unrelated to the overall governance and culture of the organisation, especially accountability mechanisms both within and outside the organisation.

The effects of ethics on governance in sports organisations

Personal ethics

So far, we have described ethics in general. In the following sections we shall look in detail at the different types of ethics that individuals and organisations can exhibit in sport and how these impact on governance.

Personal ethics are concerned with an individual's morality and their view of what is right and wrong. To some extent, the law can establish rules about what is 'wrong'. However, standards of behaviour are much more determined by social attitudes of morality and good conduct, even though the attitudes of individuals often differ on whether a particular action is 'wrong' or unethical.

Ethical personal behaviour helps to build trust and is commonly associated with the Nolan Principles, discussed in Chapter 2 (pages 36 to 39), in particular integrity (honesty) and transparency.

Theory in action

In May 2015, a 47-count criminal indictment was presented to a court in New York charging 14 defendants with racketeering, wire fraud and money laundering conspiracies, among other offences, in connection with the defendants' participation in a 24-year scheme to enrich themselves through the corruption of international football.

The indictment alleged that, between 1991 and 2015, the defendants and their co-conspirators corrupted the enterprise (world football) by engaging in various criminal activities including fraud, bribery and money laundering. Two generations of senior football officials were charged with abusing their positions of trust for personal gain, frequently through an alliance with unscrupulous sports marketing executives who shut out competitors and kept highly lucrative media and marketing contracts for themselves through the systematic payment of bribes and kickbacks. All told, the football officials were charged with conspiring to solicit and receive well over US$150 million (£110 million) in bribes and kickbacks in exchange for their official support of the sports marketing executives who agreed to make the unlawful payments.

The indicted and convicted individual defendants face maximum prison terms of 20 years for the conspiracies, money laundering and obstruction of justice charges.

In the first case brought to trial as a result of the this investigation, two former South American football officials were found guilty by a New York City jury on multiple corruption charges in December 2017. The two individuals, former Brazilian FA president Jose Maria Marin and former South American confederation president Juan Angel Napout, are yet to be sentenced.

Business ethics

Business ethics relate to an organisation's standards. The standards adopted significantly impact the governance of an organisation, not to mention affecting the organisation's dealings with its stakeholders. Business ethics are shaped by the culture of the organisation, which can vary significantly depending on where in the world the organisation is based or operating.

There is a connection between business ethics and the different approaches to governance. If a business has a shareholder/member approach to corporate governance, it puts the interests of shareholders ahead of the interests of anyone else. If it adopts a stakeholder approach to governance, it will act in an ethical way that takes into consideration the needs and concerns of other stakeholders.

Theory in action

The Cycling Independent Reform Commission (CIRC) was established by the Union Cycliste Internationale (UCI) in February 2014 'to conduct a wide ranging independent investigation into the causes of the pattern of doping that developed within cycling and allegations which implicate the UCI and other governing bodies and officials over ineffective investigation of such doping practices'.

Part of the CIRC's mandate was to consider potential unethical governance practices by the UCI, and those individuals running it at the relevant time. This is an example of what they found:

- From the late 1980s, the UCI grew rapidly as an institution and vested extensive powers in the office of president, which created an entity run in an autocratic manner without appropriate checks and balances. Internal management bodies appear to have been devoid of any real influence and the governance structure allowed the president to take a particular direction almost unchallenged.
- There was a lack of transparency and oversight in respect of financial matters, including in respect of expenses and approvals for some costly projects.
- Decisions taken by the UCI leadership in the past have undermined anti-doping efforts, which in turn severely damaged the credibility of the UCI and therefore the reputation of the sport of cycling. This was caused by a lack of proper institutional checks and balances within the UCI, meaning the leadership of the organisation was not subjected to the rigorous scrutiny and application of the rules and best practice that they should have been.

To address these specific findings regarding the lack of organisational ethics in the UCI, the CIRC made the following recommendations:

- Better control and accountability for UCI in the form of its overarching management body, which has effective financial control over all actions, commissions and bodies of UCI.
- The Ethics Commission should be revamped to ensure it is independently appointed and that people who are cited are obliged to cooperate.
- Everything that occurs during management committee meetings should be recorded in the minutes.

Professional ethics

Professional ethics emanate from professional bodies that require all of their members to comply with their standards. Unlike personal and business ethics, a key element of professional ethics is that there is a body which investigates failures to comply with the relevant codes and sanctions where appropriate.

Fair play ethics

Fair play is an ethical concept uniquely applicable to sport, but reflects values that are equally applicable to everyday life. Fair play is a positive concept and involves more than just playing within the rules – it is a way of thinking, not just a way of behaving. It incorporates fair competition, respect, friendship, team spirit, equality, sport without doping, respect for written and unwritten rules, and concepts such as integrity, solidarity, tolerance, care, excellence and joy.

The importance of implementing a code of ethics

A code of ethics in a sports organisation is important as it will inform the conduct of all participants and the culture of the organisation by instilling values of integrity, fairness and transparency, and an appreciation of acceptable conduct.

By setting out in writing in the form of a code, promoting what defines the most important core values for behaviour and conduct within a sport, and (reflecting the highest possible ethical values) there can be no doubt as to what is expected by all participants, whatever their role.

A code of ethics in sport must cover four key virtues towards all stakeholders: fairness, integrity, responsibility and respect. Some sports bodies also emphasise the need for openness and transparency on both a corporate and personal level. A number of sports organisations already have codes of ethics in place, including the international federations for swimming and football, and the IOC.

It is possible to distil common themes from those established codes to provide a model code adaptable to any kind of sports organisation:

- *Integrity* – acting with impartiality, objectivity, independence and professionalism.
- *Equality* – inclusive sport for all and no discrimination of any kind or on any basis (race, sex or religion).
- *Corruption* – the giving and receiving of gifts and hospitality must be closely monitored; a zero-tolerance policy to any secret payments/commissions.
- *Match-fixing and betting integrity* – a prohibition on any form of match or event manipulation, and restrictions on the extent to which participants can bet on sport and the use of inside information.
- *Doping* – all participants must comply with the WADA Code or other applicable anti-doping regulations.
- *Use of the organisation's resources* – any funds given to the organisation must be used for the sporting purpose intended, not for personal enrichment or gain.
- *Awarding of events* – there must be complete transparency, integrity and fairness in bidding processes for the hosting of events (at whatever level).
- *Conflicts of interest* – an individual's duty must be to the organisation and the sport. Any potential personal gain (financial or otherwise) must be declared and prohibited where it would damage the image of the sport and/or integrity of the governance of the sport.
- *Obligation to report potential breaches of the code* – the code of ethics should require participants to report any information relating to a potential breach/ violation of the code using the reporting mechanisms outlined in Chapter 9 (pages 179 and 180).
- *Bringing the sport into disrepute* – a 'catch-all' provision to apply to any conduct which may not be covered, or fall squarely, within the conduct and

expectations already listed; such conduct must be controlled to uphold the integrity of your sport. It covers types of fair play conduct both on the field, such as improper conduct towards match officials and feigning injury, and off-field behaviour, for instance, abusive posts on social media.

Once the values, provisions and offences of a code of ethics have been decided (following consultation with all of a sport's stakeholders) and drafted into a written, published document, your organisation must implement the code. This should be communicated through education and monitored (including through enforcement).

Chapter summary

- Integrity is the quality of being honest and having strong moral principles.
- Both WADA and UKAD are being held more accountable in their respective roles within the anti-doping movement.
- An emerging threat to the integrity of sport in respect of doping is gene doping, which is the transfer of nucleic acid sequences and/or the use of normal or genetically modified cells to enhance sport performance.
- The threats to sport from the integrity of betting are far broader than just 'match-fixing' and are now more commonly referred to as 'the manipulation of sports competitions'.
- Each participant in a sport must Recognise, Resist and Report approaches to manipulate sports competitions.
- Ethics is a system of moral principles that affect how people and organisations make decisions and behave.
- The welfare of the participants must be front-and-centre of the governance of any sports organisation.
- The duty of care is an obligation to safeguard your participants from harm while they are in your care, using your services, or exposed to your activities. This can be a legal, regulatory and/or moral (ethical) duty.
- Social media can be a powerful tool for all stakeholders in your sport, but must be managed proactively and sensibly.
- Culture is what an organisation does, why it does the things it does and how it goes about doing those things.
- A code of ethics in a sports organisation is important, as it will inform the conduct of all participants and the culture of the organisation by instilling values of integrity, fairness and transparency and an appreciation of acceptable conduct.

9
Compliance and legislation

■ Introduction

Never in the history of sport has the sector been subject to more laws and regulation from the UK, Europe and internationally. As a result, those responsible for compliance in a sports organisation have become of up-most importance to the successful running of the organisation.

This chapter not only identifies those vital legal and regulatory requirements that apply to sports organisations, ranging from equality and date protection, through to financial requirements in terms of both money laundering and solvency, but also outlines some of the most well-recognised processes and procedures with which to achieve compliance.

■ Compliance rules and regulations

Discrimination and equality

The UK has a wide-reaching legislative regime when it comes to discrimination and equality, including in the sports sector, of which organisations must be aware. The European Convention on Human Rights (ECHR) is where much of the UK and European law in this area comes from, with the articles of the ECHR relevant to sport being:

- *Article 4* – prohibition of slavery and forced labour (the treatment of players and restrictions on transfers);
- *Article 6* – right to a fair trial (a participant's rights during disciplinary procedures and hearings);
- *Article 8* – right to respect for private and family life (duty upon sports organisations to keep personal information on competitors protected and confidential);
- *Article 9* – freedom of thought, conscience and religion (sports organisations to have an awareness of religious events like holy days when scheduling sporting events);
- *Article 10* – freedom of expression (coverage by the press of off-field activities); and

- *Article 11* – right to freedom of peaceful assembly and association (athletes seeking to organise themselves collectively so as to best protect their rights in some form of union).

The Equality Act 2010 incorporates all aspects of the UK's obligations pursuant to the ECHR and EU law, and consolidates all the different laws and regulations in this area in UK law. The Equality Act 2010 is structured on two key tenets: the protected characteristics and the type of discrimination.

The protected characteristics under the Equality Act are:

- age;
- disability;
- gender reassignment;
- race;
- religion or belief;
- sex; and
- sexual orientation.

The main forms of discrimination under the Equality Act 2010 are:

- *direct discrimination* – one person treats another less favourably because of a protected characteristic;
- *indirect discrimination* – treatment which may be neutral on its face but which discriminates in practice against members of a group who share a protected characteristic;
- *harassment* – unwanted conduct towards a person which is related to a protected characteristic; and
- *victimisation* – a person is treated less favourably on the ground that they have done a protected act.

If there is evidence of discriminatory practices against a protected characteristic, the accused party can avoid sanction under the Act if the practice can be justified as a proportionate means of achieving a legitimate aim.

Theory in action

In *Willey and Sharpe v England and Wales Cricket Board Limited*, heard by a specialist employment tribunal, age discrimination claims were brought by two first-class cricket umpires who has been forced to retire by the England and Wales Cricket Board (ECB) upon becoming 65 years old. The tribunal began by stating that the two umpires were, because of their age, treated less favourably (in other words, sacked) than the ECB would treat someone of a different, lower age group. The less favourable treatment was the dismissal pursuant to their contracts.

The question was whether the ECB could convince the tribunal that in all the circumstances, their treatment was a proportionate means of achieving a legitimate aim.

The ECB put forward two allegedly legitimate aims: intergenerational fairness/succession planning (Aim One) and the preservation of dignity (Aim Two).

Importantly for the outcome of the case, the tribunal found that a compulsory retirement age was appropriate and reasonably necessary to pursue these aims. They made this founding principally on grounds of certainty and predictability, both for those already on the elite umpires list and those with aspirations to join it. Mr Willey and Mr Sharp were not able to advance less discriminatory ways of achieving the aim that would cause anything but 'chaos'.

The tribunal also considered it significant that there were other routes available to the two of them to remain in the game (for example, as a mentor, match liaison officer or scorer) after being retired as an umpire.

The final issue that the tribunal had to be satisfied on regarding Aim One was whether the age of 65 was justified, given that it had been abolished by statute as being a compulsory retirement age. This was problematic for the tribunal, but they did, in the end, decide it was justified given the state pension age and legitimate expectations, among other things. The ruling on Aim One was determinative in the case and the umpires' claim was dismissed.

Those who can be held liable under the Equality Act 2010 are employers (with sports governing bodies being treated no differently than any other employer), bodies who can confer a relevant qualification (those who provide sports organisations who issue licenses to participate), employment services providers (e.g. vocational training) and service providers and associations. In addition, employers can be held vicariously liable for acts of discrimination by their employees to other employees.

Theory in action

Section 12 of the Equality Act 2010 applies to discrimination on the basis of sexual orientation. One important ruling which interpreted the law broadly emanated from another EU member state: *Associtia Accept v Consiliul National Pentru Combaterea discriminarii*. A Romanian football club was held liable for the homophobic remarks of one of its major shareholders about the possible transfer of a professional footballer, who it was alleged was homosexual, following a complaint by a non-governmental organisation that promotes and protects lesbian, gay, bisexual and transsexual rights in Romania.

Disability discrimination is treated slightly differently from the other protected characteristics in the Equality Act. The question to ask is: did the disabled person get treated unfavourably because of something arising in consequence of their disability?

The further additional requirement for organisations when it comes to disability is under s. 20 of the Equality Act, which imposes a duty to make reasonable adjustments. This must be applied equally to both participants and supporters.

Sex discrimination is the protected characteristic which has the most sport-specific amendments, including a statutory exemption under s. 195. An example of sex discrimination in sport was when the governing body of judo was ruled to have acted in a discriminatory manner by refusing to allow a qualified female to referee bouts between men. The Employment Tribunal added that it was not necessary for the female referee to show that her job prospects had been affected by the discriminatory conduct; it was sufficient that it was simply discriminatory in nature.

The s. 195 exemption allows sports clubs that are 'associations' under the Equality Act 2010 to organise separate sporting events for men and women if they choose to, where:

■ physical strength, stamina or physique are major factors in determining success or failure; and
■ one sex is generally at a disadvantage in comparison with another.

A further issue relevant to sports governing bodies when it comes to sexual discrimination is the topic of single-sex private sports clubs. These have attracted significant adverse publicity, in particular in golf. A guidance note on the Equality Act indicated that member clubs may, in certain circumstances, restrict its membership to people who share a protected characteristic. However, this is not advisable or ethically defensible, and therefore not something an organisation should encourage.

Separate to claims under the Equality Act, a sports organisation should be aware of potentially discriminatory conduct by participants which must be provided for in regulations, policed and sanctioned. In recent years, there have been a number of high-profile examples of racial discrimination on the pitch in football, which the FA has had to deal with. These include alleged racial abuse from Luis Suarez to Patrice Evra and the use of the 'quenelle' anti-Semitic gesture by Nicolas Anelka. Another example of a high-profile case that led to a criminal investigation involved John Terry's race-related scandal in 2011, when allegations were made that he had racially abused Anton Ferdinand on the pitch during a match.

These cases show how delicate an approach has to be taken by sports governing bodies when dealing with discrimination allegations, particularly those based on race. This becomes even more precarious when the police and criminal law are involved.

Data protection
Significant advancements in the field of information and communication have radically increased the ease with which data may be collected, transmitted, stored, manipulated and, most importantly, disseminated. These developments, together with a general increase in awareness of fundamental rights, particularly the right to privacy, have led to legislative changes and the emergence of a new regime of privacy protection.

Overview of the General Data Protection Regulation
The most significant development in this area that affects organisations, regardless of the sector, is the General Regulation of the European Parliament and the Council on the protection of natural persons with regard to the processing of personal data and on the free movement of such data, (GDPR). It examines the nature and scope of the regime and the rights of data subjects. It also provides information on the obligations of controllers and processors and summarises the restrictions on the transfer of personal data outside the EU.

The GDPR replaced the Data Protection Directive when it became directly applicable from 25 May 2018. The reform was intended to respond to new technological challenges and to put in place a harmonised framework for the protection of personal data.

The GDPR will apply to an organisation if it:

- alone or with others determines the purposes for processing personal data relating to living individuals (known as acting as a data controller) or processes personal data relating to living individuals strictly in accordance with the instructions of another (known as acting as a data processor); and
- is 'established' in the EU, meaning that the business exercises real and effective activity through stable arrangements in the EU – including through a branch or subsidiary.

Assuming the organisation was subject to the previous legal regime in this area or compliance, and so will also be subject to GDPR, the key changes in the GDPR include:

- *Governance* – organisations have increased responsibility and accountability on how they control and process personal data.
- *Consent* – a more active consent-based model is introduced by GDPR. Wherever consent is required for data to be processed, it is defined as 'freely given, specific, informed and unambiguous'. In other words, consent must be explicit, rather than implied.
- *Transparency* – organisations have increased transparency obligations.
- *Data processors* – organisations processing data on behalf of other companies are required to comply with a number of specific data protection related obligations.
- *Security* – there is no definitive standard to adhere to when it comes to data security. Rather, GDPR requires controllers and processors to evaluate risks

involved with their processing activities and implement appropriate measures to prevent loss and unauthorised access to data, such as pseudonymisation, encryption or restricted access.

■ *Enforcement* – stronger enforcement means non-compliance could lead to much heavier, turnover-based sanctions. For the most serious breaches, the sanctions available are a fine of €20,000,000 or up to 4% of total worldwide annual turnover.

Data Protection Principles

There are seven Data Protection Principles that underpin the new law:

Principle one – lawfulness, fairness and transparency

Lawfulness requires a data controller to satisfy at least one 'processing condition' when processing personal data. These include explicit consent, necessity for performance of a contract with the data subject, necessary for compliance with a legal obligation to which the controller is subject, or necessary for the purposes of a legitimate interest of the controller. Going forward, data controllers will need to tell data subjects what conditions they are relying on for each of their processing activities. There is a supplemental list of processing conditions for sensitive data, which are very restrictive and will in most instances require explicit consent. Fairness and transparency is where privacy policies and data capture notices come in. An increased amount of information will need to be given and must be presented in a clear and concise manner, and tailored for the specific audience.

Principle two – purpose limitation

Personal data should be collected for specific, explicit and legitimate purposes, it should not be processed in a manner incompatible with those processes.

Principle three – data minimisation

Personal data should be adequate, relevant and limited to what is necessary in relation to the purpose for which processed.

Principle four – accuracy

Personal data must be accurate, up-to-date and rectified or deleted if not.

Principle five – storage limitation

Personal data must be kept in a format which enables the identification of individuals for no longer than necessary to achieve the purpose.

Principle six – integrity and confidentiality

Personal data should be stored in a secure and confidential way.

Principle seven – accountability

Data controllers must continuously assess risk, implement appropriate policies and procedures and keep them under review as to suitability and effectiveness.

The role of the data protection officer

A sports organisation (whether a processor or controller) is required to appoint a data protection officer (DPO) if it:

- is a public authority or body;
- undertakes regular and systematic monitoring of individuals on a large scale;
- processes sensitive categories of data on a large scale; or
- processes data relating to criminal convictions/offences; or
- considers appointing a DPO is necessary following its own internal risk assessments.

A DPO needs to have expert data protection knowledge (with reference to the type and complexity of processing carried out by the organisation) and must act independently (although it can be an internal appointment).

If the sports organisation does not fall into any of the above categories, then it should still designate at least one person who is familiar with GDPR who can assist with compliance, but avoid labelling them as DPO to ensure they are not subject to the strict DPO regime.

Transferring data outside of the EU

Transferring personal data outside of the jurisdiction of the GDPR (the European Economic Area) will be particularly relevant to NGBs and national Olympic committees, as they will potentially be transferring data internationally.

Fortunately, the requirements of the GDPR in this respect remains much the same as under the previous regime. Organisations will still be able to transfer personal data outside of the EEA where it is going to an 'adequate country' (i.e. one which the EU Commission has approved as having appropriate safeguards in place), and where the organisations puts in place appropriate safeguards, such as binding corporate rules, model clauses or relies on the US privacy shield for US transfers.

Other grounds also apply, such as explicit data subject consent (but noting the more stringent consent requirements) or where the transfer is necessary for the performance of a contract.

This will still apply as and when the UK eventually leaves the EU, as the UK Parliament passed the Data Protection Act 2018 (replacing the Data Protection Act 1998) ensuring the standards set out in the GDPR have full effect in the UK.

Money laundering

Money laundering is the process of disguising the source of money obtained from serious crime or terrorism so that it appears to come from a legitimate source.

Businesses can be used for money laundering, which is a criminal offence in most countries.

In the UK, Part 7 of the Proceeds of Crime Act 2000 (POCA) sets out money laundering offences and those offences resulting from a failure to act on a suspicion of money laundering. Directors and executives should be familiar with this legislation and know what red flags to look out for, especially when people from outside the sport suddenly want to invest in it.

There is also another offence under POCA which applies to sports organisations, where an individual knows or suspects that a money laundering investigation has begun, or is about to begin, in respect of another, and that individual makes a material disclosure to any other person which is likely to prejudice the investigation, or interferes with relevant material.

Committing any offence under POCA is extremely serious and could lead to a prison sentence. The offences are punishable by a maximum of 14 years' imprisonment, a fine or both for individuals including directors, managers and officers of any organisation. There are also unlimited fines for corporate entities.

Simple steps an organisation can take to prevent money laundering include:

- employing a specialist outside organisation to undertake a money laundering risk assessment; and
- undertaking a proportionate level of due diligence for sponsors and other commercial partners in the sport. Organisations may wish to extend that to cover those who own the clubs in their sports.

Theory in action

Mr Mazhar Majeed bought semi-professional football club Croydon Athletic in 2008. He reportedly boasted of having invested vast sums of money in the club, particularly in terms of infrastructure.

In November 2011, Mr Majeed was jailed for his role in a high-profile international cricket match-fixing scandal involving the Pakistan senior national team. The matter came to light as a result of a newspaper sting operation which offered Mr Majeed a large cash payment in return for information on when no-balls would be bowled.

During this criminal investigation, it was alleged that Mr Majeed had a track record of money laundering through the club, with customs and tax officials believing 'substantially' more than £20 million was laundered through Croydon Athletic. Official company accounts stated that only tens of thousands of pounds had been 'invested' by Mr Majeed.

Mr Majeed was later sent back to prison for two years for tax evasion by deliberately under-declaring income of £259,000 from his property development and rental business.

There are three money laundering offences in POCA relating to the direct handling of the proceeds of crime, all of which require either knowledge or suspicion of money laundering. These can be committed by any person. It is an offence to:

■ conceal, disguise, convert or transfer the proceeds of crime, or to remove the proceeds of crime from the jurisdiction of England and Wales;
■ enter into, or become concerned in an arrangement, in which a person knows or suspects the retention, use or control of the proceeds of crime (aiding and abetting); or
■ acquire, use or possess the proceeds of crime (handling).

Bribery and corruption

Bribery and corruption in sports organisations has been covered extensively in the media in recent years. As a result, the sector has never been subject to more scrutiny to be clean. Organisations must know the applicable laws, and have internal regulations and policies to minimise the major criminal, financial and reputational threats that come with bribery and corruption.

Each country has its own laws when it comes to individuals or organisations committing offences linked to bribery and corrupt conduct/practices. The UK Bribery Act 2010 and the United States' Foreign Corrupt Practices Act (FCPA) are the most powerful pieces of legislation as they have extra-territorial effect, meaning they apply beyond national borders.

The Bribery Act 2010 largely abolishes the existing common law and legislative offences in the UK against bribery and corruption, and introduces four new criminal offences:

1. bribing – offering, promising or giving a financial or other advantage (active bribery);
2. being bribed – requesting, agreeing to receive or accepting a financial or other advantage (passive bribery);
3. bribery of foreign public officials; and
4. organisations failing to prevent bribery by an associated person.

Individuals found guilty of one or more of the first three offences can be punished by up to ten years' imprisonment and/or an unlimited fine. If an organisation commits the fourth offence by failing to prevent the individuals within the organisation from committing acts of bribery, it can face an unlimited fine, plus untold damage to its reputation.

A consequence of the Bribery Act is that UK companies must have internal controls sufficient to prevent bribery by any of its employees or agents, and to detect bribery when it does occur. This will defend an organisation against a charge of a failure to prevent bribery, as the Bribery Act acknowledges that it is impossible to prevent it at all times.

There are six principles to consider when putting 'adequate procedures' in place within a sports organisation to ensure it complies with the Act. These are:

1. proportionality;
2. top-level commitment;
3. risk assessment;
4. due diligence;
5. communication; and
6. monitoring and review.

When it comes to monitoring, and ensuring there is an ethical approach taken by your organisation, a comprehensive and robust (yet still proportionate) anti-bribery and corruption policy should be in place which restricts the following actions by all participants, including board members and other executives:

- prohibition on any acts of bribery or corruption;
- prohibition of any payments of made to facilitate any transactions;
- gifts or hospitality can only be offered or received where it is transparent, proportionate, reasonable and for a legitimate business purpose;
- expenses incurred must be reasonable and for a legitimate business purpose;
- no political donations on behalf of the organisation;
- no charitable donations other than with the consent of the board;
- prohibition on any act to fix, manipulate or ensure a specific outcome in the sport for financial gain and/or competitive advantage which negatively impacts on the integrity of the sport;
- duty on individuals to do their part in preventing, detecting and reporting any possible acts in the policy; and
- duty not to threaten or retaliate against another individual who has refused to commit bribery or who has raised concerns under the policy.

This is more detailed and wider in scope than the Bribery Act; therefore training and the communication of this policy will be crucial to its success in ensuring individuals' compliance.

Insolvency

As discussed in Chapter 1 (pages 14 and 15), companies can get into financial difficulty for a number of reasons. If your organisation gets into that position, it is important that the board and other executives are aware of the laws on insolvency and comply strictly with them. Otherwise those individuals could face both civil and criminal liability.

The principal law in the UK dealing with this issue is the Insolvency Act 1986. That Act does not define the term 'insolvency' itself, but embodies the concept in the phrase 'unable to pay its debts', which can mean one of four things:

1. failing to comply with a statutory demand for a debt of over £750;
2. failing to satisfy enforcement of a judgment debt;
3. the court being satisfied that the company is unable to pay its debts as they fall due (the 'cash flow' test); or
4. the court being satisfied that the liabilities of the company (including contingent and prospective liabilities) exceed the assets of the company (the 'balance sheet' test).

If a company is 'unable to pay its debts' under any of the tests set out above, any creditor (a person your organisation owes money to), among other potential stakeholders, may petition for the company to be placed into compulsory liquidation.

The latter two tests are the most common grounds for a business being liquidated/wound-up (closed down). Crucially, a board must be aware that a seemingly successful and stable organisation can go out of business due to the cash flow of the business being neglected. Always remember, cash is king! Therefore, the finance director or treasurer (which is most likely for the majority of sports organisations being run by volunteers) must, for example, not just issue invoices to members, but ensure they are paid promptly, so that the organisation can pay any people to whom it owes money.

Whistleblowing/reporting

Whistleblowing is a term commonly used when someone who works in or for an organisation raises a concern about possible fraud, crime, danger or other serious risk that could threaten participants, stakeholders, the public or the organisation's own reputation. It can act as an early warning system about improper or illegal behaviour within the organisation.

The need for whistleblowing arises when internal channels are not able to unveil the potentially damaging activity, because the individuals responsible can avoid detection and/or others with suspicions/knowledge of the conduct do not have sufficient trust in your organisation to tell it.

In the UK, the Public Interest Disclosure Act 1998 (PIDA) protects 'workers' from being subjected to any detriment on the ground that they have made a protected disclosure.

'Workers' are defined more broadly than just the employees of your organisation, and arguably could include other participants, as PIDA covers individuals who have entered into works under any contract (whether express or implied) whereby the individual undertakes to do or perform personally any work or services for another party to the contract.

A 'worker' under PIDA will be protected by law if they report any of the following matters in relation to your organisation:

- a criminal offence (such as bribery or corruption);
- that someone's health and safety is in danger;

- a miscarriage of justice;
- that the organisation is breaking the law (alleged discrimination, for example); or
- the 'worker' believes someone is covering up wrongdoing within the organisation.

The term 'whistleblower' often has negative connotations; therefore, to encourage people to use mechanisms made available by an organisation, it is better to describe such individuals as 'reporting persons'.

Theory in action

Reporting persons have recently played a vital part in uncovering ethics scandals in sport. One such individual was the former head of Moscow's anti-doping laboratory, Grigory Rodchenkov, who blew the whistle on the institutional doping taking part in Russian sport.

In the Oscar-winning documentary film on the Russian scandal, *Icarus*, Rodchenkov revealed how he implemented an elaborate scheme allowing Russian athletes to dope throughout the 2014 Winter Olympic Games in Sochi, Russia, all while avoiding detection. He said the order to cheat originated at the very top of Russian politics.

Compliance processes and procedures

Reporting mechanisms

When discussing the duty of care report, there are several instances where the need for confidential channels of reporting is stated. This may not only be for such issues as allegations of discrimination or having mental health difficulties, but may also be used to report approaches to engage in corrupt practices (such as match-fixing).

Views differ in the sporting community about the best system to adopt when offering participants the opportunity to report any information regarding any of these issues.

An entirely anonymous reporting system, such as that operated by the IOC with their Integrity and Compliance Hotline, means that the sports organisation (and law enforcement body in some circumstances) may not be able to follow up with or check the accuracy/reliability of the information provided by a participant, or indeed any other person outside the sport (such as a fan or member of the public). In addition, the sports organisation cannot monitor whether participants are complying with their duty to report.

At the other end of the spectrum, in an ideal world, participants should feel comfortable enough to approach their issue with someone with the sport. However, there have been too many instances where that information is not then kept confidential, or is not acted upon, and therefore there has been a fundamental breakdown in trust.

An acceptable middle ground for your organisation may be to guarantee anonymity to the person who provides the information should charges be brought, and formal evidence required, but only up to and including a trial or hearing. In sport, this approach has already been taken by (CAS) and deemed acceptable.

Here are a number of questions to consider, to help shape the approach an organisation should take to reporting mechanisms and requirements:

- *Who is the target audience for the reporting mechanism?* The mechanism could be made available just to participants, all of the stakeholders in the sport or the public as well.
- *What information does the reporting mechanism want to receive?* This comes back to the breadth of topics the organisation happy for the target audience to provide information on.
- *What type of reporting mechanism?* Consideration needs to be given to anonymity, confidentiality and whether it will be a one-way or two-way dialogue. If it is going to be anonymous, is it possible for the organisation to do this without the assistance of, say, law enforcement?
- *What communications channels should be available for reporting?* This refers to the need to decide whether it will be telephone, email and/or in person (an ombudsman).
- *Is the proposed reporting mechanism legal?* There are many legal requirements when it comes to the handling of information and data, so it would be advisable to obtain specialist legal advice at an early stage when planning the mechanism.
- *Who will manage the reporting mechanism?* The organisation will have to undertake risk and resource assessments to decide whether it can deliver and manage the mechanism internally, or whether it will have to be outsourced to a company specialising in such services.
- *Are the system and security requirements clearly identified?* System security and backups will have to be assured. This has come very much to the forefront of participants' concerns given the actions in recent years by the Fancy Bears group, who hacked the systems of sports organisations and leaked confidential medical records to the global public.
- *How will information be handled and what is the information flow process?* This is about making the reporting person comfortable about how the information will be used and to whom it will be passed.
- *Who will receive training about the reporting mechanism and how?* The groups that may receive training include the target audience and those managing the mechanism and how the information may be used.
- *How will it be marketed?* This concerns ensuring the target audience know about the existence of the mechanism and also how to use it.

■ *How will we measure the value of the reporting mechanism?* It is difficult to measure the effectiveness of reporting mechanisms; however, the frequency of use, intelligence value of the information and awareness among the target audience are all options.

Control functions

For operational risks, financial reporting risks and compliance risks, suitable internal controls should be designed and implemented. Such controls need to be embedded within an organisation so that they become part of the norm. However, given the diverse size and complexity of organisations in the sports sector, the cost and effectiveness of controls should be assessed relative to the benefits they provide so that they are proportionate.

Controls within an organisation are those that are concerned with the management of business risks other than strategic risks. Internal control functions can be classified into three main types:

1. *Preventive controls* – these are intended to prevent an adverse risk event from occurring – for instance, to prevent opportunities for corruption by having robust ethics regulations in place and monitoring the use of development finance given to regions/clubs;
2. *Detective controls* – these detect risk events when they occur, so that the appropriate person is alerted and corrective measures taken – this is best achieved by having a thorough incident plan; and
3. *Corrective controls* – these deal with risk events that have occurred, and their consequences – these may be disciplinary sanctions including suspensions and financial penalties.

One area of an organisation that will require internal controls is financial matters. The finance director/treasurer of the organisation must have clear and proportionate policies in place, not only for the organisation itself, but also for the money given out to its members, to ensure it is used for the purposes intended. FIFA has been remiss about this in the past, with leaders of national federations misappropriating funds meant for football development purposes.

Operational controls should be designed to prevent failures in operational procedures, or to detect and correct operational failures if they do occur. In sport, this can mean ensuring that competition management IT systems run without glitches and participants' data is kept secure and safe from cyber-attacks.

A sports organisation must also have compliance controls in place so that it complies with all the relevant laws and regulations. This will include people within the organisation regularly attending seminars and training, and ensuring information about legislative and regulatory developments is disseminated throughout sport, especially to the board.

Incident planning

The final part of this chapter assists with what you should do should the controls and other compliance processes in place not take effect swiftly enough, and an incident arises.

When this happens, apart from dealing with it and hopefully remedying the issue, one vital issue is communication. The objectives of communication when an incident arises are twofold: to reassure and allay the inevitable fears of stakeholders, and to control the flow of information to the public. There should be a spokesperson chosen from with your organisation who has strong communication skills and good relationships with the media.

What you must not do when an incident arises, especially concerning serious matters such as allegations of corruption, is to deny them blankly before a proper investigation is carried out. This approach has been prevalent in sports organisations because the sport in question does not want sponsors and other commercial partners to abandon them, or for the senior executives to be forced to resign.

A 'no comment' response to questioning can be equally as damaging. In addition (although it seems self-evident), one should never lie, as lying about an incident can cause more long-term damage than the incident itself.

One task for an organisation when an incident arises will be to establish an organised approach to obtaining, checking and disseminating information. At all times you must act within your powers and be alert to the rights of any person of interest, should an investigation be required. Equally, your organisation must not turn a blind eye to alleged misconduct, even by senior officials within your sport.

Relationships and co-operation with outside stakeholders, such as law enforcement, must also be considered carefully. In this regard, an organisation should at all times act with the utmost integrity, and engage fully and frankly with such bodies.

Chapter summary

- Ethics is a system of moral principles that affect how people and organisations make decisions and behave.
- The welfare of the participants must be front-and-centre of the governance of your sports organisation.
- The duty of care is an obligation to safeguard your participants from harm while they are in your care, using your services, or exposed to your activities. This can be a legal, regulatory and/or moral (ethical) duty.
- The UK has a wide-reaching legislative regime when it comes to discrimination and equality covering 'protected characteristics' including age, disability, gender reassignment, race, religion or belief, sex and sexual orientation.

■ Data protection and compliance with the new comprehensive regime is imperative for your sports organisation to maintain positive and trusting relationships with your stakeholders and avoid potentially very punitive fines.

■ Social media can be a powerful tool for all stakeholders in your sport, but must be managed proactively and sensibly.

■ A code of ethics in your sports organisation is important, as it will inform the conduct of all participants and the culture of the organisation by instilling values of integrity, fairness and transparency and an appreciation of acceptable conduct.

■ The UK Bribery Act 2010 means you must have internal controls sufficient to prevent bribery by any of your employees or agents, and to detect bribery when it does occur.

■ Reporting mechanisms should allow stakeholders to raise a concern about possible fraud, crime, danger or other serious risk that could threaten participants, other stakeholders, the public and/or your organisation's reputation.

■ Suitable internal controls need to be developed and implemented to manage operational, financial reporting and compliance risks.

10
Funding and other sources of income

Introduction

This chapter addresses the increasingly tough financial climate sports organisations are operating in, and suggests avenues through which to counter it, so as to become (self) sustainable in order to resource long-term good governance.

Sources of funding and income

Prior to the establishment of sports councils in 1972, the Central Council of Physical Recreation was the principal body offering grants to sports. The situation changed in 1972 when sports councils were formed in each of the home countries to oversee and fund sport (Sport Northern Ireland was established in 1973). Since then, a range of funding opportunities have been created, aiming to deliver sports policy and strategy for community and elite sport, facility development and wide policy benefts such educational attainment and community cohesion.

Public funds

Exchequer funds, raised through taxes, are awarded to sport through each of the respective home country government departments for sport. In all cases, non-departmental or government-sponsored bodies (the sports councils) were established to invest public money into sport.

The five sports councils, in delivering sports policy through this investment, set out investment principles or eligibility criteria which must be met for organisations to receive funds. These are subject to change, particularly as governments and sports policies shift. For example, in 2005, after being awarded the right to host the London Olympics and Paralympics, Gordon Brown announced an additional £300 million to fund British sports and athletes that would be competing in the Games. This included sports such as handball, which had not previously met performance criteria to be eligible to receive funds. However, after 2012, UK Sport funding principles for 2013–17 (the Rio cycle) were adjusted and handball, basketball, wrestling and table tennis had their funding reduced to zero. Basketball and table tennis subsequently challenged the decision and were supported through the Rio cycle.

In 2016, after the Rio Olympic and Paralympic Games, UK Sport again reviewed its investment in sports for the Olympic and Paralympic Games in Tokyo under its No Compromise funding system. As a result, all funding was removed for seven sports deemed unlikely to win medals in 2020 – archery, badminton, goalball, fencing, table tennis, weightlifting and wheelchair rugby. Despite appeals and support from other NGBs, they were unable to overturn the decision.

UK Sport's No Compromise approach has been the subject of criticism with some claiming it does not facilitate any legacy from 2012 or enable the development of sports with the potential to reach new audiences (such as basketball). However, defenders of the system, including ministers, point to unprecedented medal success since 2008 as a direct result of investment focused solely on sports and athletes with the potential to win medals. During the London cycle, UK Sport invested £341 million of Exchequer and National Lottery funds; this rose to £347 million between 2013 and 2017. A total of £345 million was awarded for the 2017–21 Tokyo cycle.

The home country sports councils have each developed their own investment priorities which extend across community sports development as well as high-performance sport. While UK Sport focuses solely on Olympic and Paralympic medal success, the home country sports councils will invest in sports and athletes just below World Class Programme levels that can succeed at the Commonwealth Games.

All sports councils offer Exchequer and Lottery grants in different forms and have created funding programmes that are tailored to specifc groups and purposes. Some of these are listed in the next section.

National Lottery and small grants

The National Lottery was established in 1994 with the licence awarded to Camelot to run it on behalf of the government. Sports councils were appointed as Lottery distributors in 1997 and each home country sports council has since awarded grants to NGBs, clubs, community groups and other organisations as part of their strategic investment programmes.

The type of funding programmes change over time. Table 10.1 shows some of the grant schemes available in 2017.

The Directory of Social Change has developed a website which allows organisations in the voluntary sector to research potential funders. These include grantmakers, companies and trusts that donate or fund voluntary initiatives, sporting and non-sporting. Organisations must register to access the information.

National governing bodies also offer their stakeholders the opportunity to apply for funding, with the Football Foundation investing £40 million per year into football facilities and the RFU also making facility grants available to community clubs.

Table 10.1: Sports councils and lottery programmes

Sports council	Lottery programme
Sport England	Small grants – £300–£10,000 Active Aging Fund – £50,000–£500,000 Community Asset Fund – to enhance active spaces in the community
Sport Wales	Community Chest – up to £1,500 for community sport Development Grants – up to £25,000 to develop activity in communities
Sport Northern Ireland	Active Awards (Exchequer) – £1,000–£10,000 for grass-roots community sport Active Spaces – £10,000–£120,000 for small-scale capital projects
sportscotland	Awards for All – £500–£10,000 for projects that help improve local communities through sport UK Coaching Certifcate subsidy – funding for coaches working towards the UK Coaching Certifcate

Membership and associated revenue

National governing bodies, regional and county associations, and clubs that offer membership will invariably rely on this income not only to provide membership services, but also to help sustain and develop other aspects of their services. For example, for the 2012–17 Rio cycle, all sports in receipt of funding from UK Sport had to resource some of their World Class Programmes themselves. Some, including British Judo, included some of their membership revenue in their submission to UK Sport as part of their World Class Programme funding.

Sports organisations have become much more adept at building business models that measure the value of the membership services and associated revenue. This helps ensure the cost of services does not exceed related income. In many cases, sports bodies are creating a range of membership packages that generate revenue.

National and local sports bodies also seek to understand the profile of their members in the same way a supermarket does, as members are perceived as consumers of products and services. It is thus possible to target groups with the most relevant services, for example, family membership (sailing) or sport-related insurance (cycling). This tailoring of products and services not only better serves the members but also allows the organisation to generate revenue through different schemes and offers.

Diversification of revenue streams

Given the continuing tough global economic conditions, it is inevitable that public funding for sport will decrease. Indeed, the UK Government made this point explicitly in their latest strategy for sport and physical activity called *Sporting Future: A New Strategy for an Active Nation* released in December 2015: 'It is vital that organisations that rely heavily on a single source of income take active steps to diversify their income to insulate themselves from the risk of changes to that source of income'. This single source of income is often an over-reliance on the public sector and public funding.

Not only is the diversification of revenue streams becoming a necessity, but empirical research by Wicker and Breuer in 2013 showed that the higher the level of revenue diversification in a sports organisation, the higher the total revenues and the profit of the organisation. Other important findings from that research included:

- Sport governing bodies which attach importance to increasing memberships in sport clubs generate fewer total revenues, make less profit.
- Organising competitions has a significant negative effect on the total revenues of sport governing bodies – it seems that the organisation of such smaller events is cost intensive and that insufficient revenues can be generated, probably due to the local character of the events, fewer spectators, and a lack of media exposure – nevertheless, such smaller events like district or regional championships must be organised by the governing body because it is part of its core business.
- On the contrary, the hosting of major sporting events had a positive effect on the financial condition of sports organisations.
- Paid staff have a significant positive impact on total revenues – the more paid staff are employed at a sport governing body, the higher the total revenues that are generated.

The principal implication of this research for the management of sport governing bodies is that governing bodies increase their level of revenue diversification if they want to improve their financial condition and decrease their financial risk.

Alternative income streams

In the Sport and Recreation Alliance and Sport England's 2017/18 *Sports Club Survey Report*, the ways in which those surveyed had increased their revenue included:

- increase membership fees;
- offering sponsorship opportunities;
- accessing community grants;
- hiring our club facilities;
- holding sponsored events;

- undertaking crowdfunding campaigns;
- accessing social finances; and
- using community shares.

The report also says, 'there are other types of financial support that have not traditionally been explored or used effectively by the sport and physical activity sector. Individual giving, through donations, investments or legacies, corporate giving through partnerships and other types of Corporate social responsibility (CSR) activity, along with trusts and foundations all offer further potential sources of income that organisations should be exploring as part of their push to become more financially sustainable. The fact that very few consultation responses mentioned these highlights how underused they currently are by the sector'.

This sub-section shall now look at some of these initiatives in further detail, as well as other alternative income streams utilised by organisations in the sector.

Membership fees

A large proportion of sports organisations rely heavily on income generated from membership fees, so it is important to set these at the right price. Ideally membership fees should cover the day-to-day financial running costs of the organisation. Additional income generated can be used to improve and develop the organisation, as well as build up a sinking fund to cover unexpected events.

Raising membership fees can be an emotive issue so ensure the members know exactly what they are getting for their money and let them know how the organisation is funded overall. Often a rise in membership fees is more acceptable if members are better informed about the overall financial position of the organisation.

Sponsorship

Sponsorship can be a great way to generate income and form a partnership with a local business or organisation. Sponsorship is not free money. It requires time and resources to be successful and it should be seen as a two-way mutually beneficial relationship between an organisation and the sponsor.

The different types of sponsorship a sports organisation can offer include:

- sponsorship fee for sponsoring the club kit, match, equipment and so on;
- provision of resources, such as volunteers helping out the organisation at an event; and
- provision of products or services: for example, an electrical company providing energy efficient lighting or a local builder providing some facility maintenance work.

Fundraising

Raising money from fundraising and social events can be a great source of income as well being an excellent way to bring members together. By involving members other than the committee to organise events, it can give them the opportunity to feel they are doing their bit to support the organisation.

Commercial activities

Increasing income into an organisation through selling products or services can be achieved from both within and outside a sports organisation. From within the organisation, it is about encouraging members and other users to spend more. For example, could you encourage more people to visit by making the organisation more family friendly, or can you encourage parents to stay throughout kids' sessions by offering free wi-fi and selling refreshments? There is also the need to 'make your assets sweat', namely utilising facilities to the fullest by making them available to the local community. This also opens up the possibility to register as a charitable organisation and the many benefits that come with that. In addition, more people using the facilities will increase promotion and awareness of the organisation.

Monetising data

One of the most recent income streams is the use of a sport's data and making it an official and enforceable IP right through entering into commercial arrangements to that effect. Fast and accurate data is vital to modern sport. This unique breadth and depth of data can be used by rights holders to provide more content for sponsors, teams and media partners, bringing commercial benefits for all involved. Through controlling data centrally, a rights holder can increase and improve the consistency of data used in coverage for competitions. Organisations can grow by expanding their official data reach with fans, media and commercial partners] through competition management, statistics driving applications or allowing it to be used by the betting industry.

In-kind support

While the largest NGBs are able to secure sponsorship deals with big brands, the vast majority of sports organisations, national and local, face significant challenges. Commercial organisations may seek to align their brand with sports, but a simple exchange of branding opportunities for a cash sum is less common as companies want to engage actively in the sponsorship process.

One example of a sports body and commercial organisation activating a partnership is the British Paralympic Association (BPA) working with Sainsbury's. The supermarket chain created adverts that involved high-profle Paralympians such as Ellie Simmonds and David Weir, blended with Sainsbury's shopping aisles and customers. This raised the profle of the athletes and Paralympics GB as well as Sainsbury's and its commitment to Paralympic sport.

In-kind support will often mean less financial support but the provision of services, expertise or equipment which would otherwise cost an organisation a lot of money. One example is the provision to UK Sport and funded sports of specialist technical expertise by BAE Systems. As the offcial research and technology partner to UK Sport, BAE Systems facilitates access to 18,000 engineers with specialist knowledge that can help certain sports gain a competitive advantage. These include laser technology for cycling, taekwondo and pentathlon pistol shooting. Buying in such technological expertise would be very expensive for UK Sport and the sports themselves, but BAE has gained signifcant reputational beneft from their work in assisting GB medal success.

Obtaining public funding

All publicly funded programmes, whether they are Exchequer or Lottery funds, require organisations to apply in some way. This may be online, via a dedicated panel or in a comprehensive submission. It is always useful for sports bodies to be able to simply articulate their vision or mission and priority goals, and to be able to evidence their impact. The production of an application will likely be led by a staff member or senior volunteer but, for the most strategically signifcant awards, the board should retain oversight.

Mutual beneft and shared goals

By setting the vision, values and strategic direction of the organisation, the board will be better able to assess whether there is potential mutual beneft and shared goals with other bodies. NGBs have long been the primary agencies through which sports councils funding was channelled in order to increase participation in sport. The RFU's Women's Rugby Strategy aims to increase women and girls' playing the sport to 100,000. As Sport England has prioritised groups that do not participate regularly, including women, there is a natural alignment between the RFU's and Sport England's strategic aspirations.

Not all NGBs have been able to demonstrate the same level of progress in attracting disadvantaged groups to their sport. As a result, Sport England restructured its funding streams to release money to different organisations including non-sporting bodies. NGBs in England can access funding to serve their core market (those who are already engaged with the sport and participate regularly) however, NGBs will have to demonstrate with robust evidence and greater innovation how they will reach non-traditional participants if they want Sport England to fnance other programmes, such as schemes for older people or those from lower socio-economic groups.

Some of Sport England and Sport Wales's funding streams actively seek new partners such as the Girl Guides, BAME sports organisations and local health boards. This has opened up funding for non- sporting organisations that use sport to achieve other outcomes with vulnerable or disadvantaged groups.

In all cases, applicants must be able to demonstrate that they have sound governance processes (they are constituted) and provide information about their structures and fnances as well as their proposed projects. This information helps sports councils make funding decisions against their own risk strategy and risk appetite, ensuring public money is going to organisations that can effciently receive and manage funds.

Conditional funding requirements

Having successfully secured funding, organisations will be expected to meet not only the project or programme outcomes (such as reducing mental health issues in teenagers) but will have to meet conditions of grants set out in the funding agreement. National sports organisations in receipt of sports council funds will usually have to demonstrate compliance or implementation with the:

- Equality Standard for Sport;
- Standards for Safeguarding and Protecting Children in Sport;
- Companies Act and Charities Act; and
- Data Protection Act (2018) and General Data Protection Regulation (2018).

Specifc conditions can also be added to a funded body's agreement depending on any issues or risks identifed. For example, NGBs may have specifc conditions relating to the achievement of the requirements set out in sports councils' respective governance codes. Any failures to meet specifc conditions can result in the suspension of funding.

Reporting on compliance with funding agreements

Any partnerships with commercial organisations will have tailored reporting processes that assure both parties that their contribution is meeting expectations. For example, a company may want access to elite athletes at certain events to promote their partnership, while the sports body will expect the company to deliver on its commitments, be they financial, equipment or other tangibles, at the agreed time.

Sports councils have established assurance frameworks and dedicated resources to the monitoring of the organisations they fund. Apart from those who receive small grants, recipients of larger awards can expect to have to submit information about governance, financial reporting, policies, business plans and staff structures.

sportscotland states that it will only invest in SGBs that:

- have been assessed as fit for purpose through an independent audit;
- apply the principles of good governance as laid out in the SGB Governance Framework; or
- actively demonstrate their commitment to equity, child protection and drug free sport.

Recipients are therefore expected to demonstrate that these requirements have been met. Independent audits have been used by all sports councils as a means of gathering information on site through external auditors. This enables a more tailored approach to partner assurance and provides a higher level of detail in respect of a funded body's governance and internal control.

Sports bodies that receive public and Lottery funds have found some methods of assurance onerous and time consuming; however, it is widely believed that governance requirements in particular have helped strengthen national sports organisations in terms of governance and financial management.

Financial reporting

Chapter 6 (pages 118 and 119) covers financial reporting in depth. Increasingly, funders expect sports bodies to be able to produce high-quality, accurate financial reports as part of any funding agreement.

Principle 3 of the Code for Sports Governance – Policies and Processes sets specific requirements as follows:

Requirement 5.4: Each organisation must prepare annual accounts which:
a. comply with legal Requirements and recognised accounting standards
b. give specifc disclosure of income received from public investors and clearly account for the expenditure of such funding
c. are audited.

Requirement 5.5: The audited annual accounts must be published on the organisation's website.

Financial reports will usually be required by sports councils on a quarterly basis and show clearly how public and Lottery funds have been spent. This must be on the outputs listed in the funding agreement, or the sports council can demand repayment. Similarly, any concerns regarding financial probity are likely to be investigated swiftly.

As sports organisations – clubs, community groups and NGBs – are now defned as micro-businesses or small and medium sized enterprises (SMEs), the expectations of stakeholders have changed. Running a small business means efficiency, customer service and a professional outlook, which is what members, partners and volunteers expect when they join or connect with a sports organisation. As public funds diminish, good governance and skilled leadership will help ensure an organisation is well placed to take advantage of other opportunities with commercial partners, trusts or donors.

▨ Chapter summary

■ While UK Sport focuses solely on Olympic and Paralympic medal success, the Home Country Sports Councils have each developed their own investment priorities which extend across community sports development to high-performance sport. Sports Councils invest Exchequer and National Lottery funds in community organisations as well as NGBs and national sports organisations, such as Coaching UK.

■ To receive public and National Lottery funds, national sports bodies must demonstrate compliance with legislation, including the Data Protection Act 2018, and relevant frameworks including the Code for Sports Governance and the Equality Standard for Sport.

■ Given the continuing tough global economic conditions, it is inevitable that public funding for sport will decrease and diversification of income will become a necessity.

■ Alternative income streams that sports organisations should explore include sponsorship and other commercial activities, including crowdfunding and hiring out club facilities.

11
Finance

Introduction

This chapter details the role that finance plays within organisations and how a large percentage of business practices and operations are underpinned by finance and financial decision making. Effective financial decision making, based on sound financial information, can be the difference between good and poor business performance. Key topics covered in this chapter include financial compliance to legal requirements, financial controls, the importance of effective financial reporting and ensuring budgets align with organisational strategy.

Financial compliance to legal requirements

Financial probity dictates that organisations must exhibit undeviating honesty, integrity and competence in financial matters. Organisations must be fully accountable to their public funders for the management and use of funding, demonstrating how they have applied it to achieve the purposes for which it was given. They must therefore account for every public penny, with annual accounts including sufficient disclosure of public income and expenditure. Larger organisations (including NGBs of sport, national partners and others) must make independently audited accounts available to stakeholders and the public.

All accounting designations are the culmination of years of study and rigorous examinations, combined with a minimum number of years of practical accounting experience. There are regulatory bodies that set accounting standards and the people that work for these regulatory bodies are accountants themselves with recognised professional qualifications. In terms of the profession of accounting, there are basic accounting principles that have been followed by accountants for many years and understood and accepted by practising accountants. In summary, the major principles applied by accountants historically were:

■ prudence;
■ accruals;
■ going concern;
■ consistency;

- substance over form; and
- separate determination.

The principles above were originally set out in Statement of Standard Accounting Practice (SSAP) 2 *Disclosure of Accounting Policies* and in the Companies Act (1985). However, Financial Reporting Standard (FRS) 18 *Accounting Policies* has since replaced SSAP 2. Financial Reporting Standard 18 *Accounting Policies* has been mandatory since 2001: it sets out the principles to be followed in selecting accounting policies and the disclosures needed to help users to understand the accounting policies adopted and how they have been applied (Accounting Standards Board, 2000). FRS 18 in particular defines accounting policies and estimation techniques used in implementing those policies which should also be consistent with accounting standards. An organisation must also consider the appropriateness of accounting policies to its particular circumstances against the objectives of relevance, reliability, comparability and understandability. The objective of FRS 18 is that all material items are categorised and conform with giving a true and fair view, that the policies adopted are reviewed regularly to ensure they remain appropriate and that the financial statements and the information disclosed enables users to understand the accounting policies adopted and how they have been implemented (Accounting Standards Board, 2000). Accounting policies are concerned with:

1. recognising;
2. selecting measurement bases for; and
3. presenting assets, liabilities, gains, losses and changes to shareholders' funds.

The accounting policies do not include estimation techniques, but such techniques are documented within FRS 18 to implement the measurement aspects of accounting policies. Estimation techniques include methods of depreciation and estimating the proportion of trade debts that will not be recovered, while measurement bases can be adopted to accommodate historical cost systems. Put simply, accounting policies determine which facts about an organisation are to be presented in financial statements, and how those facts are to be presented, while estimation techniques are used to establish what those facts are. In the UK, all private limited companies, at the end of their financial year, must prepare full statutory annual accounts and a company tax return in line with the accounting policies outlined above. There are exemptions to this if a company is classed as 'dormant' or 'small' or is registered as a charity. However, even companies such as this still have to file information relating to financial performance through an annual return, abbreviated accounts or, at the very least, provide a breakdown of income and funding streams. This information also has to be consistent with the relevant accounting policies and standards.

Financial controls

Financial controls are processes, policies and procedures that are implemented to manage finances. They play a role in achieving an organisation's financial goals and meeting obligations of corporate governance, fiduciary duty and due diligence. Controls may be implemented with accountabilities, responsibilities and automation. The following are illustrative examples of financial controls with supporting information.

Accounting standards

Adopting an accounting standard, with knowledgeable staff who are accountable and responsible for its implementation, is particularly important when considering the different types of organisations across different sectors (public, private and voluntary) and different sizes (small, medium and large). Despite the influence of accounting standards, not every standard will fit with each organisation, so it is important that staff are knowledgeable about each one and can align them with best practice within their organisation.

Financial statements

Executive leadership such as the CEO and chief finance officer (CFO) are accountable to deliver timely and accurate financial statements such as statements of comprehensive income (income statements), cash flow statements, statements of financial position (balance sheets) and statement of changes in equity. Effective financial reporting allows for effective decision making in line with business objectives. A not-for-profit organisation, for example, might focus purely on balancing the books and making sure that expenditure is covered by income and funding each year. A larger organisation might use effective financial information to fund realistic expansion through methods such as borrowing, while even larger, major organisations may attempt to stretch their profit margins as far as possible to reinvest in future business strategies.

Operating metrics

Executive leadership such as the CEO, CFO and chief operating officer are accountable for delivering timely and accurate operating metrics such as profit margins. Defining the appropriate metrics for your organisation is important. There are many variables to measure financial performance, including the profit before and after tax, how much cash is available to an organisation and what money they owe to creditors; however, not all are relevant, depending on the type and size of the organisation you are involved in.

Policies

Policies are in place in areas such as general ledger, chart of accounts, recognition of revenue, reconciliations, invoicing, payment processing, inventory and asset management. Knowledgeable accounting staff, managed by the executive team, are responsible for implementing policy and should also make sure that policies are aligned with business objectives.

Segregation of duties

A clear segregation of duties exists between areas such as sales and revenue recognition. Segregation of duties is the principle that no single individual is given authority to execute two conflicting duties. It is a basic type of internal control that is used to manage risk. In many cases, segregation of duties is required by law or standards in areas such as accounting, corporate governance and information security. There are numerous examples of segregation of duties including purchase orders and approvals, payments and bank reconciliation, and expenses and expense approvals. It is also of vital importance that there are clear responsibilities such as a person who is responsible for sending account statements to customers each month.

Audit trail

Audit trails are created and retained for events such as approvals, financial transactions and updates to financial documents.

Information security

Access to financial software and documentation is restricted to authorised personnel.

▨ Role of an external auditor

All company accounts must be audited unless the company is:

- a small company as defined in s. 382 of the Companies Act;
- a dormant company as defined in s. 1169 of the Companies Act; or
- a subsidiary company fulfilling certain criteria in s. 479A of the Companies Act.

Auditors are appointed by an ordinary resolution of the shareholders. Directors may also appoint auditors in certain circumstances and there is currently no limit on the length of an auditor's appointment. In private companies, where no alternative auditor is appointed at the end of each financial year, the auditor in office is deemed to be reappointed. However, in public companies, auditors need to be reappointed every financial year. The UK Corporate Governance Code currently stipulates that FTSE 350 companies should put the external audit contract out to tender at least every 10 years.

The Competition and Markets Authority also published in September 2014 a final order requiring FTSE 350 companies to put their audit contracts out to tender every 10 years and to give more powers to audit committees in relation to the appointment of the auditor (for example, it must be the audit committee which initiates and supervises the competitive tender process). The order applies to financial years commencing on or after 1 January 2015. Further changes, some of which are subject to consultation at the time of writing, will result from the UK implementation of the Regulation (EU) 537/2014 and amendments to Directive 2014/56/EU by 17 June 2016.

Who can be an external auditor?

Due to the sensitive nature of the auditing role, there are some restrictions as to who can be an auditor for particular companies. The auditors of a company must be:

- appropriately qualified; and
- members of a recognised supervisory body and eligible for appointment under the rules of that body.

A person cannot be an auditor of a company if they are an officer or employee of the company being audited, or the partner or employee of such an individual. A partnership in which an officer or employee of the company is a partner also cannot act as an auditor. There are no legal restrictions on the non-audit work that auditors can do for a company whose accounts they audit. However, the Financial Reporting Council's (FRC) *Ethical Standard 5 – Non-audit services provided to audited entities* sets out the approach to be adopted by audit firms in relation to non-audit services. As part of the FRC consultation described above, the FRC is proposing to introduce a revised Ethical Standard (2016) which will apply to all audit and other public interest assurance engagements performed under the FRC's performance standards. The UK Corporate Governance Code requires the audit committee to develop and implement policy on the engagement of the external auditor to supply non-audit services. In addition, the audit committee should explain to the board how auditor objectivity and independence are safeguarded.

The importance of effective financial reporting

The concept behind financial management is not the simplistic idea that you need to manage profit, but more importantly how to monitor, evaluate and control the income and expenditure of an organisation. It is important for you to understand the changing values of the three sectors (public, private and voluntary) and their respective objectives (to make a profit, to increase participation) and to recognise that a large number of sport services are provided to achieve social objectives, which operate at a loss and which will normally require a government subsidy.

Users of financial information

It is important that the financial performance of the organisation is communicated effectively to the appropriate audiences. Financial information will be useful to a wide variety of stakeholders, who will often span several sectors and each will have slightly different needs for the information. For example, Malcom Glazer (the owner of Manchester United FC) will want to know how much profit his company has made, to ensure that he can afford the necessary interest payments on the loans he took out to finance his takeover in 2005. Sheffield City Council will want to know how much subsidy it has to provide in order to keep all of its leisure services running across the city, so that council taxpayers get value for money.

Effective decision making

Managers require financial information so that they can make future plans for the organisation. As such, it is vital that the financial information recorded is both correct and effective. At management level, an effective decision can only be made with an appropriate grasp on the financial position and performance of the organisation. Decision making is a difficult process that involves many risks and uncertainties, so having effective financial information is vital for managers. Effective financial reporting more often than not will lead to effective decision making that can have a profound impact on business performance. Effective decision making means that:

- organised and systematic decision making leads to better decisions;
- without a well-defined process, you risk making decisions that are based on insufficient information and analysis;
- many variables affect the final impact of your decision; and
- if you establish strong foundations for decision making, generate good alternatives, evaluate these alternatives rigorously and then check your decision-making process, you will improve the quality of your decisions.

Ensuring budgets align with the organisational and finance strategies

A key point about budgeting is that it is an ongoing process rather than a time-limited one-off event. The actual mechanics of drawing up the numbers involved in a budget are just a small part of the overall budgeting process. By bearing in mind that budgeting is designed to help an organisation with planning, decision making and control, it is possible to appreciate that budgeting is a continuous part of business life. This point is reinforced by viewing budgeting as steps in a logically sequenced planning process, and by making sure that your budgets align with strategy.

Define your business objectives

The first question to ask when involved with any financial business planning is: 'In monetary terms, what are we trying to achieve?' This question should provide a clue: most sane business people would not answer by saying 'making a loss'. Losses are made in business but it is inconceivable to imagine that managers set out deliberately to make losses. Losses normally occur when there is a mismatch between what was planned and what happened in reality. Organisational objectives will vary according to the nature of the business. A community sports club that exists for the benefit of its members may desire nothing more than to break even or to make a small surplus to maintain its existing facilities. A more complex organisation such as a professional football team needs to balance the requirements of producing a successful team on the pitch (utility maximisation) with the requirements of being a commercial franchise (profit maximisation). Whatever the objectives of an organisation, they need to have certain qualities that enable them to be measured. These qualities are contained within the mnemonic 'MASTER':

- Measurable – for example, making a profit of £3 million in the financial year, or simply to break even;
- Achievable – the organisation must have the capability to attain its objectives; capability means staff, other resources, and competitive advantage;
- Specific – objectives must be specific (£3 million profit), not just 'to do well this year';
- Time limited – objectives must have a stated date for being achieved;
- Ends related – objectives must relate to achieving outputs (ends) rather than describing means (how); and
- Ranked – ideally objectives should be ranked in priority order.

An example of an objective meeting the MASTER mnemonic might be: 'our first priority is to achieve a net profit of £3 million in the financial year 1 April 2017 to 31 March 2018. This target is considered to be attainable as the organisation has increased its capacity and the market is expanding.' It is also important to conduct and audit of resources alongside the budget. The audit of resources is a 'reality check' on the objectives. Its purpose is to ensure that the objectives and the resources required to achieve them are internally consistent. Where there is a discrepancy between the objectives and the resources available to achieve them, two courses of action are possible. First, the objectives can be changed to be compatible with the resources. Second, the gap between the resources available and the resources required can form the basis for prioritising capital investment such as increasing the capacity of a stadium, or identifying training and development needs to ensure that staff have the skills to deliver what is required of them.

Operationalise strategies

Having defined what you want to achieve and confirmed that you have the resources to deliver the objectives, the budgeting process evolves to consider the day-to-day tactics to use to meet the objectives. In private health and fitness clubs, these might include marketing plans, pricing policies, customer care protocols and opening hours. If organisational objectives can be regarded as 'what' we wish to achieve, then operational strategies can be regarded as 'how' we plan to achieve the objectives. Thus a football club aiming for an average match day turnover of £300,000 might set out to achieve this via operational strategies for spectators, corporate hospitality customers, programme sales, half-time draw tickets, catering and beverage sales, merchandising sales and car parking.

Allocate responsibility

The successful achievement of objectives does not occur by chance, or as a result of a mechanical exercise. Sport is primarily a service industry and the most important people in determining the extent to which objectives are met are an organisation's staff. In order for people to see where their contributions fit into an organisation's overall plan, they need to have agreed responsibility for particular areas of work. Agreed responsibility is particularly important in situations where staff can be rewarded, or indeed punished, on the basis of their performance. For example, basic performance for a sales adviser in a health club might be 20 new peak time members per month, with incentives available if the basic target is exceeded. By contrast, a private sector company managing a leisure facility on behalf of a local authority might be punished by deductions from its management fee for not meeting the terms of its agreement, for example, cleanliness standards. If it is known and clearly stated 'who is going to do what and by when', then there is the basis for a meaningful comparison of actual performance with planned or expected performance.

Analysis of variance

Incorporating the principles outlined above and treating budgeting as a continual process that is aligned with organisational objectives also allows for a clearer understanding when comparing budgeted performance to actual performance. Variance analysis is an important component of the budgeting process. It allows managers to see whether or not they are likely to achieve their objectives, and it also allows them to react more quickly to external changes in the marketplace.

The information in Table 11.1 relates to a hypothetical budgeting case study of a small event hosted by a local swimming club and compares its actual performance in hosting the event versus what it budgeted before the event took place. Table 11.1 is an example of how such a comparison might be presented to the managers of an organisation.

The layout of Table 11.1 has a deliberate structure to it and each component is explained in turn below:

- 'Actual' income and expenditure refers to entries made to an organisation's accounting system which are supportable by documentary evidence such as invoices, receipts, staff time sheets and so on. 'Actual' figures are drawn from the financial accounting systems and can be supported by an audit trail of evidence.
- 'Incurred' (or 'committed') expenditure refers to expenditure that relates to the financial period in question that we know has been made, but as yet has not been billed for. This sort of data can be picked up from documentation such as

purchase order forms. In order to produce timely budget reports, it is sometimes not possible to wait until all of the paperwork relating to expenditure in a period has been received. Thus, in order to reflect a more realistic picture of events, the 'Incurred' column is used to log known expenditure that is not formally in the books of account. The 'Incurred' column tends to be used for expenditure only – it would be unusual to have incurred income.

Table 11.1: Actual versus budget comparison

INCOME	Actual	Incurred	Total	Budget	Variance	Direction	Note
Spectator tickets	1,450		1,450	1,350	100	F	1
Other ticket sales	250		250	0	250	F	
Sponsorship	1,700		1,700	1,800	–100	U	2
Catering	220		220	200	20	F	
Merchandising	3,750	0	3,750	3,450	300	F	3
Total income	3,750	0	3,750	3,450	300	F	
EXPENDITURE							
Volunteer kit	700		700	600	100	U	4
Pool hire	2,500	0	2,500	3,000	–500	F	5
Marketing activities	136		136	140	–4	F	
Administration	342	50	392	400	–8	F	
Total expenditure	3,678	50	3,728	4,140	–412	F	
SURPLUS / DEFICIT)	72	–50	22	–690	712	D	6

- The 'Total' column is simply the sum of the 'Actual' and the 'Incurred' columns.
- 'Budget' refers to the approved budget for a given financial period.
- 'Variance' is the difference between the 'Total' column and the 'Budget' column.
- 'Direction' is a reference to whether the variance on any given line of the budget is favourable (F) or unfavourable (U). One characteristic of good information is that it is relevant to the intended recipient. For non-finance specialists, spelling out whether a variance is favourable or unfavourable is a helpful aid to understanding the underlying meaning of the figures.
- 'Note' is a cross-reference to a written qualitative explanation of a variance. Numbers in isolation do not explain a variance, therefore, it is sometimes useful for a written explanation to accompany some of the more significant variances.

To illustrate how qualitative explanations can help to explain the meaning of variances, Worked Example 11.1 shows an example of the notes that might have accompanied the actual versus budget comparison in Table 11.1. Note how it is written in the form of a report and can easily be cross-referenced to Table 11.1.

Worked Example 11.1: Example of an event budget report

Event Budget Report

To: Swimming Committee
From: Event Manager
Date: 10 September 20XY
Re: Actual v Budget Notes

Note 1: Spectator ticket sales
Spectator ticket sales (580 at £2.50) were 40 ahead of target (540 at £2.50). More spectator ticket sales have been achieved by encouraging people who attended the event in the past to return this year.

Note 2: Sponsorship
Following the renegotiation of last year's agreements with our club's partners, we were able to secure £1,700 in sponsorship (£100 below our target). This unfavourable result was due to one company having to reduce its involvement due to market pressures.

Note 3: Total income
Total income is £300 ahead of target following strong spectator ticket sales. However, it is not all net gain (see Note 6 below).

Note 4: Volunteer kit
The increase in event size necessitated an increase in the number of volunteers and therefore an overspend of £100 against budget. Our club policy is to reward these volunteers for their time with an event T-shirt and we purchased 20 additional items at a cost of £5 per item.

Note 5: Pool hire
Pool hire costs were £500 below budget due to an improved discount from the facility. We have reached an agreement to pay this set fee for the next five years.

Note 6: The bottom line
The event had been due to record a loss of £690 following an agreement at the last annual general meeting. However, strong ticket sales and a significant reduction in pool hire costs (due to the five-year agreement) mean that the event has made a small surplus of £72. This surplus will be reinvested into the swimming club to provide support to transportation costs for away galas.

Signed

Event Manager

Any chairperson/director reading the above report would be able to grasp the basic point that the event performed ahead of budget and had secured future discounts for the benefit of the club. At this stage the actual versus budget comparison would be noted and no action would need to be taken, other than to congratulate and encourage those responsible for delivering the better-than-planned-for performance.

Chapter summary

- It is vital that accounts are filed and disclosures made relating to income and funding streams.
- Financial controls, their processes, policies and procedures are central to good governance and should be implemented to manage finances effectively and transparently.
- An external auditor has a central role in providing transparency and it is important to have an external body/person sign-off the financial accounts of an organisation.
- Effective financial reporting ensures that the correct information is being utilised when considering organisational strategies.
- Once financial reporting has been completed, internal budgets can be aligned with organisational strategies in a cyclical process.
- Finance and financial management is vital to an organisation and organisations need to operate within the resources allocated to them to be in a position to continue trading.
- Budgeting can help in this process by expressing in financial terms where a business hopes to be at some time in the future.

12
Preparing for and conducting meetings

Introduction

This chapter will set out the relevant provisions of UK law that apply to company meetings, identify potential issues which may exist in addition to these obligations, and provide practical guidance as to how to prepare for, run and follow up company meetings.

The majority of sports organisations in the UK are incorporated as private companies limited by shares. As a result, the principal piece of legislation in the UK applicable to company meetings is the Companies Act 2006 (CA 2006). A failure to comply with CA2006 can lead to various penalties, ranging from fines to potential criminal charges.

However, it is often not as straightforward as simply knowing the relevant provisions of CA 2006 and applying them. Anybody responsible for the organisation and conduct of company meetings must also be aware of any provisions in relation to company meetings arising from a particular company's Articles of Association, (pre-CA 2006) memorandum and other internal documents (such as standing orders).

Where the sports organisation is not incorporated (a club, for example), all matters relating to the holding of meetings will be found in the governing document of the organisation (the equivalent of the articles and memorandum) and in any standing orders.

A failure of the board or members (as a collective) to act in accordance with any internal governing documents will not render a decision or act invalid in the eyes of the law; however, it may allow a director or member to bring an action against the company for breach of contract.

Before meetings

Notice
The correct serving of notice ahead of a company meeting is extremely important because it can render a meeting, and the decisions taken at it, invalid.

General

In order for a meeting to be convened validly, a notice of meeting must be issued to all of the individuals who are entitled to receive it, as well as any directors who are not also members who are entitled to attend by virtue of the organisations constitution. The latter will be relevant in a sports organisation that has appointed independent non-executive directors.

The overarching principles regarding a notice are that it must:

■ be clear and concise;
■ comply with all legal requirements; and
■ comply with any relevant provisions in an organisation's internal governing documents.

Legally required content

A notice for a general meeting must include as a minimum:

■ the time, date, day and place of the meeting;
■ the general nature of the business to be dealt with at the meeting;
■ the full text of each special resolution to be proposed; and
■ how a member can exercise their right to appoint a proxy to attend and vote on their behalf.

Recommended additional steps

As a matter of good practice, your organisation should take the following steps in respect of a notice:

■ Get it dated and signed by a person within your organisation to issue it (usually the secretary).
■ The draft of any documents to be discussed and/or approved at the meeting should be appended to the notice (such as new Articles of Association).
■ It should be approved preferably by the board, or, if not, a senior executive, before being sent out to members.

Validly serving notice and time periods

Notice of members' meetings must be given in hard copy, electronic form or via a website, and it must be served (or 'called') with at least 14 clear days' notice of the proposed meeting for the organisation, unless a particular company's articles require a longer period.

The so-called 'clear day rule' means the day that notice is given and the day of the meeting are both excluded from the calculation.

Not only do you have to give 14 clear days' notice, but you must also take into account the deemed day of delivery to the recipient, which varies depending on the method of service used:

■ *Post*: Deemed date of delivery is 48 hours after it was posted. The notice must be properly addressed, pre-paid and posted to an address in the UK. The company may be asked to prove this if any member disputes whether notice has actually been served. Your organisation should post notices using some form of registered post with a proof of postage.

■ *Email*: Deemed date of delivery is 48 hours after it was sent. The email must be properly addressed. As a matter of good record keeping, and in case of any dispute, you should request a read receipt.

Section 307(4)–(6) of CA 2006 permits meetings to be held on short notice. However, to take advantage of the short notice provisions, notice of some period must still be given.

One further instance where the period of notice may differ from 14 clear days is where the sports organisation proposes a motion to remove a director(s). In this situation, although only an ordinary resolution is required in terms of the requisite majority, 'special notice' must be given. This means at least 28 clear days' notice of the meeting at which the motion is moved must be given.

Agenda

The agenda is the document which sets out the items, matters and/or topics to be discussed during a meeting, and the order in which they will be discussed.

Any documents to be discussed at that meeting should also be enclosed or attached to the agenda. This may require liaising with other people on the board of the sports organisation, or part of the administration, who are responsible for matters such as finance, marketing or membership.

The agenda should ideally be issued to the members about one week before the meeting to provide adequate opportunity for the members to review them, and will typically include:

■ any apologies for absence received prior to the agenda being sent;
■ the draft minutes of the last meeting as to be approved at the meeting;
■ the opportunity to discuss matters arising from the draft minutes, for instance, the progression of any action points;
■ discussion of the business to be discussed at the meeting – this will mean sending the latest drafts of any relevant documents (including presentations, reports or resolutions);
■ any other business – this can be contentious if the business raised cannot be discussed during the time remaining for the meeting. Because of this, the chair may refuse to put matters under this heading to the vote until the next meeting; and
■ the date of the next meeting.

The agenda acts as a of roadmap for the chair of the meeting and therefore the business to be discussed should be listed in a logical order (usually importance). In addition, given it is there to assist the chair and the smooth running of the meeting, the agenda should be agreed with the chair prior to it being sent to the members.

Proxies

Where your sports organisation is a company, there is a statutory right for the members that the notice for the meeting informs them that they can appoint a proxy. This right cannot be excluded by any decision of the company or any provision of the company's constitutional documents.

A member would appoint a proxy where they cannot attend a meeting themselves but wish to have someone in attendance to speak and vote on matters on their behalf.

When the proxy is sent out with the notice, it must contain the terms of the right to appoint, the scope of which can be set by the individual member.

It should also contain a deadline by which the proxy should be returned, either by post or electronically (if the constitution of the organisation allows). Otherwise, proxies can be submitted right up to the start of the meeting (which is not desirable from a practical perspective).

Practical preparation

Once the notice and agenda has been sent to the members, prior to the meeting, the other preparatory steps are largely practical.

Having received acceptances of attendance and any proxies, the secretary should ensure that the room booked for the meeting is suitable in terms of size and facilities (number of chairs and refreshments), that any computer or audio-visual equipment is working and that paper and pens are readily available.

As for the taking of minutes, before the meeting, the secretary must decide how they will take their notes (pen and paper, laptop computer, tablet or smartphone). The secretary should also have a backup in case the original method fails.

The secretary must also have the following prepared to take to the meeting:

- a copy of the organisation's constitutional documents;
- the minute book;
- the agenda an any supporting documents – including spare copies; and
- a copy of CA 2006.

The secretary should also have a pre-meeting conversation with the chair, who must be told of any apologies and proxies received (as this will be vital to the calculation of the quorum) and if any questions have been sent in advance by the members, so the chair can prepare.

During meetings

On the day

On the day and during the meeting, the overarching consideration for the organisation from a governance perspective is that everything that takes place is legal and valid.

Arguably the most important task during the meeting is that accurate notes are taken for the minutes. This is discussed in further detail on pages 210 and 211.

The chair may also require some assistance during the meeting. This may be by providing advice on request about procedure, the internal rules and legislation governing the meeting, or by informing the chair if any agenda items have been overlooked.

Members at the meeting should be vocal if they believe something the other members are proposing to do is either contrary to the organisation's constitutional documents, or is potentially unlawful.

Third parties who have been invited to contribute to the meeting (usually from within the organisation but who are not members and are not entitled to attend on any other basis) should be available on the day of the meeting and brought in when appropriate. For example, the treasurer of the sports organisation may have produced a finance report for the members and be invited to explain it further or answer any questions from the members.

At the end of the meeting all papers that form part of the organisation's official records, and any papers that are in any way confidential, must be removed from the room and any copies destroyed.

Establishing and achieving quorum

A quorum is the number of people required to be present to conduct valid business at a meeting. It is the responsibility of the chair of a meeting to ensure there is a quorum before the meeting proceeds to business. Whether or not a quorum is achieved must be noted in the minutes.

The number of individuals required for a quorum is usually found in an organisation's constitution. If the articles do not provide otherwise, two 'qualifying persons' (an individual who is a member or their validly appointed proxy) must be present at a meeting to constitute a valid quorum.

In addition, the constitutional documents should be checked to determine whether members present by proxy may count towards the quorum. The documents may provide that a quorum consists of persons 'present in person or by proxy'. If, however, the quorum provision in the articles refers to persons present 'in person', then the individual must attend the meeting in person to count towards the quorum.

Voting rights

Once the quorum has been established for a general meeting, the most important part of the meeting is discussing, and voting on, the business set out in the agenda.

General

The right of a member to vote at general meetings is usually governed by the company's Articles of Association. Part 13 of CA 2006 sets out the law in relation to the different voting procedures.

Each fully paid-up member of a sports organisation should have a vote. Members will be able to cast their votes at meetings either by a show of hands or by a poll. Subject to what is stated in an organisation's constitution, unless a poll is demanded, the default position is that the decision on a resolution proposed at a meeting will be decided on a show of hands.

The procedure and counting of the votes cast is controlled by the chair of the meeting.

Different types of voting (resolutions)

An ordinary resolution is a decision passed by a majority of the members. This applies to the majority of an organisation's business proposed at a meeting.

A special resolution is a decision that requires a 75% majority to be passed. In CA 2006, this threshold is reserved for such important matters as amendments of an organisation's articles or the organisation wanting to change its name.

Different methods of voting

On a show of hands, every member present at the meeting, or their validly appointed proxy, has one vote. Those in favour of a particular resolution will raise their hand in favour of the resolution. Once those hands have been counted, the chairman will request those opposing the resolution to raise a hand and those votes will be counted. A declaration by the chair that a resolution has or has not been carried, and that being recorded in the minutes, shall be conclusive evidence of the decision.

A vote by way of a poll is a vote by the members on paper. The result of a poll vote is arguably more accurate as individuals may vote more honestly. It is therefore increasingly being viewed as best governance practice which your organisation should implement.

Pros and cons of the different voting procedures

For sports organisations, the main advantages of voting on a show of hands are speed and ease. Conversely, if there are any disaffected members who choose not to attend in protest, then those members who attend and vote are given a disproportionate degree of power over the affairs of the organisation.

After meetings

Basic elements of minute taking

The minutes of a meeting must be a true and accurate record of what took place on the day, as they provide a transparent audit trail for all current and future stakeholders in the sport.

Overall, minutes must reflect accurately what was discussed and decided at a meeting. They must give sufficient detail yet remain concise to ensure the members not only read but properly review them after the meeting.

Prior to the meeting, read the agenda, as you can use that to formulate an outline to take your notes during the meeting. However, be prepared for the discussions during the meeting not to stick strictly to the agenda.

Preparing formal minutes is a skill which takes time and practice. All minutes must include:

- the name of the company;
- the place where the meeting was held;
- the day, date, time and duration of the meeting;
- the names of those present and in attendance;
- any apologies received for being absent;
- the approval by the membership of the previous minutes;
- details of the discussions during the meeting (if appropriate, a numbering system should be used for each substantive item of business);
- (legally required) the signature of the chair on the final version of the minutes.

If possible, it is recommended that an audio recording of the meeting is taken, to cross-check against the notes taken. Depending on the number of people attending, and the size of the room, most smartphones can accurately and audibly record a meeting. Note that if you are going to record the meeting, you should inform the people in attendance prior to the meeting beginning and explain to them why you are recording. If anyone objects, you must not record the meeting.

Once the minutes have been prepared in draft form from the notes taken during the meeting, these should be circulated to the attendees, both within a reasonable period of time after that meeting, and within a reasonable period of time before the next meeting.

Importance of a transparent audit trail

The importance of minutes as an official record of the organisation's business conducted at meetings cannot be underestimated.

The agreed and signed minutes must by law be kept at the organisation's registered office, or a place notified to the Registrar of Companies, for 10 years from the date of the meeting.

In addition, the records must be open to the inspection of any member of the company without charge and any member is entitled to a copy of the minutes on payment of a reasonable fee (as decided by the organisation).

In a worst-case scenario, the minutes could become key evidence in any legal dispute that arises between the members.

Other post-meeting actions

In addition to dealing with the minutes, the secretary of your organisation must be mindful of the following:

- Notify departments and relevant personnel in the organisation of any decisions that affect them or they need to take action in relation to.

- Make a note of any item that has been deferred to make sure it is not overlooked.
- File a copy of the meeting agenda and supporting papers – destroy unused spare copies.
- Enter any minutes approved and signed in the company's minute book.

Vitally, after the meeting, the secretary must know of any deadlines imposed by CA 2006 to file documents with Companies House. Certain members' resolutions and agreements that affect an organisation's constitution must be filed with Companies House within 15 days of being passed. The company and any directors in default are liable to a fine if these resolutions are not filed. For sports organisations, special resolutions are likely to be the only matter needing to be filed as a legal requirement.

Annual general meetings

Importance of annual general meetings
Annual general meetings (AGMs) are a special type of meeting of all the members of an incorporated association which should, as a matter of best practice, be held annually. This requirement will often be mandated in an organisation's constitutional documents, which will also state the time of year to hold the AGM.

The purpose of an AGM is to:

- comply with legislative requirements;
- present the financial accounts to the members;
- report to the members on the organisation's activities;
- ensure committee rotation happens in an orderly manner;
- consider and vote on rule changes and other recommendations; and
- allow the members to ask questions and provide feedback to the committee.

The AGM is the primary forum where the members of the sport can hold the directors/executives to account – be they remunerated, voluntary or non-executives – get their questions answered and/or grievances aired.

Conducting the AGM
To conduct an effective AGM, the first step, given it is the most important members' meeting of the year, is ensuring there is sufficient space for all of the members who may wish to attend. This means finding a suitable venue as soon as possible.

As for other meetings, the secretary of the organisation must check the following prior to the AGM:

- Check the organisation's constitutional documents for the number of persons required for a quorum.

- If a quorum is not present at the start of the meeting, check whether the constitutional documents permit the chair to delay the meeting for a period of time.
- Check the constitutional documents to ensure that the directors and/or other executives may attend and speak, and whether the chair may permit non-members also to attend and speak – the important phrase there is 'may permit', as non-members who could disrupt the meeting should be excluded.

The chairman should allow, and indeed actively encourage, the members of the organisation to debate on any matter to be raised at the meeting, to ascertain the views of the membership. However, this has to be managed carefully by the chair, by keeping speakers on topic and limiting the amount of time each member can speak on a particular topic.

Given the passion of members of a sports organisation, it is highly possible that discussions at the AGM will become heated and require the management of the chair. Some guidance on how best to deal with an obstructive or disorderly member(s) is as follows:

- Ask the member to desist from their monologue and to ask any question they may have.
- Offer the member a separate discussion and a chance to air their grievance outside the meeting.
- Adjourn the AGM for a short period to try to establish a basis for continuing the meeting in good order.
- Finally, if the shareholder continues to act in a disorderly fashion, the chair should ask them to leave the room.

When it comes to formally discussing the proposed resolutions, ordinary resolutions can be amended at the AGM, while special resolutions should not be amended at the meeting itself except in very limited circumstances.

Chapter summary

- For a meeting of your organisation to be validly convened, the notice must be clear and concise, comply with all legal requirements and any relevant provisions in your organisation's internal governing documents.
- Notice of members' meetings must be given in hard copy, electronic form or via a website, and must be served with at least 14 clear days' notice.
- The agenda provides the items, matters and/or topics to be discussed during a meeting, and the order in which they will be discussed.
- There is a statutory right for the members of your organisation to appoint a proxy to vote on their behalf, and this must be stated in the notice for a meeting.

- The knowledge of the quorum required for the organisation, and the calculation of it, is vital as the quorum is the number of people required to be in attendance to conduct valid business at a meeting.
- Ordinary resolutions are decisions passed by a majority of the members, and apply to the majority of your organisation's business. A special resolution is required for important decisions where a 75% majority is required.
- Resolutions can be voted upon by a show of hands at the meeting or a poll.
- The minutes of a meeting must be a true and accurate record of what took place on the day, as they provide a transparent audit trail for all current and future stakeholders in the sport.
- After a meeting, the secretary of the organisation must know of any deadlines imposed by CA 2006 to file documents with Companies House.
- AGMs are a special type of meeting of all the members of an incorporated association and should be held annually.
- The AGM is the primary forum where the members of the sport can hold the directors and executives to account, and get their questions answered or grievances aired.

13

Advanced stakeholder engagement

Introduction

This chapter outlines the different stakeholders that sports bodies engage with inside and outside the organisation, and how communications can be shaped to engage with them most effectively.

Acknowledging and giving such groups a meaningful voice provides some checks and balances on the concept of the autonomy of sport.

Influential stakeholder groups in sport

In Chapter 5 (pages 102 to 107) we looked at some of the key stakeholders for sports organisations. The Sport and Recreation Alliance describe stakeholders as, 'people, groups, or organisations that have a direct or indirect stake in an organisation because it can affect or be affected by the organisation's actions, objectives, and policies'.

The first section of this chapter not only identifies the key stakeholders, but most importantly those that are, or should be, influential on a sports organisation.

Members/shareholders

Members of sports organisations are undoubtedly the principal concern for the majority of sports organisations, given they are historically the stakeholder group that fund the organisation. The rights and powers of members are usually set out in the organisation's constitutional documents. However, in modern governance theory, this group has to take a wider view of what constitutes success for a sports organisation and explicitly take into account their views.

Players and other participants

Those operating on or around the field of play in sport (players, referees, coaches) are the ones who generate the unpredictable drama that lead to the enjoyment for all other stakeholders and drive value and commercial opportunity. However, throughout the history or sport, right up until the present day, in general the players and other participants are given little or no say in the governance of sport and are routinely ignored, or even worse trodden upon.

With the recent Duty of Care report, and other scandals involving the abuse of athletes and other participants, there is finally some recognition that without them there is no sport, and therefore they should be listened to. This may be through a formal union, such as the Professional Footballers Association (PFA), or through another form of organisation whereby athletes' come together for a common cause, such as Global Athlete. The IOC has recently given further credence to the athletes' voice through the Athlete365 initiative; however, many doubt whether this will lead to a meaningful say in the actual running and decision making of the most powerful sports organisation in the world.

Commercial partners

Sports organisations and participants build relationships with commercial entities to attract revenue and other forms of funding. Such partners are becoming increasingly interested when it comes to good governance in the sector. Recent scandals have seen sponsors, for instance, threaten to walk away from a sport as they do not want to be associated with corruption. Activism by commercial partners can be a highly influential driver for change and should be consulted.

Funding bodies

As the reliance on public funding continues, as outlined at numerous junctures in this handbook, it goes without saying that the bodies administering this funding are a vital stakeholder. This is even more so the case given the governance requirements imposed upon sports organisations, if not complied with, has led to the direct suspension or withdrawal of funding in recent years. Arguably such bodies have never been so influential, and this is only likely to increase as time moves on.

Fans and supporters

Fans and supporters should be considered separately to the members of a sports organisation as they will often not be one or the same. There will usually be far more fans of a sport than members of the governing bodies within that sport.

The challenge with engaging fans in decision making is that there will often be a diverse range of opinions just within this one stakeholder group. However, fans and supporters are the ones who will often have the most emotional connection to the team, which can be positive or negative, depending on your view. For instance, fans will often blindly pay money to the club in various ways while being activist when it comes to the ownership of 'their' club.

In football for example, given the disparity in wealth between the upper echelons of the game and the vast majority of football clubs, those lower down the pyramid have often found themselves in great financial trouble in overreaching to reach the 'promised land', and therefore in some situations supporters collectively have come together to run their club, or at least have a seat on the board.

According to the Working towards a framework for modern sports governance report for the Parliamentary Assembly of the Council of Europe 'Notably the millennials and younger generations active on social media are vocal in appealing to the governing bodies for sports governance reforms, with integrity concerns, etc. They want to see that sport echoes the values they associate themselves with. This new group is emerging strongly as a new key stakeholder in the field of sports governance and integrity'.

The community

Sports teams and clubs are often closely tied to the community local to them. Indeed, members of the community influence sport in a number of ways. Teams and clubs aim to attract participants, spectators and volunteers from their community, building relationships with them by providing news to media, holding events to attract parents, schools and participants, or taking part in community projects.

The community is also an important stakeholder for teams planning to build new sports facilities or hold major events, particularly if they are in sensitive areas. A mass-participation road race, for example, can cause traffic disruption to a community, while a proposed new stadium in a residential area may create parking problems, noise and other forms of nuisance to the community.

UK Corporate Governance Code

The Companies Act 2006 makes clear that, while boards have an overarching duty to promote the success of the company for the benefit of its members as a whole, directors should take account of a range of stakeholders in making decisions.

While most sports organisations, including those registered as a company limited by guarantee, do not have shareholders, the Corporate Code's main principle would still apply when the board has to consider its relationship with members. This role for the board is reinforced in the various sporting codes including the Code for Sports Governance, which states under Principle 3 that organisations shall be transparent and accountable, engaging effectively with stakeholders and nurturing internal democracy. The accompanying requirements include the following:

3.1 Each organisation shall publicly disclose information on its governance, structure, strategy, activities and financial position to enable stakeholders to have a good understanding of them.

3.2 Each organisation shall publish:
- in the case of organisations which employ more than 50 staff, the total remuneration paid to its senior management team; and
- the remuneration (if any) paid to each of its directors (except for members of the senior management team who are ex officio directors).

3.3   Any information disclosed shall be fair, accurate and presented in an understandable manner.

3.4   Each organisation shall develop a strategy for engaging with, and listening to, its stakeholders (including elite athletes where appropriate) which the board shall contribute to and review at least annually.

3.5   Each organisation shall be expected to carry out a regular staff survey (including their volunteers) at least once a year and:

■   act on the results internally, communicating clearly to their employees and volunteers how such actions are to be taken; and

■   make topline data available to Sport England to collate the results for the purpose of developing a greater understanding of the sport workforce.

These requirements reflect many aspects of the UK Corporate Code, especially in relation to senior staff and director remuneration. There are many ways boards can seek stakeholder and member views: annual surveys, consultations, advisory groups, committee meetings, general meetings, roadshows or regional meetings.

The stakeholder voice in decision making

How the voice of influential stakeholder groups is reflected in the decision making by sports organisations will reflect how serious a particular organisation is about taking a stakeholder-inclusive approach rather than a member or executive centric one.

For instance, just because there are statements made by an organisation that stakeholder groups sit on certain committees, this does not mean this is in any way meaningful when it comes to decision making and the governance of the sport in question. Therefore, the rights of influential stakeholder groups should be entrenched in key constitutional documents.

Indeed, the Sport & Recreation Alliance is of the opinion that the board of a sport should make sure stakeholder views are at the core of the organisation's long term vision and mission.

ICSA and Investment Association paper

In 2017, the ICSA and the Investment Association published a paper titled *The stakeholder voice in board decision making* to help boards think about how to ensure they understand and weigh up the interests of their key stakeholders when taking strategic decisions. The 'core principles' of this approach were stated as follows:

1.   Boards should identify, and keep under regular review, who they consider their key stakeholders to be and why.

2.   Boards should determine which stakeholders they need to engage with directly, as opposed to relying solely on information from management.

3. When evaluating their composition and effectiveness, boards should identify what stakeholder expertise is needed in the boardroom and decide whether they have, or would benefit from, directors with directly relevant experience or understanding.
4. When recruiting any director, the nomination committee should take the stakeholder perspective into account when deciding on the recruitment process and the selection criteria.
5. The chairman – supported by the company secretary – should keep under review the adequacy of the training received by all directors on stakeholder-related matters, and the induction received by new directors, particularly those without previous board experience.
6. The chairman – supported by the board, management and the company secretary – should determine how best to ensure that the board's decision-making processes give sufficient consideration to key stakeholders.
7. Boards should ensure that appropriate engagement with key stakeholders is taking place and that this is kept under regular review.
8. In designing engagement mechanisms, companies should consider what would be most effective and convenient for the stakeholders, not just the company.
9. The board should report to its shareholders on how it has taken the impact on key stakeholders into account when making decisions.
10. The board should provide feedback to those stakeholders with whom it has engaged, which should be tailored to the different stakeholder groups.

Council of Europe's Committee on Culture, Science, Education and Media report

In its report, *Working towards a framework for modern sports governance*, the Council of Europe's Committee on Culture, Science, Education and Media believe the stakeholder voice is a key part of one of three pillars to achieve a broad-based (inclusive) governance framework for sport: 'inclusive action and cultivating governance culture through knowledge-sharing, involvement in policy making and communication of a broad range of stakeholders and diverse societal groups, and cooperation with multi-stakeholder platforms.'

Despite external stakeholders becoming better at holding sports organisations to account, the committee believes there is still much work to be done: 'The sports movement, from the top to the bottom, will have to get its house in order and reform its functioning in terms of checks and balances, transparency of procedures or accountability. However, the stakeholders – be it governments, public actors, international organisations or sponsors – should also assert more external pressure and demand bolder reforms'.

Communicating with stakeholders

The board has overall responsibility for stakeholder strategies: identifying key stakeholders and planning how the organisation will build effective relationships; and risk management, which includes the risks associated with strategic partnerships and communications.

The Institute of Business Ethics in its 2016 report *Stakeholder Engagement – Values, Business Culture and Society* states that a company that seeks to build a positive relationship with a wide range of external stakeholders must be clear what its values are, and its own behaviour must be consistent with the message it gives to stakeholders. A company claiming values that it does not adhere to will be found out and exposed quickly.

A sports organisations' annual report has historically been considered a key communication tool to engage with all stakeholders as it comes from the board and contains information on an organisation's performance, it strategy and any changes to the governance structure or practices in the past 12 months. The annual report is still important, but it can now be supplemented all year round with other methods and channels, which may in fact have greater impact.

Suitable channels of communication

In the late twentieth century, most communication with stakeholders, including members and funders, would have been by letter. Since the arrival of the internet and electronic communications, the way in which people consume information has changed radically. In 2016, the *Harvard Business Review* reported that more than 100 billion emails are sent every day and, with two billion Facebook users, there can be no doubt that online communication has overtaken all other forms across the world. The speed with which communication methods change is highlighted by the fact that email is now perceived in the private sector as less efficient and, for people under the age of 30, less desirable. However, it remains the principal method of communication for many sports organisations to their members, staff and funders.

Developing appropriate methods and tools to communicate

Emails: information contained in an email can be legally enforceable and sports bodies, in particular their staff and volunteers, should be clear about the implications of such communication. A supplier, funder or member can rightfully assume that the content of the original email from an authorised person constitutes a binding agreement. To protect the organisation, offers and terms of proposed agreements communicated via email should explicitly state that they are subject to any relevant conditions, as well as to the further review and comment of the sender's colleagues, for example, a director or the board. If a formal contract is attached to an email and this document has been prepared in accordance with the organisation's procedures and controls, the recipient can feel confdent it represents the totality of the offer's terms and conditions. This might include a membership offer or terms of agreement for a supplier. Creating clear divisions of responsibility and delegated authority will help ensure no staff member or volunteer makes decisions, enters into agreements or commits the organisation beyond the limits of their authority. Internal controls such as delegated financial authority policies and service contract procedures are essential as they apply to decisions and their communication.

Online meetings: for the board, it is usually preferable to meet in person where dialogue and debate can take account of body language and nuance. However, with many volunteers facing time pressures, offering remote access can help ensure more frequent participation by busy board members. Using some of the many online meeting tools now available, it is possible to include several board members from different locations.

The organisation's Articles of Association determine whether a meeting can be held remotely. That should not be an issue for more recently incorporated companies as the Model Articles, available from Companies House, will apply. Provided they have not been amended by the company's bespoke articles, the Model Articles allow directors to deal with their board meetings remotely. Directors of a company incorporated before 1 October 2009 will not be able to hold their meetings remotely unless the company has either updated its articles to enable board meetings to be held in this way or adopted the new Model Articles. The old default articles, known as 'Table A', did not give directors the ability to hold meetings other than in person.

In addition to an organisation's articles allowing for meetings to be held remotely, they should also allow for the board to establish specific committees to engage with key stakeholder groups. Such committees will have the benefit of enabling a more in-depth assessment than the board itself has time for, and providing a means of identifying emerging stakeholder-related issues that should be brought to the attention of the board while ensuring a fair representation of stakeholders without making the size of the board too unwieldly and therefore ineffective.

Social media: social media is the use of web-based and mobile technologies to create interactive platforms via which individuals and communities share, create, discuss and modify user generated content. Examples include:

- blogging and networking via users' own websites;
- networking sites – Facebook, LinkedIn, Twitter;
- sharing sites – YouTube, Flickr, Pinterest, Google+; and
- review sites, publications, third party blogs – Blogspot, WordPress, industry forums.

The open nature of social media will raise questions for the board that should be considered as part of the organisation's overarching communication strategy. These should not be dealt with in isolation from the other policies and procedures (email, internet, anti-bullying, data protection, codes of conduct and so on that protect and promote the organisation.

While some social media accounts can be created in the name of the organisation, others will be held in the name of individuals or teams. It is also likely that the people who work or volunteer for an organisation will have their own personal online accounts. It is easy to see how lines between what is work-related or personal can become blurred.

Not all board members will be experts in (or even comfortable with) social media, but there are legal, stakeholder and communications risks factors of which the board should be aware. Legislation that applies to social media activity includes:

- Malicious Communications Act 1988/Communications Act 2003;
- Protection from Harassment Act 1997;
- European Convention on Human Rights – Articles 8 and 10; breach of confidence;
- Contempt of Court Act 1981;
- Defamation Act 1996;
- Fraud Act 2006;
- Data Protection Act 2018; and
- General Data Protection Regulation (2018).

In managing the risks, the board should be assured that there are policies and controls in place, and that staff, athletes, coaches, volunteers, board members and other internal stakeholders are fully apprised of these. Put simply, when using the organisation's systems to correspond externally, whatever is written, whether via email, on a web forum or using social media, the individual needs to be aware that he or she is corresponding on behalf of the organisation.

Guidelines and policies do not need to be long or complicated, but they do need to:

- set out the benefits and risks associated with using social media;
- link to disciplinary rules and disrepute clauses;
- refect the rights of free speech;
- ensure trademarks/usernames are registered; and
- explain how negative, inaccurate or defamatory comments will be handled.

Guidelines need not be limited to individuals but can also be created and shared with stakeholders, such as clubs.

Theory in action

England Athletics have produced the *England Athletics Club Guide to Social Media*. This resource is available to affliated clubs to help them make the most of their online presence, particularly using social media resources such as Facebook, Twitter and Instagram, but also advises how to do so safely.

The guide includes:

- practicalities of setting up a club social media presence on a number of platforms including Facebook, Twitter and Instagram;
- how to use them effectively to publicise the club;
- specifc guidance on functionality that can be useful for clubs, such as how to use Facebook Groups for smaller closed communication, such as with club committees or a coaching team;
- what not to do: how social media can damage your impact, credibility or leave clubs exposed on welfare related grounds; and
- suggested social media usage guidance for clubs to give members.

Changing message according to audience

Having identifed key stakeholders, the board can delegate the design of a detailed stakeholder plan, including methods of communication, to staff or a sub-committee. The plan should contain the key messages the organisation wishes to convey to each stakeholder, bearing in mind this will not necessarily be the same message to everyone.

Creating relevant messages for key stakeholders

Members: while members will often be interested in elite success, results from national championships and other competitions, they will also be seeking reassurance that the organisation is being well run. Governance, equality, safeguarding and other areas of business should all feature on the organisation's website, while updates or features can be communicated easily through social media. Members will understandably want to know if there are any member-specifc discounts, offers, initiatives or opportunities, as any customer would.

Technology has advanced to a level where sports bodies can monitor what web pages were visited, for how long and whether the visitor clicked through to related features and pages. This provides essential feedback on the level of interest in a story, policy or update as well as the visitor numbers to any protected member areas on a website. As a result, the organisation can assess if there are particular areas of interest for members and visitors, leading to the creation of similarly tailored products or information in future.

Governing bodies are not required to publish board or committee minutes online, but it is good practice to do so. This can be a summary or an action log that sets out the important decisions and subsequent actions. Publishing the full transcript might influence the contribution made by board members as, knowing their discussions will be published in full, it might deter a free and frank exchange of views. Those elected by a constituent group may be particularly affected if the issue of confict of loyalty arises, as members of the constituent group may expect their position to be promoted and protected at board level (despite the legal implications of a director or trustee doing so).

Commercial partners: sponsorship agreements and commercial partnerships need to be nurtured so that both parties maximise the benefit of the relationship. As well as information on the outputs from their support – for example, the impact of any programmes run in association with their brand – partners will also be interested in the reach achieved by communications, in particular social media activity. Monitoring and reporting on tweets, retweets, exposure and related content can be valuable for the sports body and partners as a means of fnding new customers and also understanding what content appeals to them.

Before engaging with a sports organisation, commercial partners will undertake due diligence to ensure they are entering into an agreement with a sports body that operates with integrity, is financially secure and is able to deliver what it claims to the sponsor. This is not where the commercial partner's interest in governance will end; they will be alert to any potential scandals or negative media about the sports organisation and related sponsorship activity.

Funders: sports councils make explicit demands on the organisations they fund in terms of governance information as well as reports on the delivery of the sporting outcomes specifed in funding agreements. Sports councils are not regulators but will request access to information such as quarterly financial reports, board minutes and minutes of other committees. Unless these are specified in the funding agreement, the sports organisation can decide whether to release redacted (edited) or complete copies of such information, if at all.

Beyond the reporting processes, funded bodies will want to create communications plans that present their vision and goals, their structures, governance and people in the best possible light. These plans are more often created by a staff member or a sub-committee whose primary function is communications, and the board should satisfy itself that stakeholders have been prioritised with key messages appropriate to the audience. Reactionary communications rarely present the best of an organisation, and reputational damage is too often the cost paid for failures to plan.

Best practice with electronic communications
The need for clarity in policy and process has already been discussed earlier in this chapter and, as well as the risk of individual failures, every organisation, regardless of size, should develop robust data protection and business continuity procedures to protect information.

Accessibility

The Equality Act 2010 requires website owners to ensure that their websites are accessible to users with disabilities. Section 29(1) of the 2010 Act says that:

> A person ... concerned with the provision of a service to the public or a section of the public (for payment or not) must not discriminate against a person requiring the service by not providing the person with the service.

Accordingly, neglecting to provide a service to a disabled person that is normally provided to other persons is unlawful discrimination. This applies to commercial web services as much as to services that are not web-based.

For instance, visually impaired visitors may use speech synthesiser software to read the text in the HTML code of web pages and translate it into audible speech. However, many websites include images that contain text as part of a pre-rendered picture file. These may be unreadable by the software if the text is not embedded in the image properties or alternatively available in text somewhere on the website. This could render the content inaccessible to visually impaired users, and could therefore be discriminatory for the purposes of the 2010 Act.

Sections 20 and 29(7) of the Equality Act specify a duty for service providers to make reasonable adjustments to enable disabled persons to access their services. This applies as much to website accessibility as it does to providing participation opportunities.

The Web Content Accessibility Guidelines (WCAG) are a series of guidelines for improving web accessibility. Produced by the World Wide Web Consortium (W3C) the WCAG are the best means of making websites useful to all users. Although they are not an all-inclusive list of issues facing web users with disabilities, they are internationally recognised and adopted standards. The guidelines explain how to solve many of the problems that your users with disabilities face and can be viewed at www.w3.org/WAI/intro/wcag.php.

The guidelines are a good indicator of what a court would reasonably expect website owners and businesses to follow to ensure that websites are as accessible as possible and in line with the Equality Act. At the most basic level of compliance (priority 1), these include suggestions such as:

- providing text to accompany non-text elements (such as pictures or graphical buttons for navigating);
- document organisation for sensibly ordered readability without the need for the accompanying style sheets;
- making sure all information conveyed through coloured content can be inferred or is available without colour;
- clearly and simply labelling the website's content; and
- clearly delineating changes in the natural text of the document to other content, such as captions.

Compliance with both the priority 1 and 2 checklists is recommended. The priority 2 checklist includes:

- ensuring the foreground and background colours have suffcient contrast for those who struggle with differentiating colours;
- using an appropriate markup language rather than images to convey information;
- using header elements to convey structure;
- using style sheets to control the layout and presentation;
- clearly identifying the target of each link;
- providing further information about layout (for example, a sitemap);
- using navigation mechanisms in a consistent manner;
- providing metadata to add semantic information to web pages; and
- dividing large blocks of information into more manageable blocks when possible.

Accessibility should be addressed at the web design stage because many fundamental design decisions have an impact on accessibility. Although it is not a common basis for legal action, website accessibility is important, both from the perspective of legal compliance and because a more accessible website has a greater potential user-base.

Benefits of using electronic communications with members and other stakeholders

As technology advances and more people of all ages are familiar with web or mobile communications, this opens up a number of engagement opportunities. This can include members feeding back directly to a consultation on Facebook, live action being streamed from an international event or reports and updates being shared in seconds via Twitter.

Reducing the amount of paper, ink and printing machinery will be an obvious benfit to a sports organisation, especially clubs and community groups with limited resources. Using online communications also takes far less time – one email to 2,000 members is obviously quicker for a staff member or volunteer than writing, printing and posting the same information. Provided there is a sufficiently robust process for the management of communications, sports bodies should seek to maximise their presence by investigating and adopting the tools available.

Social media as a marketing and engagement tool

The immediacy, affordability and reach of social media make it ideal for voluntary organisations trying to communicate with a broad range of stakeholders. For NGBs and larger organisations, the benefits include:

- exposure for governing bodies (London 2012 was the first 'Twitter' Games);

- interaction with fans – online communities;
- medium for supply of information – facts, fixtures, travel information; and
- marketing the experience and brand.

Even for clubs and smaller organisations, social media can promote sporting and non-sporting opportunities, including events or facility hire.

Tools such as Facebook and Twitter can create discussion and feedback opportunities. For example, the British Parachute Association used Facebook to consult its members on a new mission and organisational values. This enabled immediate feedback from members that helped shape the final versions.

According to World Rugby, the 2017 Women's Rugby World Cup was the most socially engaged World Rugby event of 2017, generating record video views, social engagement rates and website traffc, inspiring a new, younger audience. The statistics show just how powerful online platforms can be:

- 45 million views across official tournament platforms, making it the best-performing World Rugby event of the year and the biggest since the Rugby World Cup 2015;
- 73% of social media engagement was with people under the age of 24, with a 53/47% audience split between female and male fans, highlighting the appeal of the action to both females and males;
- 63,000 uses of the hashtag #WRWC2017 in total, with 50,000 new fans joining World Rugby's social media communities; and
- 600,000 unique users visiting the tournament website over the duration of the tournament from 223 different territories, generating four times as many page views as the 2014 Women's Rugby World Cup.

This information informed the 2017–25 women's rugby strategy, which aims to build a stronger and sustainable women's game.

Chapter summary

- Sports organisations must be aware that there are certain stakeholders who are most influential and must be given a meaningful say in how the organisation is governed.
- There are many ways boards can seek stakeholder and member views: annual surveys, consultations, advisory groups, committee meetings, general meetings, roadshows or regional meetings.
- When it comes to communicating with stakeholders, both the message and the channel though which it is delivered must be carefully considered and tailored for each stakeholder group.
- Sections 20 and 29(7) of the Equality Act specify a duty for service providers to make reasonable adjustments to enable disabled persons to access their services. This applies as much to website accessibility as it does to providing

participation opportunities. The Web Content Accessibility Guidelines (WCAG) are a series of guidelines for improving web accessibility and can be downloaded for free.

■ Social media provides a vital communications tool, but organisations must stay abreast, and meet the obligations of, relevant legislation.

Directory of web resources

Better Boards, Stronger Sport: http://www.sportireland.ie/Governing_Bodies/
NGB_Support_Kit/Better-Boards-Stronger-Sport-Toolkit/

British Cycling Independent Review Panel Report: www.uksport.gov.uk/~/media/
files/resources/cycling-independent-review-panel-report.pdf?la=en

Charity Commission Model Articles: www.gov.uk/government/publications/
setting-up-a-charity-model-governing-documents

Child Protection in Sport Unit – Standards for Safeguarding and Protecting
Children in Sport: https://thecpsu.org.uk/media/1040/english-standards.pdf

Community Interest Companies Regulator Model Articles: www.gov.uk/
government/publications/community-interest-companies-constitutions

Companies House Model Articles: www.gov.uk/guidance/
model-articles-of-association-for-limited-companies

Consolidated minimum requirements for the implementation of the IOC's
basic principles of good governance: https://www.olympic.org/good-governance

Cycling Independent Reform Commission report: www.uci.ch/mm/Document/
News/CleanSport/16/87/99/CIRCReport2015_Neutral.pdf

Duty of Care in Sport: Independent Report to Government: www.
sportresolutions.co.uk/uploads/related-documents/Duty_of_Care_Review_-_
April_2017__2.pdf

England Athletics – Club Guide to Social Media: www.englandathletics.org/
library-media/documents/England%20Athletics%20Introduction%20to%20
Social%20Media%20-%20PDF.pdf

Equality in Sport – Equality Standard for Sport: www.equalityinsport.org.

European Convention on Human Rights: www.echr.coe.int/Documents/
Convention_ENG.pdf

Financial Reporting Council – Guidance on Audit Committees: FRC Guidance
on Audit Committees

Financial Reporting Council – Guidance on Board Effectiveness: www.frc.org.
uk/Our-Work/Publications/Corporate-Governance/Guidance-on-Board-
Effectiveness.pdf

Governance and Leadership Framework for Wales: http://sportwales.org.uk/
media/1602095/4180_sra_governance_and_leadership_frameworks_for_
wales_english_translation_opt1_v6_-_final.pdf

How can FIFA be held accountable? Roger Pielke Jr: https://pdfs.semanticscholar.
org/e527/8db428041dd0bed7b4a310daefd7754ae9dd.pdf

Institute of Business Ethics – Business Ethics and Sport Governance: www.ibe.org.uk/list-of-publications/67/47

International Paralympic Committee – Layman's Guide to Paralympic Classification: www.paralympic.org/sites/default/files/document/120716152047682_ClassificationGuide_1.pdf

IOC's Basic Universal Principles of Good Governance of the Olympic and Sports Movement: https://www.olympic.org/good-governance

Join In – volunteering: www.joininuk.org

Northern Ireland Code of Good Governance for the Voluntary and Community Sector: www.volunteernow.co.uk/fs/doc/publications/revised-code-of-good-governance-jan16.pdf

Olympic Agenda 2020: https://stillmed.olympic.org/Documents/Olympic_Agenda_2020/Olympic_Agenda_2020-20-20_Recommendations-ENG.pdf

Olympic Charter: https://stillmed.olympic.org/Documents/olympic_charter_en.pdf

The Principles of Good Governance for Sport and Recreation: www.sportandrecreation.org.uk/pages/principles-of-good-governance

Scottish Governing Bodies' Governance Framework: https://sportscotland.org.uk/media-imported/1480369/governance-framework-web-final-feb-2015.pdf

Spirit of 2012 – volunteering principles: www.spiritof2012trust.org.uk/our-volunteering-principles

Sport England – Accessible Facilities Design Guidance: www.sportengland.org/media/4508/accessible-sports-facilities-2010.pdf

Sport England – Active Lives Survey 2015–16: www.sportengland.rg/media/11498/active-lives-survey-yr-1-report.pdf

Sport England Clubmark: https://www.sportenglandclubmatters.com/club-mark/

Sport Wales' Club Solutions: http://www.clubsolutions.wales

Transparency International – 'Fair Play: strengthening integrity and transparency in cricket': http://issuu.com/transparencyinternational/docs/2013_fairplaycricket_en?e=2496456/5641906

UK Athletics Athletes' Commission: www.uka.org.uk/media/news/2017-news-page/june-2017/23-06-17-nine-elected-to-athletes-commission/

UK Corporate Governance Code: www.frc.org.uk/getattachment/ca7e94c4-b9a9-49e2-a824-ad76a322873c/UK-Corporate-Governance-Code-April-2016.pdf

UK Sport – impact of major events: www.eventimpacts.com

UK Sport & Sport England Code of Sports Governance: www.sportengland.org/media/11193/a_code_for_sports_governance.pdf

Women in Sport – Checklist for Change: www.womeninsport.org/resources/trophy-women-2015-checklist-for-change

World Wide Web Consortium – Web Content Accessibility Guidelines: www.w3.org/WAI/intro/wcag.php

Glossary

Accountability the obligation of an individual or organisation to account for its activities, accept responsibility for them, and to disclose the results in a transparent manner.

Accruals the accruals basis of accounting requires the non-cash effects of transactions and other events to be reflected in the financial statements for the accounting period in which they occur and not during the period when the cash is paid or received.

Agenda the document which sets out the items/matters/topics which are to be discussed during a meeting, and the order in which they will be discussed.

Articles of Association a document that contains the purpose of the company as well as the duties and responsibilities of its members defined and recorded clearly.

Autonomy of sport recognising that sport occurs within the framework of society, sports organisations chart the rights and obligations autonomy, which include freely establishing and controlling the rules of sport, determining the structure and governance of their organisations, enjoying the right of elections free from any outside influence and the responsibility for ensuring the principles of good governance be applied.

Bribery the offering, giving, receiving, or soliciting of any item of value to influence the actions of a person who has a legal duty.

Cash flow statement a financial summary of all of the cash receipts and payments over an accounting period.

Child Protection in Sport Unit (CPSU) a partnership between the National Society for the Prevention of Cruelty to Children (NSPCC), Sport England, Sport Northern Ireland and Sport Wales who work with national governing bodies (NGBs), county sports partnerships (CSPs) and other organisations to help minimise the risk of child abuse during sporting activities.

Close family ties those family members who may be expected to influence, or be influenced by, that person in their dealings with the entity and include that person's children and spouse or domestic partner, children of that person's spouse or domestic partner and dependents of that person or that person's spouse or domestic partner.

Companies Act 2006 the main piece of legislation which governs company law in the UK. It is the longest piece of legislation ever enacted in the UK, with over 1,300 sections.

Consistency similar items within a single set of accounts should be given similar accounting treatment, and the same treatment should be applied from one accounting period to the next for similar items so that one year's results are comparable to the rest.

Contract an agreement between two or more parties that creates enforceable rights and obligations.

Corruption the abuse of entrusted power for private gain.

Direct discrimination where one person treats another less favourably because of a protected characteristic.

Disability physical or mental impairment that has a 'substantial' and 'long-term' negative effect on your ability to do normal daily activities (Equality Act 2010)

Disclosure and Barring Service (DBS) a government service which helps employers make safer recruitment decisions and prevent unsuitable people from working with vulnerable groups, including children, by checking the backgrounds of certain individuals.

Duty of care a legal, regulatory and/or moral obligation to safeguard others from harm while they are in your care, using your services, or exposed to your activities.

Ethics the moral principles that govern a person's behaviour or the conducting of an activity.

European sporting model a term used to describe the structure of professional sports leagues in Europe for team sports that have certain governance principles including open leagues, no salary caps and unequal revenue distribution systems. Often discussed in opposite terms to the North American sporting model.

Executive directors members of the board who are also employees and who often have specified areas of responsibility.

Fiduciary relationship a person who holds a legal or ethical relationship of trust with one or more other parties (person or group of persons). Typically, a fiduciary prudently takes care of money or other asset for another person.

Financial probity the evidence of ethical behaviour, and can be defined as complete and confirmed integrity, uprightness and honesty in a particular process.

Financial Reporting Standards a set of international accounting standards stating how particular types of transactions and other events should be reported in financial statements.

Going concern the information presented in the financial statements is prepared on the basis that the organisation will continue to operate for the foreseeable future.

Governance the process by which decisions are or are not made.

Harassment unwanted conduct towards a person which is related to a protected characteristic.

Impairment a problem in body function or structure (World Health Organization).

Independence a person is independent if they are free from any close connection to the organisation and if, from the perspective of an objective outsider, they would be viewed as independent (Code for Sports Governance; Principles of Good Governance for Sport and Recreation).

Indirect discrimination treatment which may be neutral on its face but which discriminates in practice against members of a group who share a protected characteristic.

Insolvency the inability of an organisation to be able to pay its debts.

Listing Rules a set of regulations applicable to any company listed on the UK Stock Exchange, subject to the oversight of the UK Listing Authority (UKLA).

Money laundering the process of disguising the source of money that has been obtained from serious crime or terrorism, so that it appears to come from a legitimate source.

National governing body (NGB) organisations that govern recognised sporting activities on a UK, Great Britain or home country basis.

Non-executive directors members of a board who are not part of the executive team. A non-executive director typically does not engage in the day-to-day management of the entity, but focuses on policy and strategy and holds the executive to account.

North American sporting model a term used to describe the structure of professional sports leagues in North America for team sports that have certain governance principles including closed leagues, salary caps and unequal revenue distribution systems. Often discussed in opposite terms to the European sporting model.

Olympism a philosophy of life, exalting and combining in a balanced whole the qualities of body, will and mind. Blending sport with culture and education, Olympism seeks to create a way of life based on the joy found in effort, the educational value of good example and respect for universal fundamental ethical principles (International Olympic Committee).

Ordinary resolution a decision passed by a majority of the members of an organisation.

Performance enhancing drugs substances that have the potential to enhance sport performance, represent a health risk to the athletes or violate the spirit of sport (World Anti-Doping Agency).

Protected acts making a claim or complaint of discrimination (under the Equality Act 2010); helping someone else to make a claim by giving evidence or information; making an allegation that you or someone else has breached the Act; doing anything else in connection with the Act.

Protected characteristics age; disability; gender reassignment; marriage and civil partnership; pregnancy and maternity; race; religion and belief; sex; sexual orientation.

Proxy the authority to represent someone else, especially in voting.

Prudence states that revenue and profits are not anticipated, but are recognised only when they are realised.

Quorum the number of people required to be present to conduct valid business at a meeting.

Risk the amount and type of risk that an organisation is willing to take in order to meet its strategic objectives (Institute of Risk Management).

Separate determination an accounting concept which treats a business separately from its owner. The separate entity assumption states that the transactions conducted by a business are separate to those conducted by its owners.

Shareholder someone who owns shares in an organisation. Collectively all of the shareholders own the organisation concerned.

Special resolution a decision which requires a 75% majority of the members to vote in favour to be passed.

Stakeholder a person with an interest or concern in something, especially a business.

Statement of comprehensive income (income statement) a statement showing the profits (or losses) recognised during a period. The profit is calculated by deducting expenditure (including charges for capital maintenance) from income.

Statement of financial position (balance sheet) a list of all assets owned by the business and all of the liabilities owed by a business at a specific point in time. It is often referred to as a 'snapshot' of the financial position of the business at a specific moment in time (normally at the end of a financial year).

Substance over form an accounting principle used 'to ensure that financial statements give a complete, relevant, and accurate picture of transactions and events'.

UK GAAP the overall body of regulation establishing how company accounts must be prepared in the UK. This includes not only accounting standards, but also UK company law.

Victimisation when a person is treated less favourably on the ground that they have done a protected act.

Whistleblowing/reporting telling a public or regulatory authority, or the public, that an organisation you are working for is doing something immoral or illegal.

Index